Determinants of the Death Penalty

The death penalty is a highly emotive subject which leaves few people unaffected and has been written about extensively. However, in spite of this, there has been no even-handed and comprehensive theory of the issue until now.

Determinants of the Death Penalty seeks to explain the phenomenon of capital punishment – without recourse to value judgments – by identifying those characteristics common to countries that use the death penalty and those that mark countries which do not. This global study uses statistical analysis to relate the popularity of the death penalty to physical, cultural, social, economical, institutional, actor-oriented and historical factors. Separate studies are conducted for democracies and non-democracies and within four regional contexts. The book also contains an in-depth investigation into determinants of the death penalty in the USA.

This book is an important reference for those studying the death penalty across political science, sociology and legal studies.

Carsten Anckar is senior lecturer in political science at the Mid-Sweden University and associate professor at the Åbo Akademi University, Finland.

Routledge research in comparative politics

1 **Democracy and Post-Communism**
   Political change in the post-communist world
   Graeme Gill

2 **Sub-State Nationalism**
   A comparative analysis of institutional design
   Edited by Helena Catt and Michael Murphy

3 **Reward for High Public Office**
   Asian and Pacific Rim states
   Edited by Christopher Hood and B. Guy Peters

4 **Social Democracy and Labour Market Policy**
   Developments in Britain and Germany
   Knut Roder

5 **Democratic Revolutions**
   Asia and Eastern Europe
   Mark R. Thompson

6 **Europeanisation and the Transformation of States**
   Edited by Bengt Jacobsson, Per Lagreid and Ove K. Pedersen

7 **Democratization**
   A comparative analysis of 170 countries
   Tatu Vanhanen

8 **Determinants of the Death Penalty**
   A comparative study of the world
   Carsten Anckar

Determinants of the Death Penalty

A comparative study of the world

Carsten Anckar

 Routledge
Taylor & Francis Group

LONDON AND NEW YORK

First published 2004
by Routledge
2 Park Square, Milton Park, Abingdon, Oxfordshire OX14 4RN

Simultaneously published in the USA and Canada
by Routledge
29 West 35th Street, New York, NY 10001

Routledge is an imprint of the Taylor & Francis Group

© 2004 Carsten Anckar

Typeset in Times by Wearset Ltd, Boldon, Tyne and Wear
Printed and bound in Great Britain by MPG Books Ltd, Bodmin

British Library Cataloguing in Publication Data
A catalogue record for this book is available from the British Library

Library of Congress Cataloging in Publication Data
Anckar, Carsten, 1969–
  Determinants of the death penalty : a comparative study of the
world / Carsten Anckar.
    p. cm.
  Includes bibliographical references and index.
1. Capital punishment—Cross-cultural studies. I. Title.
HV8694.A63 2004
364.66–dc22   2004001290

ISBN 0-415-33398-9

This book is dedicated to Maja and Dag Anckar

Contents

List of illustrations   ix
Preface   xiii

1 Mapping the death penalty   1
Introduction 1
Two time periods 2
The dependent variable 4
A historical and geographical overview 17
Methodological considerations 20
Six sets of explanations 22

2 Explaining the death penalty   24
The physical setting 24
The cultural setting 29
Development, security and dependency 41
Political institutions 58
Political actors 67
Historical explanations 75

3 Contextual patterns   90
Global patterns 90
The death penalty in democracies and non-democracies 102
Regional patterns 121

4 The death penalty in the USA   139
The USA as a case study 139
Mapping the death penalty in the USA 143
Physical factors 148
The cultural setting 149

Socioeconomic development 150
Level of crime 151
Political actors 151
Historical explanations 156
Multivariate patterns in the USA 158
Discussion 159

5   Determinants of the death penalty   165
Summary of findings 165
Legitimacy, diffusion and trends 168

Notes   179
References   181
Index   193

Illustrations

Figures

1.1	Structure of the dependent variable	5
2.1	Possible association between the level of crime and capital punishment	48

Tables

1.1	Development of the abolitionist movement	3
1.2	The death penalty in 1985 and 2000	12–16
1.3	The death penalty in six regional settings	18
2.1	Associations between population size, area, density, insularity and capital punishment in 1985	28
2.2	Associations between population size, area, density, insularity and capital punishment in 2000	29
2.3	Associations between ethnic, linguistic, religious fragmentation and capital punishment in 1985	38
2.4	Associations between ethnic, linguistic, religious fragmentation and capital punishment in 2000	39
2.5	Dominating religion and capital punishment	39
2.6	Islamic and Buddhist abolitionist countries in two periods of time	41
2.7	Association between socioeconomic development and capital punishment in 1985	44
2.8	Association between socioeconomic development and capital punishment in 2000	45
2.9	Association between human development index and capital punishment in 1985	45
2.10	Association between human development index and capital punishment in 2000	46
2.11	Associations between measures of security and capital punishment in 1985	53

2.12   Associations between measures of security and capital
       punishment in 2000   53
2.13   Association between dependency and capital punishment
       in 1985   57
2.14   Association between dependency and capital punishment
       in 2000   58
2.15   Associations between degree of democracy, state structure
       and capital punishment in 1985   66
2.16   Associations between degree of democracy, state structure
       and capital punishment in 2000   66
2.17   Form of government and capital punishment in 1985 and
       2000   67
2.18   Associations between leadership duration, regime stability
       and capital punishment in 1985   72
2.19   Associations between leadership duration, regime stability
       and capital punishment in 2000   73
2.20   Associations between leadership duration, regime stability
       and capital punishment in two categories of countries in
       1985   74
2.21   Associations between leadership duration, regime stability
       and capital punishment in two categories of countries in
       2000   74
2.22   Colonial heritage and capital punishment in 1985 and 2000   87
2.23   Associations between state longevity, slavery and capital
       punishment in 1985   87
2.24   Associations between state longevity, slavery and capital
       punishment in 2000   88
2.25   Association between state longevity-dichotomy and capital
       punishment in 2000   88
3.1   Dominating religion, infant mortality, number of offenses,
       degree of democracy, leadership duration, regime stability,
       colonial heritage and history of slavery as determinants of
       capital punishment in 1985   93
3.2   Dominating religion, degree of democracy, leadership
       duration, regime stability, colonial heritage and history of
       slavery as determinants of capital punishment in 1985   94
3.3   Dominating religion, human development index, degree of
       democracy, leadership duration, colonial heritage and
       history of slavery as determinants of capital punishment in
       2000   95
3.4   Religion, degree of democracy, leadership duration,
       colonial heritage and history of slavery as determinants of
       capital punishment in 2000   96

3.5 Form of government, slavery, Christianity and capital punishment in 1985 — 97

3.6 Form of government, slavery, Christianity and capital punishment in 2000 — 98

3.7 Form of government, slavery, Islam and capital punishment in 1985 — 98

3.8 Form of government, slavery, Islam and capital punishment in 2000 — 99

3.9 Insularity, index of ethnic–religious fragmentation, dominating religion and colonial heritage as determinants of capital punishment in stable democracies in 1985 — 104

3.10 Index of ethnic–religious fragmentation, dominating religion, human development index, EU trade, colonial heritage and history of slavery as determinants of capital punishment in stable democracies in 2000 — 105

3.11 EU trade and colonial heritage as determinants of the death penalty in stable non-European democracies in 2000 — 106

3.12 Population size, religion, conflict intensity, regime stability and history of slavery as determinants of capital punishment in non-democratic countries in 1985 — 108

3.13 Population size, infant mortality and history of slavery as determinants of capital punishment in non-democratic countries in 2000 — 109

3.14 Democratic countries with capital punishment at two points in time — 110

3.15 Authoritarian abolitionist countries at two periods in time — 112

3.16 Insularity, dominating religion, conflict intensity and regime stability as determinants of capital punishment in Africa in 1985 — 123

3.17 Population size, dominating religion, trade dependency, conflict intensity, degree of democracy and regime stability as determinants of capital punishment in Africa in 2000 — 124

3.18 Index of religious fragmentation and colonial heritage as determinants of capital punishment in the Americas in 1985 — 125

3.19 Index of religious fragmentation and state longevity as determinants of capital punishment in the Americas in 2000 — 126

3.20 Population size, dominating religion, degree of democracy, regime stability and history of slavery as determinants of capital punishment in Asia and the Pacific in 1985 — 128

3.21 Population size, dominating religion, number of offenses, degree of democracy and history of slavery as determinants of capital punishment in Asia and the Pacific in 1985 — 129

3.22   Population size, dominating religion, conflict intensity and
       degree of democracy as determinants of capital punishment
       in Asia and the Pacific in 2000   131
3.23   Index of religious fragmentation, GDP/cap, EC trade and
       degree of democracy as determinants of capital punishment
       in Europe in 1985   133
3.24   Number of offenses, EC trade and degree of democracy as
       determinants of capital punishment in Europe in 1985   134
3.25   Dominating religion, number of offenses and degree of
       democracy as determinants of capital punishment in
       Europe in 2000   135
4.1   Development of the death penalty in the USA since 1972   145
4.2   The death penalty in the USA since 1976   147
4.3   Association between size and capital punishment in the
       United States   148
4.4   Association between index of ethnic fragmentation and
       capital punishment in the United States   150
4.5   Association between socioeconomic development and
       capital punishment in the United States   151
4.6   Association between level of crime and capital punishment
       in the United States   152
4.7   Associations between party dominance in state legislatures,
       party affiliation of governor and capital punishment in the
       United States   155
4.8   Civil War status and capital punishment in the USA   158
4.9   History of slavery and capital punishment in the USA   158
4.10   Population size, index of ethnic fragmentation, number of
       murders, history of slavery and party affiliation of governor
       as determinants of capital punishment in the United States   159
4.11   Associations between party dominance in state legislatures,
       party affiliation of governor and capital punishment in
       36 states in the United States   161
4.12   Population size, index of ethnic fragmentation, number of
       murders and party affiliation of governor at time of re-
       enactment of the death penalty as determinants of capital
       punishment in 36 states in the United States   161
5.1   Determinants of the death penalty in eight settings   166

Preface

The death penalty is a highly controversial and much debated issue, especially in the industrialized and democratized world. This fact notwithstanding, the reader who expects to find arguments either for or against the death penalty within the frames of the present book will be disappointed. It is my firm opinion that far too many of the works related to the death penalty have been permeated with the authors' personal views on the subject. It is my sincere hope that this book will fill a lacuna in the literature on the death penalty by contributing to the empirical theorybuilding in the field. The ambition of the present book is simple and straightforward: to identify the determinants of the death penalty in the world, nothing more, nothing less.

Since this is a global comparative study, the persons to whom I am indebted are not few in numbers. Let me begin by extending my gratitude to my mentor, colleague and friend, Professor Lauri Karvonen at the Åbo Akademi University who was the one who came up with the idea of studying the determinants of the death penalty. Needless to say, the collection of the empirical material has sometimes demanded a lot of efforts. The bulk of the material has assiduously been collected by Krister Lundell and Patrik Fagerström. Not surprisingly, exact numbers of executions was extremely hard to obtain for many countries. Without the generous help of Amnesty International and especially its Finnish Head Director, Frank Johansson, the task of gathering even approximate figures would not have been completed. I also extend my gratitude to Professor Felix Bethel of the University of Bahamas for an eye-opening discussion of the death penalty in the Caribbean. Furthermore, I would like to thank Peter Burnell of the University of Warwick and Guy-Erik Isaksson and Kimmo Grönlund, Åbo Akademi, for much appreciated tips on literature and suggestions of corrections of the text. Furthermore, I wish to thank all my colleagues at the Department of political science at Åbo Akademi (no-one mentioned, no-one forgotten) for providing me with a stimulating research environment.

During the writing of this book I have enjoyed a three-year fellowship at the Academy of Finland. I am grateful to the Academy for financing the project and for giving me the opportunity to focus entirely on the book. During the same period I have enjoyed a leave of absence from my position as Senior Lecturer at the Mid-Sweden University. I especially want to thank professor Göran Bostedt for giving me the opportunity to focus entirely on this project despite difficulties in filling my vacancy.

The completion of the book has been a time-consuming effort and I thank my wife Oxana for her indulgence with my mental and physical absence. Finally, I wish to express my gratitude to my parents for providing me with the ideal milieu in which to grow up. In my childhood home, creative thinking was, and is, ever-present.

Carsten Anckar

1   Mapping the death penalty

Introduction

Ever since humanity developed the capacity to think, the relation between the individual and the society has occupied the minds of philosophers. In every society where rules are formulated, the rights of the individual must be related to the rights of the society. Logically, these rights are in a state of opposition; the more rights the individual has, the smaller the sphere of rights confined to the society and vice versa. Since the list of authors that throughout the centuries have pondered upon the relation between the individual and the society is impressive (Rousseau 1900; Locke 1967; Rawls 1971; Mill 1972; Nozick 1974; Aristotle 1991, to name but a few), it is of course an understatement to say that the literature that covers the field is abundant. With all the evidence at hand it is fair to ask what we have learnt about this relation. The answer is, unfortunately, not much. All the works cited above have left us with very few clues to the best way to arrange the relation between the individual and the state. When it comes to it, ideas of the "best" society ensue from the personal opinions of the authors.

So why then embark on a journey that evidently does not have an end? The obvious answer is to not embark on such a journey. The present work therefore does not have the ambition to dwell upon the question of how to organize the ideal society. I could easily lay down my view of the ideal ratio of the rights of the individual and the rights of the state. However, no matter what arguments I produce in favor of this ratio, they would not convince a person with another view. The aforesaid does not, however, mean that the question of the relation between the rights of the individual and the rights of the state is unimportant or impossible to grasp scientifically. It is my firm belief we need to study this relation, but we should do this by isolating interesting theoretical questions that can be answered by means of empirical studies. Within the framework of the present study I shall focus on one fundamental aspect of the relation between the individual and the state, namely the right of the state to kill its citizens.

The ultimate form of punishment, the death penalty, leaves few of us emotionally unaffected. It is one of those rare questions were individuals generally have no difficulties in taking a stand, either for or against. It would also be an understatement to argue that it is an issue which is widely debated in many parts of the world. Although the literature on capital punishment is abundant, the curious reader is struck by the fact that the bulk of it is colored by arguments either for or against the use of the death penalty. A general trend is that opponents of the death penalty use philo- sophical, moral or religious arguments when attacking "governments which kill their citizens", whereas proponents often legitimate the use of capital punishment by either referring to the expected coercive effect of the death penalty, or to the victim's "right to revenge".

It is not venturesome to state that one rarely runs across a work where this issue is treated in a neutral analytical manner. Perhaps this is only natural since we are, literally, dealing with a matter of life and death. However, within the framework of the present study, I shall not follow this tradition. On the contrary, I shall avoid all kinds of philosophical discus- sions of whether or not an entity, in this case the state, has the right to take the life of a human being. In a like manner, I shall, as far as possible, avoid touching upon the presumed consequences the use of capital punishment might have, for instance for crime prevention. The aim is, in fact, much simpler. The ambition is to *explain* the phenomenon or, in other words, to identify those characteristics which mark, on the one hand, those countries which make use of the death penalty, and, on the other hand, those coun- tries that do not. It is indeed surprising to find that such a controversial issue, which has received so much attention, has been the subject of so few scientific studies.

Two time periods

We cannot overlook the possibility that different factors might have affected the choice of countries to either allow or forbid the use of capital punishment in different periods of time. Consequently, it is of foremost importance that the study be conducted in different time periods. Needless to say, the first question we have to tackle is which time periods to study. A quick look at the history of the death penalty in the countries of the world immediately reveals that we cannot go very far back in time. For one thing, availability of data concerning the independent variables is limited. For another thing – and this is more important – there is not enough variation on the dependent variable. Until recently, very few countries had abolished the death penalty. It was not until the 1970s and the 1980s that the aboli- tionist movement really got under way. For instance, by the year 1970 only 14 countries had abolished the death penalty for all crimes.

One time period comes naturally. It is difficult to find arguments for why we should not be interested in the present situation. Thus, one time setting will be the situation in the early twenty-first century. For determining the other time periods it is reasonable to start by taking a look at the use of the death penalty over time. The aim is to find natural cut-off points, that is, short periods of time during which a large number of states have abolished the death penalty. Table 1.1 lists the number of countries that have abolished the death penalty in each year. Data has been compiled from Amnesty International's Internet site (http://web.amnesty.org/pages/deathpenalty-index-eng) and from Hood (1996: 241–244). The general trend is that the abolitionist movement has spread slowly. A few countries have abolished the death penalty every five years. A closer look at the data reveals, however, that we do indeed find some periods where many states have changed their attitude toward the use of capital punishment. One such breakpoint is evident: in 1989 four countries abolished the death penalty. This number was doubled the

Table 1.1 Development of the abolitionist movement

Year	Number of countries that abolished the death penalty completely without having reinstalled it subsequently	Year	Number of countries that abolished the death penalty completely without having reinstalled it subsequently
1863	1	1979	3
1865	1	1981	2
1877	1	1982	1
1906	1	1985	1
1907	1	1987	3
1910	1	1989	4[1]
1922	1	1990	8[1]
1928	1	1992	3
1949	1	1993	2
1956	1	1994	1
1962	1	1995	4
1966	1	1996	1
1968	1	1997	4
1969	1	1998	6
1972	1	1999	3[2]
1973	1	2000	2
1976	1	2002	2
1978	1	2003	1
		Total	69

Notes
1 Including Slovenia and Croatia, which abolished the death penalty in 1989 and 1990 respectively, but did not receive their independence until 1991.
2 Including East Timor, which abolished the death penalty in 1999 but did not receive its independence until 2002.

following year, after which the trend slowed down again. With the evidence at hand, it seems natural to use the mid-1980s as a cut-off point. Since some countries constantly tend to change their attitude toward the death penalty, the points in time need to be specified further. Therefore, values on the dependent variable reflect the situations on 31 December 1985 and 31 December 2000.

The dependent variable

At first glance, the classification of the dependent variables seems obvious. A state either allows capital punishment or does not. The natural thing would therefore be to treat it as a dichotomous, nominal variable. However, a more thorough investigation reveals that countries where capital punishment is allowed differ in many respects, and that further classification can, and should, be done. Amnesty International has, for an extensive number of years, systematically collected data from all countries in the world concerning the use of the death penalty and the organization classifies countries into four categories. The categorization is based on the one used in the regularly conducted surveys on the death penalty undertaken by the United Nations (1975, 1980, 1985, 1990, 1995, 2000). The most distinguished authority on comparative studies of the death penalty, Roger Hood, follows this classification in his worldwide studies (Hood 1989, 1996, 2002). The four categories are as follows (the quotations are from Schabas 1997a: 239–243).

Category 1: countries that are abolitionist for all crimes

This category includes "countries and territories whose laws do not provide for the death penalty for any crime".

Category 2: countries that are abolitionist for ordinary crimes only

This category includes "countries whose laws provide for the death penalty only for exceptional crimes such as crimes under military law or crimes committed in exceptional circumstances such as wartime".

Category 3: countries that are abolitionist de facto

This category includes "countries and territories which retain the death penalty for ordinary crimes but can be considered abolitionist in practice in that they have not executed anyone during the past ten years or more, or in that they have made an international commitment not to carry out executions".

Category 4: countries that are retentionist

This category includes "states that retain and use the death penalty for ordinary crimes". Countries included in this category have, as a rule, carried out executions during the last ten years.

The term "retentionist" can be construed as emotionally charged. Contrary to Amnesty International and Roger Hood, the present study does not take a stand in the debate of whether or not capital punishment should be abolished. I therefore choose to use terms which differ from the one mentioned above. Instead of "retentionist", I use phrases such as "states that make use of the death penalty", "states that apply the death penalty", "states where capital punishment exists" and so on. Applying the classification above means that the dependent variable would be structured in terms of three dichotomous variables. The scheme of classification is illustrated in Figure 1.1.

Dichotomy 1

A first distinction comes naturally; the death penalty is either allowed or not in the penal code of the country. In cases where the law provides for the use of the death penalty, further distinctions can be made.

Dichotomy 2

Another distinction is made between countries where the death penalty is applied under normal circumstances and countries where the use of the death penalty is restricted to times where "special circumstances" prevail. In most cases "special circumstances" refer to a state of war or serious conflicts.

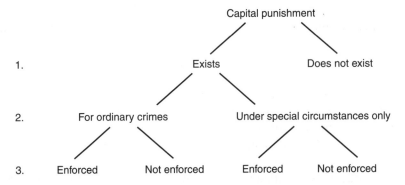

Figure 1.1 Structure of the dependent variable.

Dichotomy 3

In many countries, the constitution provides for the use of capital punishment both under normal and special circumstances. It is therefore relevant to distinguish between cases where death sentences are carried out and where death sentences are not enforced. The distinction can, in principle, be made separately for countries that make use of capital punishment under special circumstances only and countries that make use of it under normal circumstances.

A few remarks should be made about the category that consists of states that allow capital punishment under special circumstances only. In theory, it is possible to make a distinction between states that carry out death sentences and states that do not carry out death sentences in practice. However, this distinction can only be made theoretically, since there is not enough empirical evidence on how states act under special circumstances. In order to be able to make this distinction, one needs to have evidence for how each state treats the question of the death penalty "under special circumstances", such as in times of war. Furthermore, this evidence should not be dated very far back in time; preferably the evidence should not be older than, say, ten-to-fifteen years. This distinction is therefore irrelevant for the present study.

The first methodological question we have to tackle is how to treat the dependent variable. At first it seems obvious that it is a multi-nominal variable. The dependent variable has four categories: states can forbid the use of the death penalty in all its forms; states can allow the use of the death penalty under special circumstances; states can allow the use of the death penalty, but in practice abstain from implementing death penalties; and states can make active use of the death penalty. However, it is not unreasonable to treat the dependent variable as a discrete variable. It is possible to rank the categories on a scale which measures the willingness to apply the death penalty. This, however, can not be done in a totally uncontroversial manner. The two extreme values are unproblematic. States that do not allow the use of the death penalty under any circumstances are given the lowest value, whereas states that allow and make use of the death penalty are given the highest value. The two intermediate categories are more difficult to rank. Should we consider a state that allows the death penalty but where death sentences are never carried out as more or less willing to kill its citizens than a state that allows the use of the death penalty under special circumstances only?

What makes things complicated is the fact that we ought to know how countries act in those situations labeled "special circumstances". Theoretically, in these situations, a country that allows the use of the death penalty under special circumstances may either choose to make use of the death penalty or not. Similarly, a country that has a penal code that allows the death penalty but where death sentences are not carried out can choose between upholding this policy under these "special circumstances" or starting to implement death sentences. If a country that does not allow the use of capital punishment for ordinary crimes implement death sentences under special circumstances and a country where death sentences are not carried for ordinary crimes also upholds this policy under "special circumstances", we would indeed say that the former country was more willing to kill its citizens than the latter one. The problem is, of course, that we know very little about how states act under special circumstances. Another problem is that different states within the categories may choose different strategies. In other words, we are unable to answer this question on the basis of empirical evidence.

In order to answer the question we must instead consider how high the threshold for implementing the death sentences is. If a constitution does not allow the use of the death penalty, death sentences can never be imposed and much less carried out in reality. At least in peacetime, the threshold for reintroducing the death penalty is much lower in countries that are de facto abolitionist than in countries where capital punishment is forbidden except under special circumstances, since, in the former category, no change in the penal code is required. Also, it is important to emphasize that all countries that are de facto abolitionist automatically retain the death penalty under special circumstances as well. Thus, one could argue, countries classified as de facto abolitionist are one step closer in implementing death sentences than countries where capital punishment is allowed under special circumstances only. Now, empirically it is not difficult to find examples of countries that have reverted to making use of capital punishment after a long period of no executions. For instance, in 1993 the Philippines reinstalled the death penalty after having abolished it in 1987. It therefore seems natural that countries where capital punishment is allowed only under special circumstances are given a lower value than countries that are de facto abolitionist.

On the whole, the categorization makes sense. However, for analytical purposes it can be refined. Thus, the category consisting of countries that are de facto abolitionist will be merged with the category of countries that make use of the death penalty. The four categories are thus reduced to three. The reasons underlying this decision will be discussed momentarily. In addition to this major alteration of the dependent variable, I shall split up each of the three categories on a ten-degree scale.

Let us begin with the category of countries that apply and use the death penalty for ordinary crimes. Certainly, there is a marked difference between a country that has executed, say, one person for murder in a period of ten years and a country that regularly executes people for a wide variety of crimes, such as drug trafficking or rape. Therefore the category made up of countries that make use of capital punishment is divided into separate categories with reference to the number of executions carried out. However, operating with the exact number of executions carried out in a country is not possible. Data on the number of executions in each country is often unreliable to say the least. States that make use of capital punishment are often unwilling to reveal the exact number of executions that have taken place. Beginning from the 1960s, the United Nations has conducted several surveys on the use of the death penalty. However, a large number of the countries have been reluctant to give out information on the amount of executions. As Hood (1996: 67) notes: "[t]hose countries which are known from other sources to make the greatest use of executions were precisely those who most often failed to reply with the details requested by the United Nations". The surveys conducted by the UN cannot be used within the framework of this study. Instead, I shall rely on other sources. The most reliable source on numbers of executions is Amnesty International's yearly reports. It must, however, be emphasized that the figures Amnesty International provides are highly unreliable as well. For many countries it is nearly impossible to know the exact number of legal executions that have taken place.

Since data is often unavailable and/or unreliable, there is no point in operating with an assumed number of executions that has taken place. This could endanger the validity of the categorization. However, at the same time, it is necessary to account for those variations in the use of the death penalty which exist among countries that make use of it. If a country has executed, say, one or two persons in a limited number of years, it seems more than correct to separate it from a country that executes hundreds of individuals every year. I shall proceed by ranking the countries in terms of the extent to which they make use of the death penalty. Since the number of executions can vary a lot within countries we should focus on a time period of several years rather than concentrating on one year only. I have therefore chosen to calculate the average number of executions during a time period of ten years.

The absolute number of executions cannot in itself be used as an indicator of the willingness of a country to kill its citizens. The amount of executions must be related to the population of the country as well (see, for example, Hood 1996: 73). If, for instance, the Bahamas and China, both of which make use of the death penalty, execute the same number of persons each year it would indeed be fair to say that the former used the death penalty to a much higher extent than the latter, given the huge difference in size between the two countries. The obvious solution is to divide the number of executions that have taken place in a country with the size of the population. However, this strategy suffers from one serious shortcoming. As an illustration of this shortcoming, let us again consider the cases of the Bahamas and China. In 1985, the population of the Bahamas was 230,000. If there is one execution in a period of ten years, the Bahamas has an average of 0.1 executions per year. Dividing 0.1 by 230,000 gives us the value 0.0000004. China, again, had a population of 1,059,522,000, and an average number of executions of 236, which means that the corresponding value for China is 0.0000002. Based on these calculations we reach the conclusion that the proportion of the population killed by the Government of the Bahamas is roughly twice as large as the one killed by its Chinese counterpart. However, to consider the Bahamas, which kills one citizen every ten years, a country which makes more extensive use of the death penalty than China, which kills 236 persons every year, is clearly not correct. Therefore, rather than operating with the absolute size of the population I shall use the logarithmized version of population size. For the Bahamas we then receive the value 0.01 whereas the corresponding value for China is much higher, 11.27, indicating that the attitude toward the death penalty is more positive in China than in the Bahamas.

The average number of executions during a time period of ten years is divided with the logarithmized population size. For a number of countries, information concerning the number of executions is lacking for some of the years falling within this time period. In these cases, the average number of executions has been calculated based on the years for which adequate information is available. For 1985, figures cannot be drawn from a period of ten years since there is very little information regarding the number of executions. Instead, the extent of executions is based on figures from the time period 1980–1985. After this, I have looked at the distribution of the variable and made use of the deciles as a base for referring the countries in the different categories. Accordingly, we receive ten categories of countries. Countries situated in the highest decile receive the value 2.9 and countries in the lowest category the value 2.0. By using deciles as a base of categorization we escape some of the problems that arise when we are forced to operate with insufficient data. For instance, we know that both Iraq and China execute a substantial number of persons each year. However, based on the sources used, it is not possible to conclude which of the countries apply the death penalty more frequently. Concerning China, Amnesty International has only tentative figures for many years. Concerning Iraq, reliable information is even more difficult to obtain. The sources mention "hundreds of executions". Now, the exact number of executions for Iraq could be as high as China's, or even higher, or significantly lower. We do not know. Establishing exact numbers of executions under these circumstances jeopardizes the reliability of the study. Therefore, rather than trying to come up with exact numbers for countries like Iraq and China I confer both countries to the category of countries that make use of the death penalty to the highest extent, and thus refrain from making internal rankings concerning the number of executions.

When splitting up the category of countries that apply the death penalty in ten categories, I have used the number of executions as a base of classification. This means that the original category of de facto abolitionist countries, i.e. countries that have not implemented death sentences for a period of ten years or more, becomes irrelevant. There are two important arguments that favor a combination of the two categories into one. For one thing, a threshold of ten years is arbitrary. The difference between a country that has not executed anyone for a period of ten years and a country that has not executed anyone for a period of nine years is not a difference in kind, but a difference in degree. In addition, the category of de facto abolitionist countries tends to be a quite unstable one. The first edition of Hood's work was published in 1989 and the second one in 1996. Between these years, ten countries moved from the category of de facto abolitionist countries to the category of countries that make use of the death penalty (Hood 1996: 8). In the latest version of his book, Hood (2002: 13) concludes: "[t]he concept of abolitionist de facto, based purely on the criterion of the number of years without executions,... no longer has the credibility at one time ascribed to it". When applying deciles as bases of categories, the distinction between countries that have not executed anyone during a time period of ten years and the other countries is accentuated. The evidence shows that an extensive number of countries where capital punishment is allowed have not executed anyone in a time period of ten years or more. Accordingly, for the year 2000, the first three deciles cover countries where no executions have occurred. For the year 1985, such countries make up the first two deciles. Accordingly countries where no executions have occurred for a time period of ten years are given the value 2.0. After that, there is a jump to the next category of countries where the number of executions in relation to the logarithmized population size is very low indeed. For the year 2000, these countries receive the value 2.3 and, for 1985, they obtain the value 2.2. For a number of countries classified as "retentionist" in the sources used, it has not been possible to verify any executions from Amnesty International's yearbooks during the relevant time periods. Furthermore, for 1985, a number of countries have no recorded executions between 1980 and 1985 but have recorded executions if a period of ten years is applied. To avoid classifying these cases in the same category as countries where no executions have occurred for a very long time period, I have chosen to confer these countries to the category of countries that apply the death penalty but are situated within the lowest decile with regard to number of executions.

I now turn to the two remaining categories. The category consisting of countries that apply the death penalty under special circumstances only, and where the death penalty has accordingly been abolished for ordinary crimes only, can also be split up into ten categories with reference to the attitude toward the death penalty. However, applying deciles of the distribution of numbers of executions in relation to the logarithmized population size cannot be done since most of the countries situated within this category have not executed anyone during the time period of ten years. Instead it is more appropriate to try to capture a measure of how high the threshold is for applying the death penalty. Here, one could think of a number of indicators, such as the year the death penalty was abolished for ordinary crimes or the extent to which capital punishment has been applied in the past. However, since the aim of the present study is to explain the use of the death penalty in two points of time, we cannot go very far back in time when we establish the values on the dependent variable. Strictly speaking, of course, observations on the independent variable should precede observations on the dependent variable. However, concerning the death penalty some leeway must be permitted since simply regarding the number of executions in one year does not necessarily give an accurate picture of the extent to which capital punishment is applied. In addition, there is the insurmountable task of getting reliable information for all countries during one specific year.

Given these restrictions, it seems appropriate not to consider events that have taken place longer than ten years ago. The basic argument is that the psychological threshold to accept the use of the death penalty is lower in countries where executions have taken place during the last ten years than in countries where no executions have taken place during the said period of time. Accordingly, the sub classification of the category will be made with reference to number of years that have elapsed since the last execution. In other words, a country which is abolitionist for ordinary crimes only and where no executions have occurred in a period of ten years receive the value 1.0. Similarly, a country where the last death sentence has been implemented nine years prior to the relevant point in time obtains the value 1.1, a country where the last execution has occurred eight years prior to the same point in time 1.2 and so on.

The same strategy will be applied for the last category consisting of countries that have abolished the death penalty completely. If a country in this category has not executed anyone during a period of ten years, it receives the value 0.0. A country in which the latest execution occurred nine years prior to the relevant point in time receives the value 0.1 and so on. Thus, an index of the attitude toward the death penalty ranging from 0.0 to 2.9 is obtained. Values on the dependent variable in the two points of time for the countries of the world are given in Table 1.2.

Table 1.2 The death penalty in 1985 and 2000

Country	Death penalty status (1985)	Death penalty index (1985)	Death penalty status (2000)	Death penalty index (2000)
Afghanistan	Applied	2.90	Applied	2.80
Albania	Applied	2.20	Abolished OCO	1.50
Algeria	Applied	2.40	Applied	2.60
Andorra	–	–	Abolished	0.00
Angola	Applied	2.80	Abolished	0.00
Antigua & Barbuda	Applied	2.20	Applied	2.30
Argentina	Abolished OCO	1.00	Abolished OCO	1.00
Armenia[1]	–	–	Applied	2.30
Australia	Abolished	0.00	Abolished	0.00
Austria	Abolished	0.00	Abolished	0.00
Azerbaijan	–	–	Abolished	0.30
Bahamas	Applied	2.20	Applied	2.50
Bahrain	Applied	2.20	Applied	2.30
Bangladesh	Applied	2.60	Applied	2.50
Barbados	Applied	2.40	Applied	2.00
Belarus	–	–	Applied	2.80
Belgium	Applied	2.00	Abolished	0.00
Belize	Applied	2.20	Applied	2.00
Benin	Applied	2.20	Applied	2.00
Bhutan	Applied	2.00	Applied	2.00
Bolivia	Applied	2.00	Abolished OCO	1.00
Bosnia-Herzegovina[1]	–	–	Abolished OCO	1.00
Botswana	Applied	2.30	Applied	2.50
Brazil	Abolished OCO	1.00	Abolished OCO	1.00
Brunei	Applied	2.00	Applied	2.00
Bulgaria	Applied	2.70	Abolished	0.00
Burkina Faso	Applied	2.50	Applied	2.00
Burundi	Applied	2.30	Applied	2.70
Cambodia	Applied	2.20	Abolished	0.00
Cameroon	Applied	2.80	Applied	2.30
Canada	Abolished OCO	1.00	Abolished	0.00
Cape Verde	Abolished	0.00	Abolished	0.00
Central African Republic	Applied	2.40	Applied	2.00
Chad	Applied	2.30	Applied	2.40
Chile[1]	Applied	2.20	Applied	2.00
China	Applied	2.90	Applied	2.90
Colombia	Abolished	0.00	Abolished	0.00
Comoros	Applied	2.00	Applied	2.40
Conga-Brazzaville	Applied	2.30	Applied	2.00
Congo-Kinshasa	Applied	2.80	Applied	2.90
Costa Rica	Abolished	0.00	Abolished	0.00
Croatia	–	–	Abolished	0.00

Table 1.2 Continued

Country	Death penalty status (1985)	Death penalty index (1985)	Death penalty status (2000)	Death penalty index (2000)
Cuba	Applied	2.30	Applied	2.60
Cyprus[1]	Abolished OCO	1.00	Abolished OCO	1.00
Czech Republic	–	–	Abolished	0.00
Czechoslovakia	Applied	2.50	–	–
Denmark	Abolished	0.00	Abolished	0.00
Djibouti	Applied	2.00	Abolished	0.00
Dominica	Applied	2.20	Applied	2.00
Dominican Republic	Abolished	0.00	Abolished	0.00
Ecuador	Abolished	0.00	Abolished	0.00
Egypt	Applied	2.50	Applied	2.70
El Salvador	Abolished OCO	1.00	Abolished OCO	1.00
Equatorial Guinea	Applied	2.30	Applied	2.40
Eritrea	–	–	Applied	2.00
Estonia	–	–	Abolished	0.10
Ethiopia	Applied	2.20	Applied	2.30
Fiji	Abolished OCO	1.00	Abolished OCO	1.00
Finland	Abolished	0.00	Abolished	0.00
France	Abolished	0.20	Abolished	0.00
Gabon	Applied	2.40	Applied	2.00
Gambia	Applied	2.20	Applied	2.00
Georgia	–	–	Abolished	0.50
Germany	–	–	Abolished	0.00
Germany (East)	Applied	2.20	–	–
Germany (West)	Abolished	0.00	–	–
Ghana	Applied	2.80	Applied	2.50
Greece	Applied	2.00	Abolished OCO	1.00
Grenada	Applied	2.20	Applied	2.00
Guatemala	Applied	2.20	Applied	2.40
Guinea	Applied	2.20	Applied	2.00
Guinea-Bissau	Applied	2.20	Abolished	0.00
Guyana	Applied	2.40	Applied	2.40
Haiti	Applied	2.00	Abolished	0.00
Honduras	Abolished	0.00	Abolished	0.00
Hungary	Applied	2.50	Abolished	0.00
Iceland	Abolished	0.00	Abolished	0.00
India	Applied	2.30	Applied	2.60
Indonesia	Applied	2.40	Applied	2.40
Iran	Applied	2.90	Applied	2.90
Iraq	Applied	2.90	Applied	2.90
Ireland	Applied	2.00	Abolished	0.00
Israel	Abolished OCO	1.00	Abolished OCO	1.00
Italy	Abolished OCO	1.00	Abolished	0.00

Table 1.2 Continued

Country	Death penalty status (1985)	Death penalty index (1985)	Death penalty status (2000)	Death penalty index (2000)
Ivory Coast	Applied	2.00	Abolished	0.00
Jamaica	Applied	2.70	Applied	2.00
Japan	Applied	2.50	Applied	2.70
Jordan	Applied	2.50	Applied	2.80
Kazakhstan	–	–	Applied	2.90
Kenya	Applied	2.70	Applied	2.30
Kiribati	Abolished	0.00	Abolished	0.00
Korea (North)	Applied	2.20	Applied	2.80
Korea (South)	Applied	2.60	Applied	2.80
Kuwait	Applied	2.40	Applied	2.60
Kyrgyzstan	–	–	Applied	2.80
Laos	Applied	2.20	Applied	2.00
Latvia	–	–	Abolished OCO	1.60
Lebanon	Applied	2.30	Applied	2.60
Lesotho	Applied	2.20	Applied	2.30
Liberia	Applied	2.60	Applied	2.40
Libya	Applied	2.60	Applied	2.70
Liechtenstein	Applied	2.00	Abolished	0.00
Lithuania	–	–	Abolished	0.50
Luxembourg	Abolished	0.00	Abolished	0.00
Macedonia (FYR)	–	–	Abolished	0.00
Madagascar	Applied	2.00	Applied	2.00
Malawi	Applied	2.20	Applied	2.40
Malaysia	Applied	2.80	Applied	2.70
Maldives	Applied	2.00	Applied	2.00
Mali	Applied	2.30	Applied	2.00
Malta	Abolished OCO	1.00	Abolished	0.00
Marshall Islands	–	–	Abolished	0.00
Mauritania	Applied	2.40	Applied	2.00
Mauritius	Applied	2.20	Abolished	0.00
Mexico	Abolished OCO	1.00	Abolished OCO	1.00
Micronesia (Fed. States)	–	–	Abolished	0.00
Moldova	–	–	Abolished	0.00
Monaco	Abolished	0.00	Abolished	0.00
Mongolia	Applied	2.20	Applied	2.60
Morocco	Applied	2.20	Applied	2.30
Mozambique	Applied	2.70	Abolished	0.00
Myanmar	Applied	2.20	Applied	2.00
Namibia	–	–	Abolished	0.00
Nauru	Applied	2.00	Applied	2.00
Nepal[2]	Applied	2.20	Abolished	0.00
Netherlands	Abolished	0.00	Abolished	0.00

Table 1.2 Continued

Country	Death penalty status (1985)	Death penalty index (1985)	Death penalty status (2000)	Death penalty index (2000)
New Zealand	Abolished OCO	1.00	Abolished	0.00
Nicaragua	Abolished	0.00	Abolished	0.00
Niger	Applied	2.20	Applied	2.00
Nigeria	Applied	2.90	Applied	2.90
Norway	Abolished	0.00	Abolished	0.00
Oman	Applied	2.20	Applied	2.50
Pakistan	Applied	2.90	Applied	2.70
Palau (Belau)	–	–	Abolished	0.00
Panama	Abolished	0.00	Abolished	0.00
Papua New Guinea	Abolished OCO	1.00	Applied	2.00
Paraguay	Applied	2.00	Abolished	0.00
Peru	Abolished OCO	1.40	Abolished OCO	1.00
Philippines	Applied	2.20	Applied	2.50
Poland	Applied	2.60	Abolished	0.00
Portugal	Abolished	0.00	Abolished	0.00
Qatar	Applied	2.20	Applied	2.40
Romania	Applied	2.20	Abolished	0.00
Russia	–	–	Applied	2.90
Rwanda	Applied	2.70	Applied	2.60
St. Kitts & Nevis	Applied	2.20	Applied	2.40
St. Lucia	Applied	2.20	Applied	2.30
St. Vincent & Grenadines	Applied	2.20	Applied	2.50
Samoa (Western)	Applied	2.00	Applied	2.00
San Marino	Abolished	0.00	Abolished	0.00
São Tomé e Príncipe	Applied	2.00	Abolished	0.00
Saudi Arabia	Applied	2.90	Applied	2.90
Senegal	Applied	2.00	Applied	2.00
Seychelles	Abolished OCO	1.00	Abolished	0.00
Sierra Leone	Applied	2.20	Applied	2.80
Singapore	Applied	2.50	Applied	2.90
Slovakia	–	–	Abolished	0.00
Slovenia	–	–	Abolished	0.00
Solomon Islands	Abolished	0.00	Abolished	0.00
Somalia	Applied	2.90	Applied	2.70
South Africa	Applied	2.90	Abolished	0.10
Soviet Union	Applied	2.80	–	–
Spain	Abolished OCO	1.00	Abolished	0.00
Sri Lanka	Applied	2.20	Applied	2.00
Sudan	Applied	2.60	Applied	2.70
Suriname	Applied	2.20	Applied	2.00
Swaziland	Applied	2.60	Applied	2.00
Sweden	Abolished	0.00	Abolished	0.00

Table 1.2 Continued

Country	Death penalty status (1985)	Death penalty index (1985)	Death penalty status (2000)	Death penalty index (2000)
Switzerland	Abolished OCO	1.00	Abolished	0.00
Syria	Applied	2.80	Applied	2.70
Taiwan	Applied	2.80	Applied	2.80
Tajikistan	–	–	Applied	2.40
Tanzania	Applied	2.20	Applied	2.50
Thailand	Applied	2.70	Applied	2.60
Togo	Applied	2.20	Applied	2.00
Tonga	Applied	2.20	Applied	2.00
Trinidad & Tobago	Applied	2.20	Applied	2.60
Tunisia	Applied	2.60	Applied	2.50
Turkey[1]	Applied	2.80	Applied	2.00
Turkmenistan	–	–	Abolished	0.70
Tuvalu	Abolished	0.00	Abolished	0.00
Uganda	Applied	2.20	Applied	2.70
Ukraine	–	–	Abolished	0.70
United Arab Emirates	Applied	2.40	Applied	2.70
Uruguay	Abolished	0.00	Abolished	0.00
United Kingdom	Abolished OCO	1.00	Abolished	0.00
USA	Applied	2.70	Applied	2.90
Uzbekistan	–	–	Applied	2.60
Vanuatu	Abolished	0.00	Abolished	0.00
Vatican State	Abolished	0.00	Abolished	0.00
Venezuela	Abolished	0.00	Abolished	0.00
Vietnam	Applied	2.70	Applied	2.80
Yemen	–	–	Applied	2.80
Yemen (North)	Applied	2.20	–	–
Yemen (South)	Applied	2.50	–	–
Yugoslavia[1]	Applied	2.50	Applied	2.00
Zambia	Applied	2.70	Applied	2.50
Zimbabwe	Applied	2.60	Applied	2.60
Sum	Abolished: 29		Abolished: 73	
	Abolished OCO: 17		Abolished OCO: 13	
	Applied: 123		Applied: 106	

Notes

OCO = ordinary crimes only.

1 In 2001, Chile abolished the death penalty for ordinary crimes and Bosnia-Herzegovina for all crimes. In 2002, Cyprus and Yugoslavia (Serbia and Montenegro) abolished the death penalty for all crimes, whereas Turkey abolished the death penalty for ordinary crimes. In 2003, Armenia abolished the death penalty for ordinary crimes.

2 In Nepal, the death penalty was abolished for ordinary crimes at an early stage, in 1945. However, in 1985, i.e. the same year as my empirical observation on the dependent variable was made, it was reintroduced. In 1990, the death penalty was again abolished for ordinary crimes (Hood 1996: 32).

A historical and geographical overview

As has been shown, there is at present a great deal of variation as regards the use of the death penalty among the countries of the world. Historically, however, the use of capital punishment has been the rule, and exceptions from this rule have been rare. For instance, during the Middle Ages the use of the death penalty was very common indeed. With the Age of Enlightenment came the first serious critique against the death penalty in modern time. Cesare Beccaria, in particular, turned out to be very influential. As a consequence of his work *On Crimes and Punishments* (1764), the death penalty was abolished by Joseph II of Austria and by his brother Leopold, Grand Duke of Tuscany. In Russia, the Emperors Elisabeth and Catherine II also suspended the death penalty during their reigns (see Hood 2002: 9).

Although the issue of capital punishment was not totally uncontroversial before the beginning of the modern era, it was not until the late nineteenth century that the abolitionist movement really gathered momentum. In the beginning, the pace was rather slow. The first countries to abolish the death penalty were generally situated on the American continent, more specifically in South America. The first country to abolish the death penalty for all crimes was Venezuela in 1863. Costa Rica abolished the death penalty for all crimes in 1877 and, by the year 1910, Ecuador, Uruguay, and Colombia had followed the example. By that time, however, the abolitionist wave in Latin America was over. Not until 1956 did the next country in the region, Honduras, abolish the death penalty.

In Europe, San Marino was the torchbearer of the abolitionist movement. In this small mountainous republic, the death penalty was abolished for all crimes in 1865, only two years after the abolition of the death penalty in Venezuela (in Romania, the death penalty was abolished for all crimes the same year, but subsequently reinstalled in 1939). It should also be emphasized that San Marino was the first country in the world to abolish the death penalty for ordinary crimes. This happened in 1848. For many decades, San Marino and Romania were the only abolitionist countries in Europe. Not until 1928 did the next European country, Iceland, join the abolitionist movement. However, although the death penalty was not totally abandoned on the European continent, a few countries, namely the Netherlands (1870), Portugal (1867), Norway (1905) and Sweden (1921) abolished the death penalty for ordinary crimes before the outbreak of the Second World War.

Outside Latin America and Europe, the abolitionist movement is quite young. In Asia, the first country to reject capital punishment for all crimes was Cambodia in 1989. To date, only East Timor, Nepal and Turkmenistan have followed the example set by Cambodia in the region. In

Africa, Cape Verde abolished the death penalty in 1981 and did not have its first followers until nine years later, when Mozambique, Namibia, and São Tomé e Príncipe followed suit. In Oceania, many countries received their independence at a relatively late stage. The region thus got its first totally abolitionist countries as late as 1978 when the Solomon Islands and Tuvalu gained their independence. In both countries, the death penalty has been forbidden ever since the date of independence.

Table 1.3 describes to what extent the continents differ in terms of use of the death penalty. For each continent the arithmetic mean of the dependent variable is given.[1] By means of the Eta squared technique it is possible to compare the between-group variance with the within-group variance.

The results indicate that there are indeed pronounced differences between the six regions. In Asia and in Africa, capital punishment is used to a much higher extent than in the other regions. In 1985, Oceania stands out as the region with the most restrictive attitude toward the death penalty. Between 1985 and 2000 there has been a sharp decrease in the use of the death penalty in Europe, which is explained by the fall of the social-ist regimes in Eastern Europe. Accordingly, Europe now stands in the forefront of the abolitionist movement along with Oceania. In every region but one, we note a trend toward a more restrictive use of capital punishment. The exception is North Africa and the Middle East where the popularity of the death penalty remains high. Furthermore, it is well worth noting that the between-group variance has grown during the time period of fifteen years. In other words, today, the continents differ more with respect to the use of capital punishment than before. This is mostly due to the heavy decline of its use in Europe and in the Pacific region.

Death sentences are now carried out in all regions with one significant exception, namely Oceania. Africa stands out as the continent where

Table 1.3 The death penalty in six regional settings (arithmetic means)

Continent	1985	2000
Sub-Saharan Africa	2.31 (45)	1.79 (47)
America	1.47 (35)	1.28 (35)
Asia	2.37 (25)	2.28 (30)
Europe	1.15 (34)	0.42 (48)
North Africa & Middle East	2.41 (20)	2.52 (19)
Oceania	0.82 (10)	0.54 (13)
Eta squared	0.354	0.429
Sig.	0.000	0.000
N	169	192

Note
N in parentheses.

capital punishment is the most widely employed. Concerning Europe, there is a sharp difference between the former Eastern European countries and the Western European countries. Among the former Eastern European countries, Bulgaria, Croatia, the Czech Republic, Hungary, Macedonia, Poland, Romania, Slovakia and Slovenia had completely abolished the death penalty by the year 2000. In 2002, Serbia and Montenegro abolished the death penalty for all crimes. In the republics of the former Soviet Union, the use of capital punishment has been the rule rather than the exception. The first of the former Soviet republics to abolish the death penalty was Moldova, in 1995. However, in recent years the popularity of the death penalty has deteriorated in the republics of the former Soviet Union and, at present, Azerbaijan, Estonia, Georgia, Lithuania, Ukraine and Turkmenistan have also abolished the death penalty for all crimes.

It is evident that the desire of many of the former socialist countries of Eastern Europe and the Soviet Union to join the Council of Europe has had a great impact on the willingness to reject the death penalty. Following a resolution adopted by the Parliamentary Assembly of the Council of Europe in 1994, only countries that had abolished the death penalty can be granted membership (Resolution 1044 (1994) on the Abolition of Capital Punishment, paragraph 6). This decision has led to a massive abandonment of the death penalty in the Eastern European countries. It is evident that the abolition of the death penalty in Eastern Europe is a direct consequence of a desire to join in with European integration. For instance, when implementing a moratorium on capital punishment in Lithuania in 1996, President Algirdas Brazauskas explicitly stated that signing the decree "would facilitate Lithuania's integration into the European Union and other continental structures" (*Keesing's Record of World Events* 1996: 41201). These moves toward abolishing the death penalty have not always reflected the popular opinion in the relevant countries. The example of Latvia is telling. In 1998, the *Saeima* voted twenty-seven to twenty to retain the death penalty. The decision was a blow to President Guntis Ulmanis' ambition to abolish the death penalty (*Keesing's Record of World Events* 1998: 42298). The following year, however, the *Saeima* overwhelmingly voted to ratify Protocol No. 6 to the Convention for the Protection of Human Rights and Fundamental Freedoms Concerning the Abolition of the Death Penalty (ETS No.: 114), which abolished the death penalty for peacetime offenses, despite the fact that, according to opinion polls, a majority of the population opposed the abolition of the death penalty (*Keesing's Record of World Events* 1999: 42914).

It is therefore probably fair to say that pressure from Western European countries has had a profound, perhaps even decisive, impact on the decisions of the Eastern European countries to abolish the death penalty. For the moment I set the question of to what extent the choice to either employ or not employ the death penalty can be attributed to diffusion aside. I shall, however, return to this question at a later stage.

In Western Europe, capital punishment is not employed for ordinary crimes in any country, and after Cyprus abolished the death penalty for all crimes in 2002, death sentences can be passed under special circumstances in only one country, namely Greece. In Africa, a vast majority of the countries make use of capital punishment for ordinary crimes. So far, the death penalty has been totally abolished in Angola, Cape Verde, Djibouti, Guinea-Bissau, Ivory Coast, Mauritius, Mozambique, Namibia, São Tomé e Príncipe, the Seychelles and South Africa.

The death penalty is a frequent occurrence in Asia. As mentioned earlier, so far only Cambodia, East Timor, Nepal and Turkmenistan have abolished the death penalty for all crimes. Oceania, again, stands out as a highly abolitionist continent. Nauru, Papua New Guinea, Samoa and Tonga make use of the death penalty, but in none of these countries has any execution taken place for a period exceeding ten years. Nine countries – Australia, Kiribati, Marshall Islands, the Federated States of Micronesia, New Zealand, Palau (Belau), Solomon Islands, Tuvalu and Vanuatu – belong to the category of countries that have totally rejected the death penalty. In Fiji, the death penalty is allowed under special circumstances only.

Finally, as concerns America, the countries are evenly distributed among the dependent variable. In Canada, Colombia, Costa Rica, the Dominican Republic, Ecuador, Haiti, Honduras, Nicaragua, Panama, Paraguay, Uruguay and Venezuela, the death penalty has been completely abolished. Six countries – Argentina, Bolivia, Brazil, Chile, El Salvador, Mexico and Peru – have abolished the death penalty for ordinary crimes, whereas the rest of the countries make use of capital punishment.

Methodological considerations

There are two basic strategies available when we want to arrive at and ameliorate law-like generalizations about social phenomena: deduction and induction. Although this categorization is logically correct, empirical studies cannot generally be classified as either totally deductive or inductive (a subject to which I shall return shortly). That being said, it is nevertheless worth stressing that the bulk of the studies conducted in the field of social sciences tend to fall within the first category. In other words, whereas examples of deductive studies are abundant, inductive ones are few in number. The logical difference between the approaches is straightforward. When applying deduction, we depart from an existing theory, or sub-sets of theories, in the research field. In other words we have, a priori, a notion of a link between two (or more) phenomena and a logic conception of how the causal mechanism between the phenomena works. By following a line of logical reasoning from these existing theories, it is possible to derive specific hypotheses which, in turn, can be subject to empirical testing and, consequently, weaken, strengthen or refine the existing theory.

When using the inductive approach, the point of departure is the opposite. That is, we aim at arriving at generalizations of causal relations by observing the empirical reality. It has been said that the two approaches are rarely used in their original meaning. This holds true to a high extent concerning the deductive approach, and in its entirety concerning the inductive approach. A strict inductive approach, meaning that we observe the reality without any a priori assumption whatsoever is an impossibility except, perhaps, with regard to very simple and basic causal relations. An example of a strict inductive "study" could be Isaac Newton sitting under the apple tree watching the apple fall down to the ground. Drawing from this observation – according to the legend – he formulated his famous law of gravitation. Therefore it is not an overstatement to say that for generalizations derived in a strictly inductive manner, there is often an element of coincidence involved. If Newton had not been sitting under the apple tree that particular day, he would not have seen the apple fall and the credit for discovering the law of gravitation would have accrued to someone else.

Luckily, when conducting empirical research we are, as a rule, not stumbling in the dark. Although we sometimes lack a well-formulated theory about the determinants of a particular phenomenon, we still have a pretty good idea of which settings to look into for explanatory factors in the first instance. Even if this was not the case, the researcher is still likely to be able to identify a certain set of variables that can immediately be ruled out as explanations of the phenomenon he or she is about to study. The aforesaid means that an inductive study in the field of political science is never really strictly inductive. This is certainly correct with regard to the present study as well. Although no comprehensive theory concerning the determinants of the death penalty has been put forward to date, there are a number of factors that can be ruled out from the set of plausible explanatory variables. For instance, I am sure that the number of pigeons in a country is not related to the use of capital punishment. I also disregard the number of trout caught in the country and so on.

Accordingly, there is an element of deduction in every inductive study. The aforesaid suggests that the difference between deductive and inductive studies is not a difference in kind but merely a difference in degree. Some social phenomena are easier to grasp a priori than others. The crucial factor determining whether an inductive or a deductive approach is called for is, no doubt, the amount of previous research in the area. If, as a result of previously conducted research, there is already a well-formulated theory, it is natural to take it as a point of departure. The approach will consequently be deductive. If, on the other hand, we lack a general theory of the determinants of a specific phenomenon, we are left with the inductive approach. This is exactly the case concerning the prerequisites of the death penalty. The empirical evidence will (hopefully) make it possible to identify the relevant independent variable(s), and thereby to come up with a general theory, or at least a fragment of a theory, of the determinants of capital punishment. Instead of trying to put forward plausible explanations of the death penalty without any empirical support, I argue that it is more reasonable to start the quest for answers with an open mind.

However, as stated above, no empirical study is 100 percent inductive. One way of limiting the number of plausible explanatory variables in inductive studies is to look at previously conducted research in closely related areas. Based on the evidence in these studies, it is often possible to come up with an idea of in which contexts it is worth searching for explanatory variables. This, of course, means that the approach immediately comes one step closer to the deductive approach. However, one must bear in mind that knowing when a phenomenon is "close enough" is not always an easy task.

The aforesaid raises the question of whether it is relevant at all to make a distinction between deductive and inductive strategies. I argue that the answer must be in the affirmative. Although the line between deductive and inductive studies might be floating in practice, theoretically the two methods are very different indeed. One important way of distinguishing between the two approaches is how the research task is presented. In inductive studies, we begin by presenting the dependent variable. We operationalize the phenomenon and thereafter look at the empirical reality. Having done this, we proceed by identifying possible independent variables. In deductive studies we begin with selecting cases that show a variation in the independent variables. In deductive studies the variation in the dependent variable is not considered prior to conducting the empirical analyses since that would, in Lijphart's (1975: 164) words, "prejudge the empirical question".

Six sets of explanations

As I have implied already, the fact that we do not have a theory of the determinants of the death penalty does not mean that we must helplessly stumble around in the dark while hoping to come across the relevant explanatory factors. Even though we do not have a clear understanding of the causal mechanisms behind the death penalty, we still have a pretty good idea in which settings we ought to look for the relevant explanatory variables. Thus it is fair to say that earlier research has not provided us with the right variables, but with a pretty good map describing where to find the plausible explanations of the death penalty. The quest for the theory of the death penalty will consequently take place in six different settings, each providing us with a number of independent variables. For each of these settings, I briefly touch upon earlier research and try to point at logical connections to the present research problem. For some variables the theoretical arguments of the relevance for the death penalty are quite strong and the possibility to formulate actual hypotheses is, in fact, quite good. For other variables, admittedly, the logic behind the conceivable connection to the dependent variable is weaker, in some cases perhaps even fairly far-fetched. However, as the method is primarily inductive, a certain degree of trial and error must be permitted. The independent variables will emanate from the following settings:

1   physical explanations,
2   cultural explanations,
3   development, security and dependency,
4   political institutions,
5   political actors and
6   historical explanations.

2 Explaining the death penalty

The physical setting

Size

It would seem appropriate to start the quest for an explanation of the death penalty by looking at those factors that are most likely to remain unaltered over time. In most cases, physical factors precede other plausible explanatory variables in time. The physical variables of countries often go very far back in time. Another characteristic of such variables is that they generally do not change much over time. This, however, is not a rule without exception. It applies well to such physical conditions as climate and area. Arguably, the population size of countries is more sensitive to the ravages of time. The population size could at first be thought to vary a lot from year to year. This is certainly true if we look at the phenomenon asynchronically and within one single country. However, if we consider the relative differences in population size between countries, these differences over time are much less dramatic. The other size dimension, area, is even more stable than population size. However, this does not mean that area is totally static. The borders of many countries have changed throughout the past decades and centuries, mostly as a consequence of wars. In such cases, of course, the area (as well as the population size) of a country can change dramatically from one year to another. Austria of today, for instance, is comprised of only a fraction of the territory ruled from Vienna prior to the Treaty of Versailles in 1919.

Unfortunately, in most comparative studies, variables related to physical characteristics are neglected. The most cited example of a work falling within this tradition is, of course, *De l'esprit des lois* by Montesquieu (1944), where the author argued that variations in climatic conditions explained differences in types of government. Other examples are, if not abundant, at least easy to come up with. Throughout the years, many authors have dwelled upon the association between size and democracy. A persistent argument, first put forward in ancient Greece by Plato (cited in

Bratt 1951: 17; Tarkiainen 1959: 76) and Aristotle (1991: 282) is that small-ness constitutes a favorable condition for a democratic form of govern-ment. During the Age of Enlightenment, the Greek philosophers had their adherents in Montesquieu (1944, vol. VIII: chapter 16) and Rousseau (1900, vol. III: chapter 1). In modern times, Arend Lijphart (1977: 60) in particular has argued that smallness is a conducive factor for a consocia-tional form of democracy. The view that smallness is a virtue for a demo-cracy does not, however, stand unchallenged. When writing in the *Federalist Papers*, James Madison turned the argument upside down, claiming that the heterogeneity of large entities (Hamilton, Madison and Jay 1961: 83–84) counterbalanced the risk of the establishment of a perpet-ual majority oppressing a perpetual minority.

There are some theoretical arguments that justify the inclusion of size among the plausible explanatory factors of the death penalty. In their classic work, *Size and Democracy* (1973), Robert Dahl and Edward Tufte follow the footsteps of Aristotle and Plato. According to the authors, dif-ferences in size are likely to affect a variety of components in the political system, such as citizen participation, structure of the party system and system capacity. Although the link between size and the death penalty is not discussed by Dahl and Tufte, some of their arguments concerning the effects of variations in size can be thought to be of relevance for the death penalty as well. A crucial feature of small societies is that they tend to be more homogeneous and more consensual than large ones (Dahl and Tufte 1973: 91–94). If this assumption is true, this is likely to affect the attitude toward the death penalty. Theoretically, the intimacy and dependency that smallness is thought to generate might affect the willingness to apply the death penalty in two opposing ways.

One line of reasoning suggests that smallness gives rise to a restrictive attitude toward capital punishment. In small societies, people tend to know each other and rely on one another to a totally different extent than is the case in large societies. As concerns the death penalty, my argument is simple but reasonable. When people know each other well and have to rely on each other on a day-to-day basis they can be thought to resent the thought of killing a fellow citizen, who might, perhaps, be a neighbor, cousin, or a friend of a relative. Another feature of small societies is that politicians, policemen, lawyers and judges are likely to often confront the relatives of the executed criminal. The use of capital punishment can be fraught with momentous consequences in small societies. Bitterness is likely to prevail in many parts of the community, and anger and disbelief will grow in the aftermath of an execution. If there are significant ethnic cleavages in the society, capital punishment can be particularly harmful. In such cases, the killing of a citizen can be seen not only as an action against one individual, but against his or her ethnic group.

Another argument leads to the assumption that the death penalty is widely applied particularly in small entities. The argument in favor of the use of the death penalty in small or isolated entities springs from the same theoretical basis which underlay the assumption of a link between small-ness and a negative view of the death penalty. In the case of murder, the victim is likely to be known by a great many people. Consequently, the murderer is likely to be met by disgust and calls for revenge are likely to carry far. In such cases, the death penalty can be considered the only just form of punishment by large parts of the population.

Size, of course, incorporates two dimensions: population and area. The discussion so far has primarily focused on the possible effects of popu-lation size on capital punishment. At first glance, it does seem reasonable to expect that population size is more important than area. After all, Dahl and Tufte's book is primarily concerned with effects of population size (although they occasionally discuss effects of area). With regard to the death penalty, area can be of some importance as well. If a country is large in terms of area, this is likely to affect the possibility of the people, be they many or few, to know each other well. In the discussion so far I assumed that the people of a small country know each other well. However, if a relatively small population is dispersed over a large territory, the likeli-hood that they interact regularly is much lower than if an equally large population occupies a significantly smaller territory. In such cases, the con-sequences for the dependent variable are unlikely to be the same as in situations where a small population inhabits a small territory. The inclu-sion of both population and area among the explanatory variables is thus motivated.

The inclusion of both population and area inevitably leads us to a third dimension of size that is likely to affect the outcome on the dependent variable. This is actually a combination of population size and area. It is possible that we fail to detect a relation between either one of the size dimensions and the death penalty. At the same time, it is not unlikely that it is a combination of the size dimensions that is crucial. The discussion of the effects of size on the death penalty naturally presupposes that the population has to be concentrated to a certain extent; in other words, it is necessary that the population is aware of its size. The argument was that people tend to know each other better in small societies than in large ones. This was thought to have a bearing on the attitude toward the death penalty. It is nevertheless possible that the same effects of homogeneity and dependency that characterize small societies can be upheld in popu-lous countries as well. This is particularly the case if the territory is large whereby it is possible that the population is dispersed over a large territory but still continue to live in small communities. This, of course, creates the same effect as if the country in itself was very small. To overcome this problem it is necessary to combine the two size dimensions to a measure of density. This dimension is easily measured by dividing the size of the population with area. The assumption is that in countries with a high level of density the consequences for the death penalty are the same as the one expected for countries with large populations.

Insularity

In addition to size, another physical condition could be of relevance for the study. As has been said already, there is reason to expect that small entities be characterized by high levels of homogeneity. Carrying this argument further gives us reason to expect that the same thing applies for island states as well, perhaps even to a greater extent. Not only are island states often very small, they are also very often geographically isolated. This, one could argue, creates a feeling of loneliness and being left out from the world community. This is particularly the case if the distance to the mainland is very far (as is the case for the small island states in the Pacific). Island states tend to be very small indeed and, following my line of argument, it is not unreasonable to expect that this combination of smallness and isolation affect the attitude toward the death penalty.

Thresholds of size

Another issue that has to be dealt with concerns effects of thresholds. If smallness possesses some explanatory power, it is quite possible that this explanatory value does not extend beyond a certain level. When discussing the relation between size and attitudinal homogeneity, Dahl and Tufte claim that this is the case. Although the authors refrain from suggesting an exact threshold in numerical terms, they do indicate that it is probably "lower than the population of even a very small country like Iceland" (1973: 94). Consequently, Dahl and Tufte argue that their assumption of a link between size and attitudinal homogeneity only has relevance at a sub-state level. Some objections can, however, be raised against their line of reasoning. First, one should be aware of the fact that the world today looks quite different than it looked at the time of writing of *Size and Democracy*. During the 1970s and 1980s, many former colonies received their independence. These former colonies were often very small islands, indeed substantially smaller than Iceland. So, whereas Dahl and Tufte lacked the empirical data necessary for conducting research at an inter-state level, the relevant data is now at our disposal. Second, although Dahl and Tufte's work is theoretically impressive, its empirical contribution is actually rather meager. Dahl and Tufte's assumption of a threshold of homogeneity is never tested and consequently we cannot know whether such a threshold exists or not. An empirical test, in fact, seriously challenges the validity of the threshold theory (D. Anckar 1999: 41–43); still, I do not wish to rule out the possibility of a threshold operating with reference to the death penalty. It is reasonable to assume that the associations between the two size dimensions and the dependent variable are non-linear. In small entities, changes in size are likely to have a more visible effect than in larger entities. Anybody becomes aware of a change in population size by 5,000 people if the change is from 5,000 people to 10,000 people. However, if an entity grows from 50,000,000 people to 50,005,000, hardly anybody can perceive the difference. Consequently, in all statistical analyses where size is linked to the death penalty, I use the logarithmized version of population size, area and density. Concerning insularity, I apply a dummy variable where island states are given the value 1 and mainland states the value 0.

Empirical evidence

Let us then turn to studying whether there is any empirical support for the assumption of a link between physical factors and the death penalty. Tables 2.1 and 2.2 present the results of bivariate regression analyses where four independent variables are related to the dependent variable. As the results show, we can safely disregard both density and insularity as explanatory factors.

However, there is some support for my assumption that links size to the use of capital punishment. Smaller states tend to be more restrictive in the use of the death penalty than larger ones. The association is approximately the same in the two points of time. Also, population size seems to be more important than area, although it has to be said that the two size dimensions are heavily interlinked (Pearson's r is 0.85 in 1985 and 0.87 in 2000).

Table 2.1 Associations between population size, area, density, insularity and capital punishment in 1985 (bivariate regressions)

	B	Beta	T-value	R^2	N
Population (log)	0.108	0.254	3.472**	0.067	169
Area (log)	0.075	0.235	3.123**	0.055	169
Density (log)	−0.039	−0.065	−0.840	0.004	169
Insularity	0.238	−0.109	−1.412	0.012	169

Notes
**Significance at the $p < 0.01$ level.
*Significance at the $p < 0.05$ level.

Table 2.2 Associations between population size, area, density, insularity and capital punishment in 2000 (bivariate regressions)

	B	Beta	T-value	R^2	N
Population (log)	0.121	0.239	3.386**	0.057	192
Area (log)	0.088	0.222	3.137**	0.049	192
Density (log)	−0.006	−0.071	−0.982	0.005	192
Insularity	−0.116	−0.043	−0.591	0.002	192

Notes
**Significance at the $p < 0.01$ level.
*Significance at the $p < 0.05$ level.

The cultural setting

Ethnicity

The countries of the world are different in many respects. One of the differences that have caught the attention of many scholars is the distinction between homogeneous societies and heterogeneous ones. The impact of divisions on various aspects of politics is a frequently recurring subject in political science. Stein Rokkan, in particular, has ardently maintained that a variety of social and political phenomena can be explained by the formation and structure of divisions. In 1967, Lipset and Rokkan, argued in a famous introduction that the structure of the European party systems could be referred to old divisions based on region, class and religion (Lipset and Rokkan 1967). It is natural to assume that the inclination for the use of the death penalty is influenced by the degree of homogeneity in the society. Thus, the question of to what extent a society is divided by various cleavages should be tackled within the framework of this study. Now, divisions can take many forms and the question is what factors we should focus on. Since we lack a general theory of the prerequisites of the death penalty we need to approach the matter with as broad a perspective as possible.

First, it is reasonable to expect that the concept of ethnicity is important with regard to the death penalty. One could, of course, argue that the question of ethnicity is irrelevant today as the process of modernization has made it easier to migrate, not only from one country to another but also between continents. At a universal level it is probably fair to say that most countries are affected by this general lowering of the threshold to leave a place and settle down in another. The aforesaid does not, however, mean that ethnic differences are irrelevant today. It is evident that there are huge differences between countries in terms of the level of ethnic fragmentation. Although the notion of nation-state hardly fits into any of the countries today, it is, for instance, still fair to say that, while Kenya,

Tanzania and Uganda ethnically are extremely heterogeneous, Greece, Malta and Norway are quite homogenous, whereas Korea, Japan and Yemen are extremely homogeneous (Anckar, Eriksson and Leskinen 2002).

The impact of ethnic fragmentation on politics is by no means neglected in the literature. Thus, we run across studies where ethnic fragmentation is related to the level of democracy (Vanhanen 1990: 104–117; Hadenius 1992: 112–118). We also find an assumption that relates ethnic cleavages to state stability and state performance (Lane and Ersson 1994: 131–135). In yet another study the level of ethnic fragmentation is related to the level of party system fragmentation (Anckar 1998). The empirical evidence of these presumed relations are, however, quite weak, although it is worth noting that they point in the theoretically presumed direction (Vanhanen 1990: 115–116; Hadenius 1992: 115–116; Lane and Ersson 1994: 131–135, 148–149; Anckar 1998: 139–170). In other words, the more fragmented the country, the lower the level of democracy, the higher the risk of instability, and the more fragmented the party system.

Although the explanatory power of ethnicity was rather weak in the studies cited, it is possible that the ethnic composition of a country influences attitudes toward the death penalty. The theoretical argument underlying the presumed association between ethnic fragmentation and democracy departs from a quite simple assumption that kin groups favor group members over non-members. According to van den Berghe (1981: 7–19), this argument can be extended to encompass ethnic groups as well. This phenomenon which, according to van den Berghe, can be regarded as an extended form of nepotism, has implications for the political stability of societies. If the population of a country is made up of several ethnic groups, which all act in a selfish manner in trying to promote the interest of its own group members over others, conflicts are likely to emerge. If a country is fragmented, there is reason to believe that the political climate is tense. Thus, violence is expected to erupt more easily in ethnically fragmented societies than in homogeneous ones. The relation between ethnic diversity and political violence has in fact been empirically confirmed by Bingham Powell (1982: 51, 154–161). There are also a number of authors who claim that the destabilizing effect of ethnic fragmentation constitutes an impediment for the success of democracy in many parts of the world (Hannan and Carroll 1981; Vanhanen 1987: 29). All in all, then, we seem to have a firm ground on which to stand when linking ethnic fragmentation to high levels of violence and instability.

One way to uphold the social order and avoid social disturbances is to make sure that the punishments for crimes are severe. In societies marked by political conflicts, it is not unreasonable to expect that the threshold for making use of the death penalty is low. Therefore it is plausible to assume that death penalties would be applied more frequently in ethnically fragmented countries than in ethnically homogeneous countries.

Ethnicity, of course, is difficult to conceptualize. Initially, ethnicity had the same meaning as race. Over the last decades the concept of ethnicity has broadened to encompass a variety of things such as race, language, religion, national origin and physical characteristics. However, I do agree with Allardt and Starck (1981: 44) who claim that descent is the key issue. Ethnicity should be inherited from generation to generation. Applying this criterion means that religion, for instance, does not constitute an ethnic characteristic. Narrowing the meaning of ethnicity to traits of character that are inherited makes it natural to use race as an indicator of ethnicity.

If it is difficult to grasp the meaning of "ethnicity", it is even more difficult to define "race". At first it is necessary to disregard those people who are of mixed racial origin. Having done that (and thus eliminated a substantial share of the world's population, of course depending on how strictly we define "mixed racial origin") we still have to confront other problems. Africans, Asians and Caucasians can, at least in theory, be separated from each other. But how far should we go within these categories? Clearly there are differences between people belonging to the Hausa tribe and people belonging to the Ibo tribe in Nigeria. The terrifying examples of Rwanda and the Former Yugoslavia tell us that ethnic groups cannot be separated from each other simply on the basis of physical characteristics. Yet another problem is that the same ethnic cleavage can give rise to different outcomes in different parts of the world. In Spain, the cleavages between Castillians, Catalans, Basques and Galicians run deep. However, among the population of Spanish descent living in Latin America, the same cleavage base is insignificant. Instead, it is reasonable to assume that the important cleavage is the one that divides people of, for instance, European descent from Native Americans.

These problems inevitably lead to the conclusion that it is impossible to work with a universal definition of ethnicity. Instead, the best solution to empirically grasp the concept is to use self-definition as a criterion of ethnicity. As a point of departure, the assumption is made that only such divisions that are considered important in the respective country should be regarded. Countries are thought to pay attention to, and report, those cleavages in particular that are regarded as important for the specific country. Hence, the crucial factor for determining whether or not an ethnic cleavage exists in a particular country is whether or not the ethnic cleavage is considered to be important by the citizens of the country. This operationalization means that it is possible that the same ethnic cleavage can exist in more than one country but only be regarded as important within one or a few of the countries (and, consequently, not be accounted

for in the statistics of the other countries). In these (presumably rare) situations, different criteria of ethnicity admittedly apply in different contexts.

Concerning the American continent, I have made some deviations from
my general rule of strictly using those ethnic groups that the sources list.
Instead, the criteria of classification have largely been determined on a
case-to-case-basis. The basic principle has nevertheless been the same;
that is, ethnic groups are regarded as distinct if the sources used regard
them as distinct. However, within the American context I have followed
the basic guideline that people of European descent constitutes one group
and people of African descent one group. As concerns the Native population, it has been regarded as one homogeneous ethnic group in USA and
some countries in Latin America where the number of Native Americans
is low. In other countries, for instance in Peru, where Native Americans
make up the majority of the population, the various tribes have been
regarded as separate ethnic groups.

Since ethnicity is a difficult term to conceptualize, it seems reasonable
to also pay attention to a more specific dimension of ethnicity, namely linguistic cleavages. Here, too, we have some difficulties in drawing the line
between separate languages and dialects of the same language. Again, I
am at the mercy of the sources used. A language group is thus regarded as
distinct from other language groups if the sources used consider them to
be distinct (Anckar *et al.* 2002: 2–3).

In order to measure the impact of ethnic and linguistic fragmentation
on the dependent variable, we need to construct an index. The most
widely used measure of fragmentation is the index of fractionalization proposed by Douglas Rae and Michael Taylor (1970: 24–27). Their index is
calculated according to the following formula:

$$F = 1 - \Sigma p_i^2$$

where p_i is the share of persons belonging to category i.

Rae and Taylor's measure varies between 0 and 1. Values close to 0
imply a low degree of fragmentation, whereas values approaching 1
denote a high level of fragmentation.

We still have to confront the question of how to deal with persons
belonging to small ethnic or linguistic groups, in the sources used, these
are generally labeled "others". Obviously, this group should not be treated
as one homogeneous group, but rather be thought to consist of many small
heterogeneous groups. One alternative is to make the assumption that the
"others" group is maximally heterogeneous, meaning that every individual
is ethnically or linguistically distinct. This assumption is, of course, not
correct either; the group is heterogeneous but not to such an extent.
However, the application of this strategy does not affect the reliability of

the measurement since the number of persons listed in the "others" category is generally very low.

Religion

So far, I have only considered cleavages along ethnic or linguistic lines. I now turn to another base of group formation that is likely to affect the use of the death penalty, namely religion. As a result of the process of secularization, the impact of religion on society in general has been steadily declining, especially in the western world. Still, in many parts of the world, the life of the citizens is highly determined by religion. In fact, the secularization that has taken place in Western Europe during the last few decades is yet to be seen in the majority of the countries in the world. It does indeed seem odd that at the same time as the importance of religion declines within families and communities, its impact on a variety of political phenomena at an inter-state level remains intact.

There are two aspects of religion that can be considered relevant for the study of the determinants of the death penalty. First, religious cleavages are expected to affect the use of the death penalty in the same way as ethnic cleavages. In other words, we assume that if there are many religious denominations represented within a country, the country is likely to experience tensions between the various religious groups. Such tensions can, if the worst comes to the worst, erupt into acts of violence, or even civil war, as the case of Northern Ireland bluntly illustrates. Following the line of reasoning that applied for ethnic heterogeneity, we expect that there is a link between religious fragmentation and the death penalty. In a violent society, one method of controlling the amount of violence is to make use of severe punishments. Therefore, one can expect the death penalty to be in frequent use in societies marked by religious cleavages.

Contrary to the case with the operationalization of ethnic fragmentation, it is fairly easy to tackle the question of religious heterogeneity. To use Sartori's (1970) terms, religion is a concept that generally at least, "travels well", meaning that the different religions are more or less the same in every corner of the world. In other words, the different religions can be considered universal; Catholicism is Catholicism irrespective of whether we are in Latin America or in Oceania. The religions of the world can be broadly classified into six major categories: Christians, Jews, Muslims, Hindus, Buddhists and indigenous beliefs (see Nikolainen and Raittila 1970). This classification, however, is not satisfying. As we know, there are substantial differences within the categories. Take, for instance, the serious conflict between Catholics and Protestants in Northern Ireland or the clash between Shia Muslims and Sunni Muslims in some Islamic countries. Therefore the six categories have to be split up further.

Consequently, Christians are split up into Catholics, Protestants and East Orthodox Christians. As concerns Muslims, Sunni Muslims are separated from Shia Muslims. Buddhists are split up into Mahayana-Buddhists, Hinayana-Buddhists and Lamaists. Regarding Jews and Hindus, no further classification is needed. Since the six original religions do not exhaust all religions in the world, there are a few other religions that are regarded as separate categories (such as Shintoism in Japan and Taoism in China). Concerning the indigenous beliefs, these can, of course, vary quite a lot from country to country. However, the sources used do not provide us with enough information about these religions to render further categorization possible. Thus, all religions that are classified as indigenous beliefs are regarded as one homogeneous religion. Having done this categorization, it is easy to construct an index of religious fragmentation according to the same formula used for calculating the level of ethnic and linguistic fragmentation.

There is, however, another aspect of religion, which at least intuitively appears to be more important for the death penalty than the degree of religious diversity. This assumption departs from the belief that different religions take different approaches to the death penalty. Some religions oppose the use of capital punishment, whereas others accept, or even encourage, its use. One important dividing line immediately calls on our attention, namely the one between Muslim countries and Christian countries. One noteworthy difference between Christianity and Islam lies in the concept of *Umma*, the Muslim society. Islam is all-encompassing; rules for social, economic, cultural, political and religious organizations are laid out, and virtually every aspect of life is regulated by the *Sharia*. In contrast, Christianity does not aspire to encompass every aspect of life. The Kingdom of God cannot be established or maintained by political means, and Jesus Christ was accordingly never considered a political leader (Kateregga and Shenk 1983: 82). The intermixture of the religious and judicial spheres is crucial for the relation between Islam and the death penalty. It is evident that, compared to Christianity, the attitude of Islam toward the death penalty is very consistent. The *Sharia* lays down the principle of an eye for an eye. For Islam, it is thus evident that the attitude toward the death penalty goes far beyond that of a silent acceptance, as the *Sharia* clearly prescribes that the death penalty should be applied for a variety of crimes.

Although far from all Muslim countries apply the *Sharia* strictly, we can nevertheless expect Muslim countries to have a more positive view of the death penalty than countries where other religions are in a dominant position. In a like manner, we can expect Christian countries to be less favorably disposed toward capital punishment than Muslim countries. The Christian attitude toward the use of the death penalty is actually quite ambivalent. When one reads the Ten Commandments it immediately becomes clear that capital punishment is incompatible with Christianity. The sixth commandment laconically states "You shall not kill". On the other hand, the Bible also lays down the principle of an eye for an eye and tells us that "whoever shed the blood of man, by man shall his blood be shed" (Genesis 9:6). In a historical perspective, it is not an overstatement to say that the Catholic Church in particular has taken a very flexible attitude toward the sixth commandment. Let me here only mention the terrifying examples of the witch-hunts and the Holy Wars. In recent years, however, the Catholic Church has become a fierce opponent of the death penalty, which is manifested not least by recurrent protests by Pope John Paul II against the enforcement of death sentences. In the revised Catechism, the attitude toward the death penalty is critical to say the least. On the one hand, it is acknowledged that capital punishment is possible "if this is the only possible way of effectively defending human lives against the unjust aggressor". However, it is furthermore stated that "[t]oday ... the cases in which the execution of the offender is an absolute necessity 'are very rare, if not practically non-existent'" (Catechism 2267; John Paul II, *Evangelium vitae* 56).

Concerning the different Christian denominations, assumptions of if and how they differ with regard to the death penalty are not easy to make. True, fundamental differences between Protestants and Catholics can be found. One such difference concerns the attitude toward religious authorities. The Catholic Church has a rigid power structure, with the Pope on top of the worldly hierarchy. In contrast, the Protestant denominations are marked by highly egalitarian power structures, where the priests are in no way closer to God than other people of Christian faith (see Lundell 2000: 55). A famous argument, which can be traced back to Weber, asserts that Protestantism, since it incites individuality, emphasizes tolerance and stands for freedom from prejudice, constitutes a better breeding ground for a democratic form of government than Catholicism (Weber 1978; Lipset 1959: 85; Lenski and Lenski 1974: 349). The differences between the Catholic Church and the Protestant Church notwithstanding, it is still difficult to come up with reasons for why Catholics and Protestants would differ with regard to the death penalty. A reasonable assumption is thus that countries with a Christian population have a more restrictive attitude toward the death penalty than countries where other religions dominate, but that differences between Catholic countries and Protestant countries with regard to the attitude toward capital punishment are unlikely to exist.

Judaism bears many similarities to Christianity. The fundamental difference between Jews and Christians is the Christian belief that Jesus Christ was the incarnation of God. The New Testament in some cases rejects the principle of "an eye for an eye", and instead urges people to "turn the other cheek" (Matthew 5:38–39). Since the New Testament is not recognized in Judaism, one could argue that the right to make use of the death penalty is sanctioned to a higher extent in Judaism than in Christianity. Furthermore, the *Torah*, the Jewish law, prescribes the death penalty for a number of offenses (Braybrooke, 2003).

In contrast to many other religions, Buddhism does not include the notion of "god". Another distinctive feature of Buddhism is that it is extremely individualistic. The individual should strive for moral and spiritual improvement by following the *Noble Eightfold Path*. Buddhism appears to take a negative stand to the death penalty. A cornerstone in Buddhism is the *panca-sila*, or the five precepts. The first of these is the training rule of abstaining from taking life (Horigan 1996: 275), which effectively seems to ban all form of executions. Other rules against the use of the death penalty are found in the *Dharmapada*, a collection of aphorisms. In Chapter 10 we learn that "[e]veryone fears punishment; everyone fears death, just as you do. Therefore do not kill or cause to kill. Everyone fears punishment; everyone loves life, as you do. Therefore do not kill or cause to kill" (cited in Horigan 1996: 277). The negative attitude of Buddhism toward the taking of life is not only limited to humans. Indeed, a strict interpretation of the rule not to kill would, for instance, mean that for a Buddhist there is no alternative to vegetarianism (see Horigan 1996: 275).

As was the case with Christianity and Judaism, the Hindu position toward the death penalty is ambivalent. On the one hand, the ancient *Dharmasasbras* prescribes the death penalty for a wide range of crimes. The use of the death penalty is not confined to crimes resulting in the death of another human being. On the other hand, the *Mahabharatha* (Chapter 257 of the *Santiparva*) takes an opposite view toward the killing of a human being as a form of punishment. There are also additional factors in Hinduism which speak against the death penalty. One of these is the spirit of *Ahimsa*, the belief that it is wrong to hurt any living being. Another is the Hindu requirement that in order to be restored to society, criminals not only have to suffer a punishment but also expiate their guilt. Thus, it can be argued that, if the death penalty is applied, the criminal is deprived of the possibility to expiate his or her guilt (Braybrooke, 2003).

It is therefore necessary to give a qualitative assessment of religion. As a point of departure, I argue that most countries have one religion that is in a dominant position. The identification of this religion is relatively easy in most cases. The crucial factor is the number of citizens that adhere to a specific religion. For countries where more than half of the population share the same religion, it goes without saying that this religion should be regarded the most important one in the country. For countries where no religion has the support of the majority of the population, I have regarded the religion that has the largest number of followers as the dominating one. When separating the religions from each other, I have made use of the same bases of classification that applied when I calculated the index of religious fragmentation.

Empirical evidence

We are now ready to empirically assess the impact of ethnic and religious fragmentation on capital punishment. Since the ethnic and religious composition of a country is unlikely to change dramatically in fifteen years, the values on the independent variable are the same in 1985 and in 2000. Since I have assumed that both ethnic and religious fragmentation has the same effect on the dependent variable, it is also necessary to account for the overall level of fragmentation. Consequently, I combine the two dimensions of fragmentation into an index of ethnic–religious fragmentation by adding the index of ethnic or linguistic fragmentation to the index of religious fragmentation. Since ethnic and linguistic cleavages tend to go hand-in-hand, the three measures cannot be added. Instead, for each country I have chosen to consider either the index of ethnic or linguistic fragmentation. For each country, the index which yields the highest value is added to the index of religious fragmentation. Admittedly, this measure still suffers from a shortcoming in that it fails to distinguish between "cross-cutting" and "reinforcing" cleavages. The statistical references from which data on the two dimensions have been collected do not provide information on to what extent ethnic or linguistic cleavages go hand-in-hand with religious cleavages. In some countries (Sri Lanka, for example), ethnic/linguistic cleavages coincide with religious ones, whereas in other countries ethnic/linguistic and religious cleavages run across each other, as is the case, for instance, in Canada and Switzerland.

Now, consider two countries, A and B. In the former country, 50 percent of the population belongs to one ethnic group and 50 percent to another. Furthermore, suppose that half of the population adheres to one religion and the other half to another. However, the ethnic and the religious cleavages coincide perfectly, leaving us with two equally large groups that differ in two respects. Now, consider country B. Similarly to country A, it is ethnically divided between two groups, each making up 50 percent of the population. In terms of religion, the country is also split up into two equally large groups. However, this time the ethnic and religious lines cross each other perfectly, dividing the country into four equally large groups. When calculating the level of ethnic–religious fragmentation for the two countries we come up with the same result for countries A and B. Admittedly, this is a weakness for which it is hard to find a remedy. Nevertheless, I argue that by using all three measures of fragmentation, I have, to the best of my ability, covered myself against problems that occur from not knowing to what extent the cleavages are "cross-cutting" or "reinforcing".

Tables 2.3 and 2.4 provide results from statistical analyses of the impact of ethnic and religious fragmentation on the death penalty. The results indicate that there is a weak association between ethnic/religious fragmentation and the death penalty. The higher the degree of fragmentation, the stronger the inclination to make use of the death penalty. It is worth noting that the combined index of ethnic/linguistic and religious fragmentation possesses more explanatory power than its three components separately in 1985. However, in 2000, the index of religious fragmentation is a slightly more powerful determinant of the death penalty than the combined index. The strength of association was much stronger in 1985 than in 2000, which seems to indicate that the explanatory power of ethnic/religious fragmentation is declining over time.

We then turn to the other dimension of religion, that is, the dominating religion of the country. Table 2.5 gives the results of a comparison of means test between the different religions. To avoid too many categories with only a few cases, I have not split up Buddhism and Islam in their subcategories. The results clearly show that religion is a strong determinant of the death penalty. As expected, countries where Islam is the dominant religion make extensive use of capital punishment. In 1985, all of the countries classified as Islamic made use of the death penalty. In six of these countries – Brunei, Comoros, Djibouti, Ivory Coast, Maldives and Senegal – no execution had taken place for a period of ten years or more. In contrast, all countries that were abolitionist for all crimes were Christian. At the same time it should, however, be emphasized that there were still

Table 2.3 Associations between ethnic, linguistic, religious fragmentation and capital punishment in 1985 (bivariate regressions)

	B	*Beta*	*T-value*	R^2	N
Index of ethnic fragmentation	0.936	0.271	3.622**	0.074	167
Index of linguistic fragmentation	0.815	0.275	3.653**	0.076	165
Index of religious fragmentation	1.030	0.267	3.586**	0.071	169
Index of ethnic–religious fragmentation	0.636	0.290	3.910**	0.084	168

Notes
**Significance at the $p < 0.01$ level.
*Significance at the $p < 0.05$ level.

Table 2.4 Associations between ethnic, linguistic, religious fragmentation and capital punishment in 2000 (bivariate regressions)

	B	Beta	T-value	R^2	N
Index of ethnic fragmentation	0.718	0.165	2.298*	0.027	190
Index of linguistic fragmentation	0.611	0.162	2.239*	0.026	188
Index of religious fragmentation	1.060	0.226	3.197**	0.051	192
Index of ethnic– religious fragmentation	0.619	0.223	3.147**	0.050	191

Notes
**Significance at the $p < 0.01$ level.
*Significance at the $p < 0.05$ level.

more Christian countries that made use of the death penalty than there were Christian countries that had abolished it in all its forms.

By 2000, several changes had occurred. It was not only Christian countries that had abolished the death penalty in all its forms. Many Islamic countries have refrained from carrying out executions for a period exceeding ten years, and four countries with Muslim majorities – Azerbaijan, Djibouti, Ivory Coast and Turkmenistan – had abolished the death penalty completely. Of the three countries with a Hindu majority, only one makes use of the death penalty for ordinary crimes (India) whereas the other two (Mauritius and Nepal) had abolished the death penalty completely. The

Table 2.5 Dominating religion and capital punishment (arithmetic means)

Dominating religion	1985	2000
Protestantism	1.55 (35)	1.28 (38)
Catholicism	1.29 (58)	0.72 (65)
Eastern Orthodox	2.20 (6)	1.10 (12)
Judaism	1.00 (1)	1.00 (1)
Islam	2.42 (43)	2.25 (50)
Buddhism	2.35 (11)	2.23 (11)
Hinduism	2.23 (3)	0.87 (3)
Shintoism	2.50 (1)	2.70 (1)
Confucianism	2.90 (1)	2.90 (1)
Indigenous beliefs	2.42 (10)	1.77 (10)
Eta squared	0.291	0.317
Sig.	0.000	0.000
N	169	192

Note
N in parentheses.

most surprising result is perhaps the inclination of Buddhist countries to make extensive use of the death penalty. This is odd given the fact that, in the teachings of Buddha, the death penalty is rejected more explicitly than in any of the other major religions. The only Buddhist country that has abolished the death penalty for all crimes is Cambodia, whereas Bhutan, Laos, Myanmar and Sri Lanka have not executed anyone for a substantial number of years. It is also worth pointing out the change that has occurred in the group of countries where a large part of the population adheres to indigenous beliefs. In 1985, the vast majority of the countries made regular use of the death penalty. The only exception was Madagascar where no execution had taken place for ten years or more. By the year 2000, Guinea-Bissau had moved to the category of abolitionist countries and was joined here by Mozambique (which accommodates a large population with a Christian faith).

Religious fragmentation in itself does not explain variations in the death penalty. Instead the results show, with desirable clarity, that the dominating religion is a powerful determinant of the death penalty. It is also worth noting that several changes have occurred in fifteen years. In 1985, only Christian countries had abolished the death penalty completely. In 2000, a somewhat different picture emerges. Countries with a dominant religion other than Christianity also forbid or restrict the use of capital punishment. It is also worth mentioning that the abolitionist movement is riding on the crest of the wave, particularly in Catholic countries. In 1985, 29 percent of the Protestant countries were abolitionist; the corresponding value for the Catholic countries was approximately the same at 33 percent. However, in 2000, 42 percent of the Protestant countries were abolitionist, whereas the proportion of abolitionist Catholic countries had risen to 65 percent.

Although the dominance of Islam or Buddhism appears to be an extremely important explanatory factor of the death penalty, there are still countries that contradict the assumption of an association between these religions and the use of capital punishment. These countries are listed in Table 2.6. A quick glance at the Islamic countries that contradict the rule that Islam goes hand-in-hand with a favorable stand toward the death penalty reveals that they are all geographically located outside the core area of Islam, i.e. the Middle East. In these countries, the grip of Islam on society is much looser than in countries incorporating, or close to, holy locations such as Mecca and Medina. Concerning the Buddhist exceptions, common characteristics are more difficult to come up with. However, Cambodia's status as an abolitionist country is explained by historical uniqueness, more specifically with its tragic experiences in the last few decades. The case of Cambodia is discussed more thoroughly in Chapter 3 (pages 115–116).

Table 2.6 Islamic and Buddhist abolitionist countries in two periods of time

Islamic or Buddhist countries which had completely abolished the death penalty in 1985	*Islamic or Buddhist countries which had completely abolished the death penalty in 2000*
None	Azerbaijan (I) Cambodia (B) Djibouti (I) Ivory Coast (I) Turkmenistan (I)
Islamic or Buddhist countries which were abolitionist for ordinary crimes only in 1985	*Islamic or Buddhist countries which were abolitionist for ordinary crimes only in 2000*
None	Albania (I) Bosnia-Herzegovina (I)
Islamic or Buddhist countries where no executions had taken place for a period of ten years in 1985	*Islamic or Buddhist countries where no executions had taken place for a period of ten years in 2000*
Bhutan (B) Brunei (I) Comoros (I) Djibouti (I) Ivory Coast (I) Maldives (I) Senegal (I)	Bhutan (B) Brunei (I) Burkina Faso (I) Eritrea (I) Gambia (I) Guinea (I) Laos (B) Maldives (I) Mali (I) Mauritania (I) Myanmar (B) Niger (I) Senegal (I) Sri Lanka (B) Turkey (I)

Notes
B = Buddhist.
I = Islamic.

Development, security and dependency

Socioeconomic development

Although the idealist view of the pioneers of the so-called modernization school (Lerner 1958; Deutsch 1961) has been modified during the last decades, the assumption of a link between modernization and politics is ever-present in political science. For instance, studies indicate that there is an association between industrialization and urbanization on the one hand, and mass political participation on the other (Allardt and Rokkan 1970). Another finding shows that affluence in combination with other indicators of economic development constitutes the most important determinant of state stability and performance (Lane and Ersson 1994).

The most frequently cited and explored finding maintains that modernization and development lead to a better breeding ground for a democratic form of government. The assumption was first put forward, tested and confirmed by Seymour Martin Lipset (1959). Lipset operated with 15 independent variables, all of which where indicators of wealth, industrialization, education and urbanization. Separate analyses were conducted for Europe and Latin America. His conclusion was that wealth, industrialization, education and urbanization were all related to democracy. Ever since, his hypotheses have been re-tested and verified in a number of studies. In a worldwide test of Lipset's theory, Larry Diamond (1992) reached results that gave evident support for Lipset's findings. Earlier on, similar results had been obtained by Cutright (1963); Needler (1967); Olsen (1968); Flanigan and Fogelman (1971); and Bollen (1979, 1983). There is also evidence that shows purely economic indicators do not contain as much explanatory power as other indicators of development. In his impressive works of the prerequisites of democratization, Tatu Vanhanen has emphasized the importance of the struggle of power resources for democracy. According to Vanhanen (1984, 1990), a balanced distribution of power resources nurtures a democratic form of government. In his study of 132 developing states, Axel Hadenius (1992: 89) found that "the proportion of the population who can read is clearly the most decisive of the different measurements of the degree of socioeconomic development".

Even though there is strong evidence of a link between socioeconomic development and democracy, this does not necessarily mean that we should find a corresponding link between socioeconomic development and capital punishment. Some arguments that endorse the existence of such a link can nevertheless be put forward. Opponents of the death penalty often refer to it as a barbaric and cruel form of punishment. Implicitly at least, it is assumed that well-educated people would dissociate themselves from such a thing. There is also a purely economic aspect, albeit perhaps a rather far-fetched one, which speaks in favor of the presumed relation between development and capital punishment. The drift of this argument is that it is far more expensive to keep a prisoner alive in prison than it is to kill him or her. In countries where a majority of the population live under difficult conditions, and some even encounter starvation, it is not impossible that the feeding and housing of murderers is seen as an unnecessary and perhaps even provocative gesture.

Socioeconomic development comprises several dimensions. Authors generally rely on GDP/cap or GNP/cap as an indicator of economic development. Although this measure is in no way a perfect indicator of economic development (see Dogan 1994: 44–46) it is very useful indeed in situations where the research population comprises all countries in the world. Reliable information is easily obtained, and the measure is fairly robust. Admittedly, we should also pay regard to aspects other than the purely economic. One must also take into account of how the level of affluence is distributed in a country. If there are severe cleavages between the rich and the poor, this means that the society may suffer from tensions. The overall level of affluence is, of course, a necessary prerequisite of economic equality. In order to establish a welfare state, there has to be something to distribute among the population. Therefore we need a measure of income distribution. Measures of income distribution are often unreliable, particularly in a worldwide comparison. One frequently used measure is the proportion of income earned by households constituting the highest decile, i.e. the wealthiest 10 percent in a country. Another variant of this measure is the proportion of the population falling within the lowest decile (or quintile). Within the framework of the present study, income distribution is measured according to the first-mentioned strategy. Unfortunately, for many countries, data concerning income distribution is difficult to come across, and the number of missing cases is accordingly substantial.

Urbanization is another measure frequently used as an indicator of socioeconomic development. Urbanization is expected to correlate with the GDP/cap. However, compared to the GDP/cap, the degree of urbanization is a better measurement of the dispersion of economic power resources (Vanhanen 1990: 52). I therefore include the degree of urbanization among the measures of socioeconomic development.

The GDP/cap, the index of income inequality and the degree of urbanization are purely economic measures. Socioeconomic development, however, encompasses another dimension as well, namely quality of life. Although these two dimensions are linked to each other, some important differences still exist. Quality of life is a more ambiguous term than standard of living, and the operationalization is accordingly difficult, especially with regard to worldwide comparisons. Values highly appreciated in one context can be considered less important in another. Nevertheless, some general measures stand out as more or less self-evident expressions of quality of life. One such indicator is infant mortality and another is the level of education, which I operationalize by the percentage of the population that is able to read. Consequently, five variables are used to express socioeconomic development. Three of these – the GDP/cap, income distribution and degree of urbanization – are used as indicators of purely economic aspects of development, whereas the other two – infant mortality and literacy – are seen as indicators of quality of life.

Empirical evidence

Tables 2.7 and 2.8 show the results of bivariate regressions between the independent and the dependent variables in the two respective points in time. We find that there is indeed a strong association between socioeconomic indicators and the use of the death penalty. Only income inequality is irrelevant for explaining variations in the death penalty. The association between the socioeconomic variables and the dependent variable are stronger in 1985 than in 2000.

The examination conducted thus far has revealed several significant associations between independent and dependent variables. At the beginning of the chapter, I made a distinction between purely economic indicators and social indicators of development. Based on the results, it is difficult to reach a conclusion as to which of the indicators are the most important. For instance, the regression coefficients for urbanization, infant mortality and literacy are almost identical, approximately $(-)0.01$. Urbanization and literacy are expressed in percentage points, meaning that an increase in the degree of urbanization or a decrease in literacy by one percentage point reduces the readiness to resort to the death penalty by 0.01 units. The explanatory power of infant mortality, which measures the death rate of infants per 1,000 births, is approximately the same.

Due to the high level of interrelatedness of the variables, they cannot be incorporated in a multiple regression analysis. However, since both the economic indicators as well as the indicators of quality of life turned out to be relevant in the bivariate analyses, a sensible strategy is to use one single measure, which captures both dimensions of socioeconomic development. Such a measure is the frequently used United Nations' Human Develop-

Table 2.7 Association between socioeconomic development and capital punishment in 1985 (bivariate regressions)

	B	Beta	T-value	R^2	N
GDP/cap (log)	−0.226	−0.347	−4.764**	0.120	168
Income inequality	0.026	0.223	1.860	0.050	68
Urbanization	−0.014	−0.377	−5.264**	0.142	169
Infant mortality	0.008	0.406	5.719**	0.165	168
Literacy	−0.013	−0.402	−5.667**	0.161	169

Notes
**Significance at the $p < 0.01$ level.
*Significance at the $p < 0.05$ level.

Table 2.8 Association between socioeconomic development and capital punishment in 2000 (bivariate regressions)

	B	Beta	T-value	R²	N
GDP/cap (log)	−0.339	−0.327	−4.750**	0.107	191
Income inequality	0.032	0.248	2.786**	0.062	120
Urbanization	−0.013	−0.259	−3.699**	0.067	192
Infant mortality	0.010	0.307	4.442**	0.095	191
Literacy	−0.014	−0.276	−3.953**	0.076	192

Notes
**Significance at the $p<0.01$ level.
*Significance at the $p<0.05$ level.

ment Index (HDI). The only drawback is that numbers are not available for all countries of the world. Particularly for the situation in 1985, the number of missing cases is substantial. Tables 2.9 and 2.10 return the results of bivariate regressions between HDI and the death penalty in the two points of time.

The results are easy to interpret. HDI is a very important determinant of the death penalty. The variance explained by HDI is higher than the variance explained by any of the other socioeconomic indicators. Again, we note that the explanatory value of HDI is much higher in 1985 than in 2000. HDI varies between 0 and 1, and an increase of this magnitude yields a decrease in the dependent variable by almost all its range of variation.

Crime, conflict and corruption

Crime

Advocates of the death penalty frequently mention the deterrent effect capital punishment is thought to have as the most important argument for the use of the death penalty. The deterrent effect of the death penalty is a highly controversial issue and it often seems as if neither proponents nor

Table 2.9 Association between human development index and capital punishment in 1985 (bivariate regression)

	B	Beta	T-value	R²	N
HDI	−2.688	−0.508	−6.190**	0.258	112

Notes
**Significance at the $p<0.01$ level.
*Significance at the $p<0.05$ level.

Table 2.10 Association between human development index and capital punishment in 2000 (bivariate regression)

	B	*Beta*	*T-value*	R^2	N
HDI	−2.220	−0.335	−4.642**	0.112	173

Notes
**Significance at the $p < 0.01$ level.
*Significance at the $p < 0.05$ level.

opponents of the death penalty are ready to discuss the object unconditionally. It is, no doubt, essential to take a closer look at the association between capital punishment and deterrence. Proponents of the death penalty argue that the threat of being executed prevents would-be killers from carrying out capital crimes. Opponents of the death penalty, on their part, argue that the deterrent effect of the death penalty is a chimera and that the threat of capital punishment does not prevent criminals from carrying out violent crimes. Not surprisingly, the empirical evidence at hand is equivocal. A striking feature is that very few empirical studies of the deterrent effect of the death penalty have been conducted outside the USA (a few, but highly unreliable, results are cited by Hood 1996: 180–181). As stated earlier, one useful way of analyzing the deterrent effect of capital punishment is to compare homicide rates before and after the abolition of the death penalty. Such a cross-country study was conducted by Archer, Gartner and Beittel (1983). Homicide rates were compared before and after the year of abolition of the death penalty for ordinary crimes for Austria, Canada, Denmark, England and Wales, Finland, Israel, Italy, Netherland Antilles, Norway, Sweden, and Switzerland. The results showed that there was no clear-cut link between homicide rates and capital punishment.

Bohm (1999: 85–90) provides a detailed account of empirical studies conducted within the USA. The pioneering work was done by Thorsten Sellin (1959, 1967). Sellin compared homicide death rates in states where capital punishment was in place with homicide death rates in states where capital punishment was not used. In order to minimize the influence of intervening variables, Sellin compared contiguous states. His findings showed that the use of capital punishment had no deterrent effect whatsoever. The lack of the deterrent effect has subsequently been confirmed by Peterson and Bailey (1988, 1998).

The results from the studies cited above suggest that capital punishment does not have a deterrent effect. However, empirical studies which point in a different direction have also been conducted. In a famous study, Isaac Erlich (1975) found evidence of a link between execution risk and murders. Contrary to Sellin, Erlich made use of multiple regression analysis and was consequently able to control for the impact of many other variables that could affect the relation between execution risk and murders. Erlich's results were subsequently confirmed in a number of other studies (e.g. Erlich 1977; Cloninger 1977; Layson 1985), but also falsified in other studies (e.g. Forst 1977; Decker and Kohfeld 1990). The evidence thus suggests that, although the deterrent effect cannot be totally dismissed as irrelevant, there are no watertight proofs that such an effect really exists.

In fact, one cannot rule out the possibility that the death penalty has the opposite effect, namely that executions of individuals actually increases homicide rates. This is called the *brutalizing effect*. Bohm (1999: 94) lists several explanations for this presumed effect. For persons who wish to commit suicide, but are too afraid to actually carry out the suicide, the death penalty is a way of overcoming the problem. People thus commit murders in order to receive the death penalty. This is called the "suicide–murder syndrome". Another explanation labeled "the executioner syndrome" refers to situations where those executed believe their killing eliminates a problem. Others have "a pathological desire to die by execution" whereas a final category consists of those who become killers in order to gain public attention and become famous. An eventual execution is, of course, the final stage in such a process. Again, the empirical evidence is ambiguous. Bowers and Pierce (1980) found support for the brutalizing effect and were able to show that the number of homicides grew significantly following an execution in the state of New York between 1906 and 1963. Other studies (e.g. Phillips 1980; Phillips and Hensley 1984), however, point in a different direction, indicating that there is a short-term deterrent effect following an execution, but that this effect fades away as time goes by.

Even though it is more or less impossible to draw any far reaching conclusions as to whether or not capital punishment has a deterrent effect, a brutalizing effect or no effect at all on homicide rates, it is still possible to establish whether or not there is a link between the overall level of crimes, in particular capital crimes, and the use of the death penalty. The expectation is that states with high levels of crime are likely to resort to severe punishments in order to uphold law and order. In such countries, capital punishment would be seen as a means of reducing the number of crimes. In other words, where crimes in general and murders in particular are frequent, the government is thought to resort to tough measures against the criminals. In states with a low level of crime, the need to resort to the ultimate form of punishment is lower. Therefore states that are not affected by high crime rates could afford to forbid the use of the death penalty.

The question of whether there is a link between high levels of crime and the use of capital punishment is, however, more complicated than any other variable-relation discussed so far. What distinguishes the level of crime from the other potential independent variables is that we now have a problem of establishing the causal link between the independent variable and the dependent variable. If a country has a high level of crime, this might be a consequence of many circumstances (poverty, scarcity of resources and so on). We then expect this high level of crime to result in a decision to allow and perhaps make use of the death penalty. The problem is that we ought to know exactly if and to what extent the use of the death penalty deters criminals from conducting capital crimes. If there is a deterrent effect, then the use of the death penalty would reduce the number of homicides in particular and, perhaps, the level of crime in general. This problem of causality is illustrated in Figure 2.1.

A natural point of departure is that governments, when deciding whether or not to make use of the death penalty, *believe* that the death penalty has a deterrent effect. Consequently, we would expect a country to resort to the use of capital punishment more easily if the level of crime is high. If our empirical analysis shows that the level of crime is *not* related to the death penalty, a possible explanation is that countries with capital punishment have a lower level of crime due to the deterrent effect of the death penalty. In other words we measure the association at a point in time when the deterrent effect has already had a chance to affect the relation between the use of capital punishment and the level of crime. Another explanation is, of course, that there is no, and never has been, any link between the use of the death penalty and the level of crime. The problem is that it is difficult to make sure that the analysis is conducted at that particular point of time where the first relationship in Figure 2.1 is accounted for, i.e. that the level of crime constitutes a determinant and not a consequence of the use of the death penalty.

If, on the other hand, we do find an association between the death penalty and the level of crime, the picture is somewhat clearer. If the association is negative, i.e. if the use of the death penalty is associated with low crime rates, we can assume that the death penalty reduces crime (given our theoretical point of departure which states that governments of countries affected by high crime rates are particularly positive toward the use of capital punishment). If the association is positive, i.e. if the use of the death penalty coincides with high levels of crime, the conclusion must be that countries that are highly affected by crimes make use of the death penalty to a higher extent than other countries. If this is the case, it is also

Figure 2.1 Possible association between the level of crime and capital punishment.

probable that the death penalty does not have any significant deterrent effect. Such a conclusion, however, cannot be drawn with certitude since we do not know how high the crime rates would have been had the death penalty not been in force.

Now, since the object of the present study is to identify the determinants of the death penalty, we do not actually have to tackle the question of its deterrent effect. Instead, within the framework of the present study, I restrict myself to answering the question of whether countries with a high level of crime employ the death penalty to a higher extent than countries with a low level of crime. It is worth emphasizing that the result of such an analysis does not necessarily answer the question of whether or not capital punishment has a deterrent effect on the level of crime. To answer that question we need to make analyses within countries which have imposed the death penalty at some stage in their history. Only by comparing the level of crime prior to the date of installation or abolition of the death penalty with the level of crime after that date is it possible to generalize about the deterrent effect of capital punishment.

Before we can empirically assess the relation between the level of crime and the death penalty, we need to discuss measurements of crime. Now, when discussing the deterrent effect of the death penalty, scholars generally refer to homicides. It is once again worth pointing out that the issue of deterrence is not primarily in focus in the present study. However, it does seem appropriate to make the assumption that the death penalty is used as a means of dealing with high levels of capital crimes in a society. On the other hand, we cannot rule out the possibility that there is also a connection between the overall level of crime and the death penalty. If crime rates in general are high, this is likely to affect the general level of security in the country. One way to come to grips with the problem is of course to apply severe punishments. Accordingly, I expect the use of the death penalty to correlate with both the level of crime and the level of homicides, in particular with murders. The overall level of crime is operationalized as the number of offenses reported to the police per 100,000 inhabitants. The other measure used is the number of murders reported to the police per 100,000 inhabitants. Unfortunately data concerning the number of murders is not available for 1985. The number of cases for which data on total offenses was available is also rather limited for the same point in time.

Conflict

In addition to the assumed association between the death penalty and the level of crime, other aspects of security can be thought to influence the attitude toward the death penalty. Considering all forms of punishment that are used throughout the world, including various forms of corporal punishment, the death penalty is no doubt the most violent and brutal punishment that exists. The degree of violence can vary to some extent depending on the form of execution, but we cannot escape the fact that the victim is killed contrary to his or her will. Now, it is an indisputable fact that the countries of the world show a great variation in terms of how much violence they have experienced in the past. In some countries, such as Sweden and Switzerland, we have to go very far back in time to confront a generation that has experienced a war. In other countries – and unfortunately these countries are not few in numbers – violence and killing are a part of daily life.

It is highly plausible that the attitude toward the taking of a human life is dependent on how familiar the citizens are with death, and especially with the killing of human beings. People who have fought on battlefields, seen their friends and families die by the hands of fellow human beings and/or killed or taken part in killings themselves are, perhaps, not very likely to regard the death penalty as a highly cruel and unjust form of punishment. Turning the picture around, people that have grown up under secure conditions and have no experience of organized violence may have a very different attitude toward the taking of a life. For a person who has grown up under such circumstances, the killing of a human being is a brutal, execrable act that lies far beyond the power of imagination.

Finding measures of violence experience is neither easy nor impossible. There are three factors to be taken into consideration when measuring the level of violence: the intensity of the conflict, the duration of the conflict and the date of the conflict. The intensity of the conflict is perhaps the most important one. Simply put, a conflict where close to a million persons die, as was the case in Rwanda in the genocide of 1994, is much more intense than a conflict with only a couple of hundred victims. In addition to the intensity of the conflict, the duration is important. A conflict that continues for years is thought to affect the population more than a conflict that lasts for only a number of weeks. Finally, we have to pay regard to how far back in time the conflict occurred. A conflict that has taken place in the nineteenth century is less likely to have implications for the death penalty in the late twentieth and early twenty-first centuries than a conflict that has taken place in the 1970s.

Accounting for the duration and the moment of the conflict can be done relatively easy. However, the intensity of the conflict is more problematic. Fortunately, there is a solution. The Heidelberg Institute of International Conflict Research has created a database called KOSIMO (http://hiik.de/de/index_d.htm), in which the level of intensity of conflicts in the world from 1945 onwards is measured. Conflicts are classified into four categories depending on the intensity of the conflict:

1   latent conflicts, i.e. conflicts that are completely non-violent,
2   mostly non-violent crises,
3   mostly violent crises and
4   war, which is defined as "systematic, collective use of force by regular troops".

For the categorization of the various conflicts the research team has relied on an impressive number of sources.

For both practical and theoretical reasons I pay regard to conflicts that have taken place after 1945 only. On the one hand, the database used does not list conflicts beyond that year. This means that conflicts prior to that date would have to be classified into the four categories applying the same criteria, which, of course, would heavily increase the workload. Also, it is fair to assume that conflicts that have taken place prior to the Second World War are not decisive for the choice to make use of, or forbid the use of, the death penalty in the 1980s and early 2000s. Today, as well as in the mid-1980s, very few people in leading political positions can be thought to base their position toward the death penalty by occurrences that have taken place prior to the Second World War.

It is also necessary to put a limit on the duration of the conflict. This is a rather complicated matter. For instance, suppose we stipulate that a conflict must have lasted for one year in order to qualify as a "real" conflict. Accordingly, a conflict where thousands of people are killed in a few months is not classified as a "real" conflict, whereas a more drawn-out incident, which lasts for years but where relatively few persons are killed, is classified as one. Here, it is reasonable to assume that separate criteria apply for the separate categories. A war is likely to leave many unhealed wounds no matter how short its time-span. A latent conflict, on the other hand, cannot be expected to have an impact on the dependent variable if it has lasted only a few months (indeed, the concept of "latent" implies that the conflict has been going on for quite a while). It seems fair to apply separate time restrictions for the four categories. Consequently, wars and crises described as "mostly violent" are classified as such no matter how short the period of endurance. Concerning the other categories, a period of more than one year is required. Another thing that ought to be considered is the fact that several countries have been going through more than one crisis since the Second World War. For these countries, the most severe crisis determines the level of experiences with crises. We then obtain a variable, measured on the ordinal level. Countries with no experience of conflicts receive the value 0, countries where there have been latent conflicts the value 1, countries with mostly non-violent crises or mostly violent crises receive the values 2 and 3 respectively, whereas countries that have experienced wars receive the value 4.

Corruption

The concept of violence is, no doubt, important. However, it seems fair to also take notice of another aspect of insecurity. If people in general are insecure when dealing with each other and with authorities, it is quite possible that the criminal code is constructed in a more brutal way than otherwise. The argument is simple. When formal rules do not apply, people must resort to other means in a wide range of areas. In such systems, people are likely to constantly live under a feeling of insecurity. This insecurity is reflected in many areas of day-to-day life, such as in getting food on the table, arranging day care for the children or in getting the paycheck each month. Such unstable conditions often arise in situations where the powers of the government are limited and/or questioned by a large part of the population. Under such conditions, the relations between the citizens and the representatives of the government are likely to be strained. If, for instance, a crime like jaywalking can have virtually every consequence from nothing to a jail sentence, citizens are likely to regard the police and government officials as their enemies. At the same time, of course, the government is likely to feel insecure and threatened as well. As the stability of the system deteriorates, the government is likely to answer by resorting to more severe punishments for crimes. This is primarily done in order to keep the system working and, of course, in order to stay in power.

The underlying assumption, then, is that when people can rely on the authorities, the overall level of stability in the society increases. How are we then to grasp this phenomenon empirically? One useful measure is the level of corruption. If, for instance, many offenses can be overlooked in exchange for payments or by other forms of favors, this is likely to create an atmosphere of mistrust and frustration in many segments of the population. Evidently, finding reliable measures of the level of corruption for all countries in the world is not an easy task. However, a measure of corruption has been introduced by the German organization Transparency International. The organization provides a corruption perceptions index for a great many (but far from all) countries, thus making cross-country studies possible. The figures have been collected from the Internet (http://www.gwdg.de/~uwvw/histor.htm and http://www.transparency.de/documents/cpi/index.html). It should be noted that high values indicate a low level of corruption, whereas low values denote a high degree of corruption.

Empirical evidence

Tables 2.11 and 2.12 give the results of the two statistical analyses. In Table 2.11 the death penalty is regressed on the measures of security for

Table 2.11 Associations between measures of security and capital punishment in 1985 (bivariate regressions)

	B	Beta	T-value	R^2	N
Number of offenses (log)	−0.431	−0.484	−5.045**	0.235	85
Conflict intensity	0.162	0.265	3.530**	0.070	167
Corruption	−0.177	−0.430	−3.401**	0.185	53

Notes
**Significance at the $p < 0.01$ level.
*Significance at the $p < 0.05$ level.

the year 1985, while Table 2.12 gives the corresponding values for 2000. We discover that there is a strong negative association between the level of crime and the death penalty in 1985. The higher the level of crime, the lower the threshold of applying the death penalty. In 1985, 24 percent of the variation in the death penalty is explained by the level of crime, whereas the corresponding value for 2000 is approximately 9 percent. However, due to lack of data, comparisons over time should be interpreted with great caution. Surely, these results will not put an end to the everlasting discussion of the deterrent effect of the death penalty. Nevertheless, based on the empirical evidence at hand, it seems correct to conclude that countries that make use of the death penalty have a lower level of crime than countries that have abolished or restricted the use of the death penalty.

Results show that both conflict intensity and the level of corruption have an impact on the death penalty. As presumed, past experiences of conflicts as well as high levels of corruption go hand-in-hand with an extensive use of the death penalty. Corruption seems to be a very strong

Table 2.12 Associations between measures of security and capital punishment in 2000 (bivariate regressions)

	B	Beta	T-value	R^2	N
Murders	−0.005	−0.056	−0.683	0.003	151[1]
Number of offenses (log)	−0.210	−0.295	−3.875**	0.087	160
Conflict intensity	0.226	0.297	4.292**	0.088	192
Corruption	−0.197	−0.383	−4.057**	0.146	98

Notes
1 Excluding Rwanda, where the number of murders is many times higher than in any other country.
**Significance at the $p < 0.01$ level.
*Significance at the $p < 0.05$ level.

determinant of the death penalty. However, comparing the impact of corruption with the impact of the other independent variables is difficult due to the limited number of cases for which values on corruption are available.

Dependency

The 1950s saw the birth of the so-called modernization school in political science. According to the advocates of the development theory, differences in economic performance between developing countries and developed countries were only temporary. The economic development in the west, they argued, would inevitably lead to the spreading of wealth across countries, continents and cultures. David Lerner's *The Passing of Traditional Society* (1958) is frequently mentioned as a standard example of a work falling within this tradition. The dependency school arose mainly as a protest movement against this positive view of the future of the Third World. The representatives of the dependency school were mainly Latin American political scientists. They advocated the view that the structure of the international economy favored the developed nations and worked to the disadvantage of the poor states in the Third World. The development of Third World countries was dependent on the industrialized countries. While the industrialized countries could build their economy around manufactured high-quality goods, the poorer countries were destined to produce primary products. As a result of these structural differences, countries in the Third World have to rely on the export of one or a few primary products, the value of which are totally dependent on the demand of the product(s) in the industrialized world.

Although highly controversial, the dependency argument has given rise to many interesting studies about the relation between economic dependence and democracy. Kenneth Bollen (1983) found evidence suggesting that countries that were located in the economic periphery had a lower level of democracy than other countries. However, Bollen's results have subsequently been questioned by Mark Gasiorowski (1988) who, after having re-analyzed Bollen's data, concluded that "a simple, inverse relationship *does not* hold between economic dependence and political democracy" (Gasiorowski 1988: 508, italics in original).

It is fair to assume that the concept of dependence is of importance within the framework of the present study as well. It is probably fair to say that countries today are far more dependent and sensitive to the opinion of other countries than ever before. Naturally, this is primarily a consequence of the fall of the Soviet Union and its socialist satellites, which lifted the USA to the position of the only super power in the world. With the end of the Cold War, there was no longer a need for the USA to keep up suspicious but friendly regimes in all corners of the world and to turn a blind eye to various breaches against human rights. Accordingly, during the last few years many governments have discovered – often through rather painful experiences – that their room to maneuver is significantly smaller than before. The international law is today not the "paper tiger" it was sometimes described as, and it is probably fair to say that, during the 1990s, a new actor entered the arena of international politics. This actor is called "the international community". Particularly in speeches made by western politicians and in western media, this expression frequently recurs.

This form of dependence is very much related to the economic sphere. Economic sanctions are nowadays used as a weapon in order to change the mind of stubborn, hostile governments. In its most extreme form, this growing dependence on "the international community" expresses itself in times of severe breaches against human rights or when the sovereignty of states are threatened. The Gulf War and the crisis in the former Yugoslavia constitute the most extreme examples of such incidents. It has also become abundantly clear that the pressure to implement a democratic form of government has increased during the last decade. This is particularly the case with countries that are economically dependent on western powers, either as a consequence of structures in trade or by being dependent on subsidies. I argue that it is reasonable to expect that the choice of a country to either make use of, or forbid the use of, the death penalty is to some extent dependent on the opinions of other countries. However, this dependence is probably not as strong and unquestionable as the one concerning democracy. There is no consensus among the states in the western world that the death penalty should be abolished. Contrary to the question of what form of government is to be considered the most desirable, there is disagreement between the USA and the European Union on the justification for capital punishment. However, this does not mean that countries can act in total isolation with regard to the death penalty. A striking example was the death sentence imposed on Kurdish leader Abdullah Öcalan in Turkey. The reaction from the European Union was not long in coming. The message conveyed to Turkey was stated in clear terms: the execution of Öcalan will obstruct Turkey's possibilities of becoming a member of the European Union. As a consequence, Öcalan's death sentence was never carried out and, in 2002, the death penalty was abolished for ordinary crimes in Turkey.

Turning to the operationalization of dependence, we note that a wide range of measurements are possible. Four measurements stand out as the most widely used (Hadenius 1992: 93–94):

1 trade dependency (imports and exports related to GNP),
2 partner dependency (share of import or export that comes from or go to a certain country),

3   commodity dependency (the share of the largest export item(s) in relation to all export items and
4   investment dependency (the proportion of direct foreign investments in relation to the GNP).

In his study of the determinants of democracy, Hadenius (1992: 93–98) used all four measures and also paid regard to bloc dependency, that is, the proportion of trade countries have with a certain country or bloc of countries. The blocs used by Hadenius were the EC, the USA, the Soviet Union and other countries in the world (Hadenius 1992: 94).

As regards the present study, it is evident that there is no need to make use of all of the indicators mentioned above. It is evident that bloc dependency in particular ought to be important. The differing view between the leading western power, the USA, and the European Union over the death penalty means that the widely used indicators of dependence should be modified to suit the present question. It is a fact that the European Union in particular regards the question of the death penalty as important. The European Union is opposed to the death penalty and does not in any way try to conceal that it wants it to be abolished globally. The USA, on the other hand, has not entered on a similar crusade in favor of the death penalty. It has refrained from criticizing other countries for the use of death penalty but, at the same time, never attempted to encourage other countries to apply capital punishment. The aforesaid gives us reason to consider dependency to the European Union as a plausible determinant of the death penalty. Therefore one indicator of dependency is the proportion of trade countries have with the European Union. The member countries of the European Union/European Community are naturally excluded from the analyses. For 1985, I also exclude Spain and Portugal which became members in 1986.

It is plausible to assume that the association between EU trade and the death penalty is negative and much stronger in 2000 than in 1985. The negative attitude against the death penalty taken by the Western European countries is a rather new phenomenon. Only in recent years has the European Community/European Union voiced loud protests against the use of the death penalty. We therefore assume that EU trade explains some of the variation in the dependent variable in 2000 but not necessarily in 1985. Indeed, we must remember that, in 1985, many Western European countries had not yet abolished the death penalty completely, although none of them performed executions any more.

The inclusion of the proportion of trade with the European Union is theoretically indisputable. However, the theoretical reasons for including other dependency measures are less obvious. It nevertheless seems necessary to include one measure of dependency on other countries in general.

As has been considered earlier (pages 2–4), the abolitionist movement has grown significantly stronger during the last few decades. For countries heavily dependent on other countries, we can readily assume that it is "more correct" not to make use of the death penalty than to make use of it. If a country wants to be on good terms with as many countries as possible, this aim is more easily achieved if the death penalty is forbidden than if it is allowed. Among the indices described above, I therefore include trade dependency as a measure of dependency. I shall mainly follow Hadenius' operationalization of the two measures of dependency, but I choose to use GDP as a reference point instead of GNP. Accordingly, trade dependency is measured by the sum of imports and exports in relation to the GDP.

Empirical evidence

Tables 2.13 and 2.14 give the internal associations between the dependency variables and capital punishment. Overall, the dependency argument wins little support. EU trade and trade dependence, especially in 1985, fail to explain the variance in the dependent variable. In 2000, the association between trade dependency and capital punishment was statistically significant, but the variation explained was quite low, only 6 percent. Moreover, the association is positive, meaning countries with a high level of trade with foreign countries have a more positive view of the death penalty than countries with a low level.

The absence of a link between dependency and capital punishment can probably be best explained by the fact that the use of the death penalty is not globally considered a breach of fundamental human rights. As long as the leading world power continues to make use of the death penalty, this fact is not likely to change. Countries can always refer to the American example when criticized by European countries and human rights movements. Likewise, economic and/or military giants like Japan and USA, which both make use of the death penalty, have no reason to act as

Table 2.13 Association between dependency and capital punishment in 1985 (bivariate regressions)

	B	*Beta*	*T-value*	R^2	N
EC trade	0.002	0.093	1.095	0.009	139
Trade dependency (log)	0.161	0.117	1.449	0.014	153

Notes
**Significance at the $p < 0.01$ level.
*Significance at the $p < 0.05$ level.

Table 2.14 Association between dependency and capital punishment in 2000 (bivariate regressions)

	B	Beta	T-value	R^2	N
EU trade	−0.004	−0.154	−1.982*	0.024	164
Trade dependency (log)	0.266	0.245	3.442**	0.060	188

Notes
**Significance at the $p < 0.01$ level.
*Significance at the $p < 0.05$ level.

spokespeople for the abolitionist movement. Consequently, it is perhaps not an overstatement to say that the American example paves the way for the use of capital punishment in many parts of the world.

Political institutions

Form of government

When considering the question of the death penalty, people readily assume that democracies should be more restrictive in the use of this form of punishment than other political systems. However, there is no well-founded theory supporting such an argument, and the first thing we ought to ask ourselves is whether this way of arguing really has an empirical footing. Although we lack a general theory of the determinants of the death penalty, there are indeed a few arguments that allow us to expect a link between a democratic form of government and the absence of capital punishment.

If a very simple line of reasoning is allowed, we can say that what distinguishes democracies from other forms of government is the fact that in a democracy the people make the decisions. The question to be raised within the framework of the present study is, consequently, whether it is reasonable to assume that the majority of the people necessarily have a negative attitude toward capital punishment. The question is undoubtedly intriguing. In non-democracies, decisions are made by a limited number of persons; indeed, in many cases, by one single individual. In these systems, the choice to either forbid or make use of the death penalty is thus made within a narrow circle. The question to be raised is whether there is anything that indicates that these people making up an autocratic regime by necessity should take a more favorable stand toward the death penalty than the average citizen in the street in a democratic system. Now, powerful leaders come in many shapes. Not all are unscrupulous and brutal. At the same time, not everyone is just and well meaning. Nevertheless, the theoretical arguments for a direct link between the rule of the few and a positive attitude toward capital punishment do seem somewhat hazy. Likewise, as we shall see, it is hardly self-evident that the majority of the population should be opposed to the death penalty in all societies and under all circumstances.

Although it is hard to find arguments suggesting a direct link between an autocratic form of government and a positive attitude toward the death penalty, it seems reasonable to assume that indirect ones exist. Ever since the Second World War, and particularly since the fall of the communist regimes in Eastern Europe, democracy is winning, some would perhaps argue has won, status as the only legitimate form of government throughout the world. Therefore, it is probably safe to assume that countries with a form of government other than a democratic one feel the pressure of democratization from the international community. Grants of aid given to developing countries are also more and more dependent upon the measures of democratization taken. In addition to, and largely also as a consequence of, these external demands for democratization, there is a growing internal demand for democratic reforms. The internal pressure for measures of democratization presumably leads to a need for the government to ensure that its position remains unchallenged. The measures taken by the governing authorities might include hard penalties for a wide variety of crimes, especially for crimes that threaten the legitimacy of the government. The death penalty, of course, constitutes the ultimate deterrent in this case. It is also worth pointing out that democratic societies can be thought to be more stable than societies governed in other ways. The threat of political violence is not as imminent in a democracy as it is, for example, in an autocracy. There are many examples of countries governed undemocratically where violent revolutions have paved the way for democracy. However, examples where the course of events has been the opposite way are difficult to come across.

The main reason for the assumption that democratic countries in particular should take a negative stand toward the death penalty is the intimate link between this form of government and the human rights movement. One of the most frequent arguments put forward by opponents of the death penalty is that it is a barbaric form of punishment, not suitable for modern, developed societies. At the same time it must be emphasized that the abolishment of capital punishment has not always been included among the fundamental human rights. The United Nations Universal Declaration of Human Rights from 1948 does not state anything about capital punishment. The European Convention for Protection of Human Rights and Fundamental Freedoms adopted by the Council of Europe in Rome in 1950 even acknowledges the rights of the participating states to make use of the death penalty. Article 2 (1) states: "[n]o one shall be deprived of his life intentionally save in the execution of a sentence of a court following his conviction of a crime for which this penalty is provided by law". Although no explicit stands against the death penalty were taken in these two documents, one should still beware of ruling out capital punishment as a component of human rights. The two documents were produced in the aftermath of the Second World War, in which, of course, death had been ever present. Also, it is unreasonable to expect that countries, which only a few years earlier had sentenced German and Japanese war criminals to death, should all of a sudden consider this act a breach of fundamental human rights.

However, a lot of time has elapsed since the adoption of the two documents. In recent years the criticism of the death penalty has been particularly strong within the human rights movement. In 1989, the United Nations General Assembly adopted the Second Optional Protocol to the International Covenant on Civil and Political Rights, which, among other things, stated that no one was to be executed in time of peace (articles 1 and 2). The Council of Europe has now become an influential advocate for the abolitionist movement. In 1982, the Committee of Ministers adopted Protocol No. 6 to the European Convention of Human Rights, which provides for the abolition of capital punishment in time of peace. In 1994, the Parliamentary Assembly decided that only countries that had abolished the death penalty could become members of the Council of Europe (Resolution 1044 (1994) on the Abolition of Capital Punishment, paragraph 6).

As our discussion has shown, some arguments that support a link between a democratic form of government and the absence of capital punishment can indeed be put forward. What, then, about other forms of government? Can we expect to find variations as regards the use of the death penalty among all the different non-democratic political systems as well? Based on the discussion in this chapter, it is hard to come up with arguments that a specific non-democratic form of government should take a more or less negative stand against the death penalty than another non-democratic form of government. However, since no systematic research has been conducted in the field, we cannot rule out the possibility that there might be systematic differences between various political systems. Therefore I shall not only focus on the relation between democracy and the death penalty but also on whether or not there are systematic differences as regards the use of the death penalty among all political systems of the world.

Over the past few decades many scholars have discussed the prerequisites of democracy. Their focus on democracy has led to the development of various definitions of the term. A dividing line can be placed between authors who regard democracy as a qualitative, "either–or" phenomenon (and consequently operate with a dichotomous variable where countries are categorized either as democracies or non-democracies) and authors who treat democracy as a "more-or-less" phenomenon, thereby operating with a continuous variable. An example of the application of the former strategy is Lipset's seminal study *Some Social Requisites of Democracy* (1959). Nowadays, it is probably safe to say that the rule is to use continuous measurements of democracy or democratization (see Cutright 1963; Needler 1967; May 1973: 9–10; Vanhanen 1984, 1990; Hadenius 1992: 36–71). In the light of the above-mentioned studies, it also seems fair to state that measures of democracy generally include two components, one relating to elections and another to civil liberties (see Bollen 1979, 1983; Flanigan and Fogelman 1971; Gastil 1972; Hadenius 1992).

The first question I raise is to what extent the degree of democracy is related to the death penalty. In other words, democracy is considered to be a more-or-less phenomenon rather than an either–or phenomenon. In order to measure the degree of democracy I shall make use of Freedom House's yearly-conducted survey of political rights and civil liberties. Here, two scales are used to measure the degree of democracy. One scale encompasses political rights, the other civil liberties. On each scale, countries receive values ranging from 1 to 7. Strangely enough, low values indicate a high level of rights or liberties, whereas high values denote a lack of such rights or liberties. Combining the values of political rights and civil liberties gives us a measure of democracy ranging from 2 to 14.

The second question I raise is whether or not different forms of governments generate different outcomes on the dependent variable. In other words, I turn from operating with quantitative variables to operating with qualitative ones. The task is to classify nations into several categories in terms of their political system. In their extensive coverage of the countries of the world, Ian and Denis Derbyshire (1989, 1996, 1999) classify political systems into the following eight categories: liberal democracy, emergent democracy, communism, nationalistic socialism, authoritarian nationalism, military authoritarianism, Islamic nationalism and absolutism. Within the framework of the present study, I shall, with a few minor alterations, follow their categorization.

Since there are only two countries where Islam completely dominates politics and society, Afghanistan (in 2000, but not in 1985) and Iran, they are included among the authoritarian national systems. In addition, the line between democracies and emergent democracies seems to have been drawn rather arbitrarily. For instance, Morocco is included in the emergent democracies category whereas the other Islamic monarchies are confined to the absolute systems category. Likewise, Antigua and Barbuda is placed in the emergent democracies category along with countries like Liberia, Nigeria and Uganda. It should also be noted that the information the authors provide for many of the countries listed as emergent democracies is obsolete. Hence, I do not include the emergent demo-cracies category as such in my study. Instead, I once again make use of Freedom House's above-mentioned compilation. Freedom House's survey not only gives values for political rights and civil liberties but also classifies the countries based on these values into three categories: free, partly free, and not free. The classification is done by means of averaging the ratings received for political rights and civil liberties.

For my purpose, countries listed as free are, with a few exceptions, regarded as democratic. My criteria for qualification as a democratic country are, however, stricter than the ones Freedom House operates with. In order for a country to be considered democratic, the combined scoring of political rights and civil liberties must not exceed 5. For coun-tries considered partly free, several options are possible. Many of the countries possess the same qualities as the free countries, but to a lesser extent, and can consequently be regarded as unstable democracies. However, this is not true for all countries listed as partly free. For instance, in the 1985 version, Iran and Malta are both listed as partly free although the former has an overall scoring of 11 and the latter of 6. Therefore the following strategy will be employed: countries classified as partly free are considered as unstable democracies if the combined value of political rights and civil liberties is less than 10. On neither scale is a value higher than 5 accepted.[1] Countries listed as partly free and not meeting these cri-teria and countries classified as not free will be classified into the following categories: communist states, nationalistic socialist states, authoritarian nationalist states, military authoritarian states and absolute states.

The space does not allow for a lengthy description of the different systems. For a comprehensive account of the defining characteristics of the different political systems, the reader is referred to Derbyshire and Der-byshire (1989: 27–42). A few words should nevertheless be said about the fundamental grounds for the classification. Countries with extensive state ownership, where Marxism–Leninism has been adopted as the official ideology and the influence of the Communist Party is pervasive, are regarded as communist. The category of nationalistic socialist states: "display many of the attributes of a communist state but in a less developed and structured form" (Derbyshire and Derbyshire 1989: 36). Absolute systems are characterized by "the absence of any constitutional form of government, or a popular assembly or judiciary to counter execu-tive power" and "the denial of the right to form political parties or other forms of organized interests" (Derbyshire and Derbyshire 1989: 40). Authoritarian nationalistic systems display:

1 Restrictions on the activities of all political parties, or a limitation which gives undivided and uncritical support to the state; 2 An

authoritarian personal or collective executive; 3 Either the absence of an assembly to balance the power of the executive or the presence of an assembly which is essentially the servant of the executive.

(Derbyshire and Derbyshire 1989: 38)

Authoritarian nationalistic systems are distinguished from nationalistic socialist systems in that the policy orientations are not (fully) socialist. Finally, military authoritarianism "is a form of authoritarian nationalism whereby military leaders take it upon themselves to impose a government on the people" (Derbyshire and Derbyshire 1989: 39).

State structure

Federalism, it has been said, "is a difficult term to define" (Paddison 1983: 98). Lane and Ersson (1994: 164), argue that "it is not easy to pin down what federalism stands for except in a formal constitutional sense". William Riker (1964: 11) identified three necessary, albeit conceptually wide, conditions for a federal system:

1) two levels of government rule the same land and people, 2) each level has at least one area of action in which it is autonomous and 3) there is some guarantee of the autonomy of each government in its own sphere.

Needless to say, the wordings "area of action", "autonomous" and "some guarantee of autonomy" are vague and can always be discussed (e.g. Stepan 1999). Be that as it may, it should not be too venturesome to regard federalism as a form (indeed, a very strong form) of power devolution.

Since all states have to redistribute power between central and regional or local governments to varying extents, some authors argue that instead of making use of the qualitative phenomenon federalism it is more correct to use continuous measures of centralization, or its opposite, decentralization. One rather-frequently used measure of state decentralization is the division of allocation funds between the central and local governments (Lane and Ersson 1994: 164). However, reliable comparable data on this measure are hard to find, especially for worldwide comparisons. Furthermore, I argue that this measure is relevant for measuring exactly the level of centralization, but that it is an inadequate indicator of federalism. Instead, we ought to focus on the many important qualitative differences that exist between federal and unitary states. Particularly with regard to the death penalty, these fundamental differences overshadow those marginal distinctions that can be made on a quantitative scale of

measurement. Within the framework of this study, the division of allocation funds is inappropriate. It is difficult to see how the attitude toward the
death penalty could be affected by this measure. Instead, I shall focus on
aspects of federalism that can be considered to be of explicit relevance for
capital punishment.

There are many reasons for a state choosing to opt for a federal structure. Heywood (1997: 124–126) mentions three: the resentment of previously independent units of giving too much power to a national
government in the state-formation process; the existence of an external
threat, or, alternatively, a desire to play a more important role in the international arena; and finally difficulties with coping with large size.
However, the most important reason for adopting a federal constitution is
probably a desire to cope with regional diversity (for example, see Paddison 1983: 104–107; D. Anckar 1997: 48). Federalism is thus a mechanism
that should make conflicts created by such diversities manageable.

In relation to the defining characteristics of federal states, the most
important one is undoubtedly the fact that there are two levels of government. What is crucial within the framework of the present study is that
each level has extensive legislative powers. In a federal country marked by
regional diversities, the question of how to deal with the death penalty can
be far more controversial than in a unitary, homogenous country. It is not
unreasonable to expect that, in different parts of the federal state, different attitudes toward the death penalty prevail. The question of whether or
not to make use of the death penalty is not only regarded as an important
political question, but also a highly controversial one. A decision in either
direction is likely to arouse conflicting emotions in the nation as a whole,
and in those parts of the country where public opinion favors another solution, people are likely to feel slighted, and bitterness might occur. The
federal government is, again, likely to want to defuse regional cleavages.
Since the country has opted for a federal constitution, one must suppose
that regional diversity exists, and that this diversity is perceived as a threat
to the stability of the nation, at least to a certain extent.

One way of overcoming such a problem is, of course, to shift respons-
ibility to the regional level. For instance, in the USA, capital punishment is
found to be in accordance with the federal constitution but the final
decision to either allow or forbid its use is left to the individual states. The
expectation therefore is that federal states should, to a higher extent, allow
the use of the death penalty than unitary states. This expectation stems
from an assumption that, in heterogeneous settings, there are areas where
the death penalty is supported and, similarly, areas where the death
penalty is opposed. In such cases, the federal government is likely to allow
its use more easily than in unitary states. The crucial thing here is that this
permission to use capital punishment could be seen as a form of *non-*

decision making, a term used to describe, for instance, situations where politicians avoid making difficult decisions simply by neglecting them (Bachrach and Baratz 1972). It should be stressed that the federal government does not necessarily allow the use of the death penalty explicitly. Instead, it is quite possible that the units composing the federal state may act on their own behalf. This is what happened in the USA after the arrival of the first European settlers. Different laws were adopted in different colonies, and there was, from the very beginning, a great variation among the colonies in their attitude toward capital punishment (Bohm 1999: 1–2).

We then turn to the operationalization of federalism. It is perhaps surprising to learn that authors face problems when trying to conceptualize federalism, given the fact that there is actually a broad consensus on which states can be considered to be federal. For the purpose of this study, the only important aspect is whether or not the units have law-making capacities of their own. The problem with such a definition is, of course, that in all countries, sub-national regions possess at least some law-making capacity, concerning, for instance, local taxes, or decrees of various kinds. However, the crucial factor when drawing a line between federal and unitary states is the fact that, in unitary states, executive rather than legislative powers are decentralized (Derbyshire and Derbyshire 1989: 18). Federalism thus implies that law-making capacities of the units composing the federal state exist and that these powers are substantial.

It is also relevant to pay regard to whether or not countries regard themselves as federal. By using the term "federal", a state makes an explicit statement that there are significant differences between various regions of the country and that the country in question accepts this diversity of and the attendant phenomenon of a federal form of government. Therefore, I take self-definition as a point of departure. A country that has a constitution stating that a country is federal is regarded as such. However, this is not a sufficient condition. In order to be classified as a federal state, the units composing the federal state are additionally required to possess legislative powers of their own.

Empirical evidence

Let us first study the association between the degree of democracy and state structure on the one hand, and the death penalty on the other. Regression analysis is employed since the degree of democracy ranges from 2–14 and state structure can be used as a dummy variable. Unitary countries are given the value 0 and federal countries the value 1.

Results are given in Tables 2.15 and 2.16 and they show that there is indeed a clear association between the degree of democracy and the death

Table 2.15 Associations between degree of democracy, state structure and capital punishment in 1985 (bivariate regressions)

	B	Beta	T-value	R^2	N
Degree of democracy	0.137	0.606	9.852**	0.368	169
State structure	−0.239	−0.079	−1.026	0.006	169

Notes
**Significance at the $p < 0.01$ level.
*Significance at the $p < 0.05$ level.

penalty. The direction is the one presumed. In other words, the higher the degree of democracy, the lower the likelihood that the country makes use of the death penalty (again the reader is reminded that low values on Freedom House's scale denote high levels of democracy and vice versa). As concerns the relation between state structure and capital punishment, the results leave little room for doubt as they clearly show that there is no difference in the use of capital punishment between federal and unitary states. Indeed, the results point in the direction opposite to the presumed one; unitary states make more extensive use of the death penalty than federal ones.

We then turn to assessing the relation between form of government and the death penalty. This time, the form of government is used as a multi-categorical variable, and strengths of association are measured by comparisons of means tests, using the Eta squared technique. Results, shown in Table 2.17, indicate that there is indeed a strong association between the form of government and the use of the death penalty. One general law can be derived from the tables: communist states make use of capital punishment. No exceptions from this rule can be found. Nationalistic socialist as well as authoritarian nationalist states generally make use of the death penalty, but a few exceptions can be found. In 1985, for instance, Cape Verde and Nicaragua were abolitionist, whereas the Seychelles was

Table 2.16 Associations between degree of democracy, state structure and capital punishment in 2000 (bivariate regressions)

	B	Beta	T-value	R^2	N
Degree of democracy	0.161	0.552	9.116**	0.304	192
State structure	−0.250	−0.066	−0.910	0.004	192

Notes
**Significance at the $p < 0.01$ level.
*Significance at the $p < 0.05$ level.

Table 2.17 Form of government and capital punishment in 1985 and 2000 (arithmetic means)

Form of government	1985	2000
Democracy	1.06 (57)	0.87 (86)
Unstable democracy	1.90 (25)	1.34 (43)
Communist	2.46 (17)	2.62 (5)
Nationalistic socialism	2.17 (22)	2.27 (11)
Authoritarian nationalism	2.39 (16)	2.08 (22)
Military authoritarianism	2.40 (21)	2.36 (13)
Absolute	2.17 (11)	2.14 (12)
Eta squared	0.367	0.268
Sig.	0.000	0.000
N	169	192

Note
N in parentheses.

abolitionist for ordinary crimes only. In 2000, Angola, Azerbaijan, Cambodia, Haiti, Ivory Coast and Turkmenistan constitute exceptions from this rule. Military and absolute states generally apply the death penalty, the Vatican State (absolute and abolitionist) being the obvious exception. Again, there is a marked difference in the use of the death penalty between democracies and other forms of government. The death penalty is considerably more unpopular in democracies and unstable democracies than in other political systems.

Political actors

Leadership duration and regime stability

It is my firm belief that political scientists in general ought to pay more attention to actor-oriented explanations. The reason for this is obvious. Political decisions are made by individual actors and the outcome of these decisions is very likely indeed to be dependent on the preferences of these actors. Lane and Ersson (1994: 173) make the following apposite remark: "How is it possible to understand the Nazi state without Adolf Hitler, the communist state without Joseph Stalin, the Egyptian events without Nasser, Iraqi politics without Saddam Hussein and Argentina without the Perons?" Obviously there are limits on how much influence one single leader can have. The examples above nevertheless show that these limits can be stretched very far if the political leader is powerful or charismatic enough.

Perhaps the most important reason for the limited use of actor-oriented explanations in political science is the difficulty in operationalizing "actor-variables". This is natural. If we assume that political phenomena are dependent on the personal view or personal characteristics of one single actor, it is hardly reasonable to expect that we can come up with generalizations that apply in wider contexts than that of the country in which the actor in question operates. In extensive comparative studies, the actor model is, no doubt, difficult to operate with. The aforesaid does not, however, mean that actor-oriented models cannot be used in global comparisons. Any operationalization cannot, however, be very sophisticated. Naturally, all brain functions that can affect political decisions can hardly be taken into account within the framework of this study. Instead, I shall focus on two rough but easily operationalizable aspects of actor-oriented explanations. In their search for explanations of state stability and state performance, Lane and Ersson (1994: 175–184) apply two different actor-related indicators: leadership duration and orientations of political actors (on the left–right scale). The orientation of the leadership does not have to be considered at this point. This is due to the fact that it coincides with the form of government. Their influence on capital punishment has already been accounted for (pages 58–63).

In contrast, there are theoretically motivated reasons to include leadership duration in the analysis of the prerequisites of the death penalty. The basic argument is that leaders that have stayed in power for a long time are likely to feel more secure about their position than leaders that have held their positions for a limited period of time. When a new leader has gained power, he or she can be expected to be eager to consolidate their position, partly by means of strengthened measures of security. Under these circumstances, the leadership is likely to favor heavy penalties for violent crimes in particular. The death penalty can thus be seen as a useful tool to uphold the position of the newly established regime. When the leadership has been consolidated, there is no longer any need to resort to the death penalty in order to maintain this position. The need to uphold the leadership based on severe punishments or even downright terror decreases as time goes by and the leadership gains legitimacy in the minds of the citizens.

It goes without saying that this line of reasoning applies better to non-democratic countries than to democratic ones. In democracies, political leaders serve fixed terms and there is a natural rotation of leaders that does not occur in authoritarian countries. Furthermore, in many presidential systems the rotation of political leaders is often constitutionally secured through the application of rules limiting the number of (consecutive) terms a person can serve as president. For the sake of consistency, I will nevertheless include democratic countries in the analysis as well. Since different conditions might affect leadership duration in democracies and non-democracies, I will not only study the effect of leadership duration on the death penalty in the whole population, but also split up the population into two sub-categories – democracies and non-democracies – and study the effects of leadership duration on the death penalty within these categories.

The operationalization of leadership duration is relatively simple. To begin with, I choose to regard the head of the executive as the relevant political leader. This is logically justifiable: a political leader who is not in control of the executive power cannot be regarded as a very powerful leader. In the categorization I made when assessing the impact of form of government on the death penalty, states were divided into seven categories: democratic, unstable democratic, communist, nationalistic socialist, authoritarian nationalist, military authoritarian and absolute forms of government. Within each of these categories it is possible to determine which person is to be considered the leader of the executive. In the categories of democracies and unstable democracies, we make a distinction between parliamentary and presidential systems. One of the most fundamental characteristics of a presidential form of government is that the president acts as the leader of the executive (see Sartori 1994: 84). Thus, in presidential systems, the head of state coincides with the head of government. For presidential democracies the president is consequently regarded as the political leader. In parliamentary systems, the situation is different. Here, the head of state is either a monarch or a president. The political power, however, resides in the government and thus the head of government, i.e. the prime minister, must be considered the real political leader.

There are a small number of countries that make use of systems that fall in between these two categories. Such systems are generally referred to as "semi-presidential". The prototype is the French fifth republic, but other variants exist as well. The common feature of semi-presidential systems is the dual structure of authority, where a popularly elected president and a prime minister accountable to parliament share executive power. The French constitution is very specific about which of the actors, the president or the prime minister, heads the government. Article 21 bluntly states that "[t]he Premier shall direct the operation of the Government" (Blaustein and Flanz, 2003–2009). In France, the powers of the president reside to a large extent in the (in)famous article 16 which gives the president emergency powers in times of unrest. Among the established western democracies, semi-presidential systems have also been in use in Finland and Portugal. In Finland, the powers of the president were to a great extent confined to the area of foreign policy. However, the loosely written constitution made it easy for the president to become a very powerful actor in domestic politics as well. The powers of the Finnish president have been significantly reduced in recent years, and the role is nowadays mostly ceremonial (although the president is still in charge of foreign policy along with the government). In Portugal, a semi-presidential system was in use in the years following the military coup in 1974. However, Portugal's experiment with semi-presidentialism ended in 1982. Since then, the powers of the Portuguese president are very similar to the ones that presidents in parliamentary systems have (Sartori 1994: 129–130, 138, 139).

I choose to regard the prime minister as the relevant leader in semi-presidential systems. This, however, is not an easy choice. Other studies have applied different strategies, albeit sometimes with bad results. Bienen and van de Walle (1991: 17), for instance, chose to regard the president as the central figure for Finland, from a belief that "they [the presidents] seemed dominant". For the French fifth republic, the authors similarly chose to regard the president as the central figure but only until the first example of *cohabitation*, i.e. a situation where the prime minister and the president represent different political parties. I do, however, regard the relation between parliament and the government as the crux of the matter. In semi-presidential systems, the government must enjoy the confidence of the legislature. A parliamentary vote of no confidence must be seen as a sign of political turbulence. More importantly, the death penalty is an issue that is more related to the government and the legislature than to the president. To allow or forbid the use of capital punishment is a question that has to do with the law-making process, where the prime minister in all semi-presidential systems is a more powerful actor than the president. Additionally, following our theoretical discussion, capital punishment is thought to be used as a means to consolidate the position of the political leader. Presidents, of course, are far more difficult to remove from office than prime ministers, since presidents are popularly elected for a fixed term. Presidents do not have to feel insecure about their positions, and, as a consequence of that feeling of insecurity, resort to the use of capital punishment.

In the categories that are made up of different types of non-democratic political systems, it is easier to identify the relevant political actor. In absolute states, the powers of the leader (usually the monarch) are more or less unlimited. In military states, the leadership is often divided between several persons, often referred to as a "junta". In most cases, however, it is possible to identify one person as the leader of the junta. In communist states, neither the president nor the prime minister is necessarily the real leader of the country. Instead, the general secretary of the communist party is usually, but not always, the most powerful actor within the system. The two remaining categories are the nationalistic socialist and the authoritarian nationalist systems. In both of these systems, one person, often the president, holds the ultimate political power.

In order to empirically test the association between leadership duration and the death penalty, I have mainly made use of data provided by Bienen and van de Walle (1991) in their previously-cited study. To some extent, the identification of political leaders necessarily implies problems of delimitation (exemplified by Bienen and van de Walle 1991: 15–23). I have, as a rule, chosen to rely on the judgments made by the authors but, as already mentioned, for semi-presidential systems the prime minister, and not the president, will be regarded as the head of government. In addition to the data provided by Bienen and van de Walle, I have also made use of data provided by Derbyshire and Derbyshire (1989, 1999) and Schemmel (1995–2004). Following Bienen and van de Walle, I have disregarded obvious cases where a political leader only temporarily holds the position as head of government. Admittedly, the time limit for how long a leader should be in power in order to be considered a "real" leader can always be debated, and different authors would, in some cases, perhaps have come to different results. San Marino and Switzerland have been left out of the study of the association between leadership duration and capital punishment. Switzerland applies a system of a rotating presidency, which means that the head of government changes every year. In San Marino, executive power is conferred to two *capitani reggenti*, elected by the parliament from among its members. They serve a term of six months and also act as head(s) of state.

Leadership duration will be measured beginning from 1945. A substantial number of countries have gained independence later than that. Therefore, the number of years a country has been independent since 1945 is divided by the number of political leaders. Particularly in the case of democracies, it is worth pointing out that, although governments tend to resign as a consequence of parliamentary (and presidential) elections, such changes are regarded as changes in government only if the leader of the government, that is, the prime minister or the president, changes. Therefore, the five socialist governments of Spain between 1982 and 1996 are counted as one as they were all headed by Felipe Gonzales, who thus ruled without interruption.

It is evident that, along with leadership duration (which, as we have already seen, can be regarded as an indication of short-term stability), it is also useful to make use of Lane and Ersson's dependent variable, regime stability, or long-term stability. Within the framework of this study, however, regime stability is used not as a dependent but as an independent variable. The reason for why regime stability would affect the occurrence of capital punishment is actually the same that applied for leadership duration. Whenever there is a change in the regime, political unrest is a natural consequence. In countries where no regime changes have occurred for a long period of time, the society as a whole can be expected to be more stable, which means that there is little need to resort to severe punishments in order to control the population.

Even though leadership and regime stability sometimes go hand-in-hand, it is important that we are aware of the differences between the two phenomena. A regime shift almost by necessity implies a change in the leadership as well. Since we are talking about a fundamental change in the form of government, it seems natural that the leaders of the old era must change as well. However, the reality does not always support this logical conclusion. Particularly in the phase of transition from dictatorship to democracy, leaders of the old era can, at least for a while, manage to stay in power. Thus, in many of the republics that were formerly part of the Soviet Union, the old communist leaders have remained in power despite the change in form of government. A change in leadership, on the other hand, can occur independently of regime shifts. This is particularly the case in democracies where there have been numerous changes in government (Lane and Ersson 1994: 175). Indeed, the nature of a democratic form of government presupposes that political leaders can be easily removed from office.

When measuring the level of regime stability I shall depart from Lane and Ersson's work. They use constitutional longevity and regime fluctuations as measurements of regime stability (Lane and Ersson 1994: 73–79). The measure of regime fluctuations takes into account the frequency of transitions from democracy to dictatorships or vice versa. Since this question has already been dealt with extensively on pages 58–63, it will not be considered here. Thus we are left with a measure of constitutional longevity. The more constitutional changes a country has undergone in relation to the number of years of independence since 1945, the less stable the regime. Data on constitutional changes have been obtained from Arthur S. Banks Cross-National Time–Series Data Archive (CNTS) 7–2000.

Empirical evidence

Tables 2.18 and 2.19 return results of the regression analyses where the death penalty is regressed on leadership duration and regime stability. The results show that leadership duration and the death penalty are associated to some extent. However, the direction is the opposite to the one

Table 2.18 Associations between leadership duration, regime stability and capital punishment in 1985 (bivariate regressions)

	B	*Beta*	*T-value*	R^2	N
Leadership duration	0.047	0.327	4.442**	0.107	167
Regime stability	−0.023	−0.350	−4.784**	0.122	166

Notes
**Significance at the $p < 0.01$ level.
*Significance at the $p < 0.05$ level.

Table 2.19 Associations between leadership duration, regime stability and capital punishment in 2000 (bivariate regressions)

	B	*Beta*	*T-value*	R^2	N
Leadership duration	0.071	0.349	5.111**	0.122	190
Regime stability	−0.022	−0.294	−4.233**	0.086	192

Notes
**Significance at the $p < 0.01$ level.
*Significance at the $p < 0.05$ level.

expected. Countries marked by long-term leaders are more likely to make extensive use of the death penalty than countries with frequent shifts of government. This, however, is probably due to the fact that countries with frequent changes of governments are democratic countries, whereas countries where the leadership rarely changes are non-democratic ones.

Based on our empirical findings, we know that democratic countries in particular are abolitionist. The form of government thus intervenes in the association between leadership duration and the death penalty. The other independent variable, regime stability, is also associated with the dependent variable and, this time, the direction is the expected one. Countries with frequent regime changes are more likely to make use of the death penalty than countries where changes are rare.

A better strategy to including all countries in the analysis is probably to separate democracies from non-democracies. If leadership duration affects the use of capital punishment, this association should be visible, particularly among countries where shifts in governments are irregular, unexpected and often disastrous from the point of view of the existing government. In democracies, again, changes in government are the norm rather than the exception. Therefore we cannot expect a similar link between leadership duration and capital punishment in democracies and non-democracies. The relation between leadership duration, regime stability and capital punishment will be assessed in two sub-categories: one consisting of the countries earlier classified as democracies or unstable democracies, and another comprised of all countries that make use of various forms of authoritarian forms of government.

Results are given in Tables 2.20 and 2.21 and they indicate that there is no association between leadership duration and the death penalty in non-democratic countries. Within the category of democracies, however, the earlier result found at the global level are confirmed. Capital punishment occurs more frequently in democracies with durable governments. The results obtained thus contradict the assumptions put forward in the beginning of the chapter in every possible way. Leadership duration does not affect capital punishment in the category of countries where it was

Table 2.20 Associations between leadership duration, regime stability and capital punishment in two categories of countries in 1985 (bivariate regressions)

	B	Beta	T-value	R^2	N
Leadership duration, democracies	0.075	0.323	3.010**	0.104	80
Leadership duration, others	0.002	0.025	0.233	0.001	87
Regime stability, democracies	−0.012	−0.191	−1.705	0.036	79
Regime stability, others	−0.017	−0.349	−3.428**	0.121	87

Notes
**Significance at the $p < 0.01$ level.
*Significance at the $p < 0.05$ level.

expected to contain explanatory power. Instead, leadership duration is linked to death penalty in democratic countries, but in the opposite direction than the one assumed.

When cogitating over this finding, one possible explanation immediately stands out. When studying the 21 democratic countries that make use of the death penalty in 1985, we note that 15 of them make use of majoritarian electoral systems. These electoral systems are generally assumed to produce stable majority governments in contrast to various forms of proportional systems, which are thought to generate feeble coalition governments. Since majoritarian electoral systems are over-represented among

Table 2.21 Associations between leadership duration, regime stability and capital punishment in two categories of countries in 2000 (bivariate regressions)

	B	Beta	T-value	R^2	N
Leadership duration, democracies	0.076	0.279	3.251**	0.078	127
Leadership duration, others	0.006	0.052	0.405	0.003	63
Regime stability, democracies	−0.019	−0.276	−3.238**	0.076	129
Regime stability, others	−0.008	−0.141	−1.110	0.020	63

Notes
**Significance at the $p < 0.01$ level.
*Significance at the $p < 0.05$ level.

the countries that make active use of the death penalty, we obtain a statistically significant correlation between leadership duration and capital punishment. As it is difficult to find a theoretically motivated explanation for why the electoral systems would be related to the death penalty, this association will not be subject to further discussion.

Regarding the link between regime stability and the death penalty, the results are equally confusing. In 1985, there was a fairly strong association between the variables in non-democratic countries. However, among the population of democracies, no such association was found. Strangely enough, in 2000, the picture was turned upside down. Regime stability affected the death penalty exclusively in the category of democratic countries. This very strange finding is probably explained by the fact that there were a lot of newly democratized countries in 2000. Many of these countries had experienced a number of constitutional changes in recent years. Given the earlier finding that non-democracies made use of the death penalty to a higher extent than democracies, it is only fair to assume that these newly democratized countries also score higher values on the dependent values than countries that had been stable democracies for a long time.

Historical explanations

The colonial heritage

A majority of the countries that are now independent were once former colonies. Differences in colonial heritage can be thought to affect attitudes toward the death penalty. It is very likely indeed that the choice of whether or not to make use of capital punishment has been influenced by the former mother country. It is certainly not unreasonable to expect that constitution-makers have glanced at the legislation of the former mother country when making a choice to either allow or reject the use of the death penalty. Now, diffusion occurs at various levels and encompasses a wide variety of phenomena (see Karvonen 1981: 7–13). Legislative diffusion is only one variant, albeit an important one. Legislative diffusion has been studied both within nations (Walker 1969; Gray 1973) and between nations (Collier and Messick 1975).

The two most important colonial powers were Britain and France. There were marked differences in the way the two countries governed their colonies. The British actively encouraged native participation in the governing process. In many colonies, the native population were even represented in political organizations. These organizations had very little power but, due to their existence, the local elite was familiarized with the democratic form of government (Bell 1967; Bollen and Jackman 1985: 445;

Hadenius 1992: 129; Weiner 1987: 19–20). In addition, the path to independence was relatively smooth in the former British colonies, particularly in those colonies that gained independence at a later stage in time. Local political organizations also existed in the French colonies but, compared to the organizations in the British colonies, their powers were rather limited (Betts 1991; Hadenius 1992: 129). With regard to attitudes toward independence movements, the French fiercely held on to its colonies. As a consequence of this, many wounds remain open, and relations between the mother country and many of its former colonies remain strained. In general, then, the British allowed the native population to take part in the administration to a totally different extent than the French. Whereas natives constituted the link between rulers and ruled in the British colonies, the French preferred to fill these vacancies with French people (Hadenius 1992: 130).

The differences accounted for above have, no doubt, given support for an assumption that democracy has a better breeding ground in former British colonies than elsewhere. Consequently, Myron Weiner (1987: 20) found that "*[e]very country with a population of at least 1 million (and almost all the smaller countries as well) that has emerged from colonial rule since World War II and has had a continuous democratic experience is a former British colony*. Not a single newly independent country that lived under French, Dutch, American, or Portuguese rule has continually remained democratic" (italics and parenthesis in original).

The assumption that former British colonies were particularly prone to adopt a democratic form of government has, however, subsequently been falsified. Samuel Huntington, reflecting on a finding which showed that democratic countries in the Third World almost exclusively tended to be former British colonies (Weiner, cited in Huntington 1984: 206), suggested that the length of British rule, and not British rule per se was crucial for democracy. Hadenius (1992: 131–133), on his part, argues that the crucial point is the length of the period a colony has been under the rule of any country with a democratic form of government. In other words, it does not make a difference whether or not the former colony is a British one or, for instance, a French one. What is of importance is the duration of the colonial rule. A third finding indicates that the crucial point is the combination of a British (or American) colonial legacy and the geographical factor. Island states with a British, or American, legacy showed a much higher degree of democracy than any other category of countries (Anckar 1997).

Even though the colonial heritage is thought to affect the readiness of a country to adopt a democratic form of government, its implications for the attitude toward the death penalty is less evident. At this point, however, we should not overlook the possibility that the colonial past affects many areas of politics and not necessarily in the direction which, at first, seems obvious. The best example is perhaps precisely the link between colonial heritage and democracy. During the period of colonization, the form of government was the same for both colonizing powers. Indeed, the French Revolution meant that France had a longer experience of a "modern" form of democracy than Britain. Still, there were marked differences in the way democracy was exported to the colonies. As far as the history of the death penalty is concerned, a similar picture is valid for Britain and France (and for the rest of the European colonial powers). In France, the death penalty was abolished in all its forms in 1981; that is, long after the former colonies had received their independence. In Britain, the death penalty was abolished for ordinary crimes in 1973 and for all crimes in 1998. However, the last execution carried out in Britain was in 1964 and in France in 1977. Although there are no marked differences between the British and the French position toward capital punishment, we cannot overlook the possibility that the effect the use of the death penalty has had in their respective colonies is quite dissimilar.

When discussing the effects of colonialism on the death penalty, it is quite possible that the crucial thing is not which European country the former colony belonged to but, rather, whether the country in question has been under colonial rule or not. One possible argument is that countries that have been under colonial rule for a substantial period of time have been influenced by the legal system of the mother country. In quite a few cases, the colonial power has been known to influence and even dictate the constitutional design of their former colony. For instance, in many cases a democratic form of government has been seen as a direct condition for the acceptance of the secession of the former colony (Ghai 1988: 4–5; Pinkney 1993: 39–60). Perhaps it is not unreasonable to expect that there is a difference between countries that have had the opportunity to develop their own legal system and countries that have more or less adopted a constitution of a country that is geographically and culturally very distant. Within the former category of countries, one can expect that the constitution better reflects the "natural" conceptions of justice; this implying either a repudiation of the death penalty or a positive attitude toward it.

The link between the colonial past and the use of capital punishment receives some support in the African context. According to Amnesty international "[c]apital punishment as it is now practised in Africa was introduced by the colonial powers" (cited in Schabas 1997b: 33). This view was also advocated by Justice Albie Sachs of the South African Constitutional Court, who argued that the death penalty was almost non-existent in Southern Africa prior to the colonization of the continent (Schabas 1997b: 33–34).

There is also another theoretical base on which to stand when linking colonial heritage to the death penalty. Again, the assumption is made that the crucial difference is the one that exists between former colonies and countries that have been independent for a substantial number of years. This line of reasoning departs from the view that people living under foreign rule do not view themselves as totally free and certainly not independent. This, arguably, is likely to create a feeling of bitterness toward the colonial power. The people of almost all former colonies have, at various points in time, and to varying extents, felt discomfort with their position as a colony. This is demonstrated not least by the fact that so many of these colonies have opted for independence (and some even have had to fight hard to obtain it). Thus we can assume that resistance against former colonial powers have made the peoples of former colonies familiar with acts of violence and oppression, and, perhaps, prone to consider violence and corporal punishments as justified. The death penalty, therefore, should be used to a higher extent in former colonies than in countries without a colonial past.

Classifying countries in terms of their colonial past is not as easy a procedure as it may seem. It is evident that a country that gained independence in the 1970s is more likely to have been influenced by the colonial experience than a country that has been independent for more than 100 years. It is therefore reasonable to regard a country as a former colony only if it has been under colonial rule during the twentieth century. The time the country spent as a colony is of importance as well. If a country has been subject to colonial rule for a long time, there is reason to believe that the influence of the mother country is stronger than if the colonial rule only lasted for a very short period. Therefore, I stipulate that the colonial period must have lasted for at least ten years if independence was gained after 1920. If a country has been independent for a longer time than that, I require that the colonial period must have lasted for twenty years, i.e. the colonial period must have extended at least from 1900 to 1920. A few countries have been under the rule of several colonial powers during the 1900s. This is the case notably with those colonies that were transferred to other nations under the League of Nations mandate system or United Nations trusteeship system after the defeats of their former mother countries in the First and Second World War. In these cases I regard the last country that has administered the former colony as the colonial power.

Some countries are exceptional in that they have been administered by more than one colonial power at the same time (for example, Cameroon, Libya and Togo). In these cases I have regarded the country that controlled the majority of the territory as the former colonial power. A few countries have required special attention. Andorra became independent in 1993. Before that it had been under the joint rule of France and the

Bishop of Urgel in Spain. It is extremely difficult to assess which country has had the most influence on Andorra. The fact that Andorra has never been under the rule of the Spanish government but instead of the Bishop of Urgel speaks in favor of regarding France as the colonial power. On the other hand, the bulk of the population of Andorra (61 percent) is made up of Spaniards. Andorrans make up 30 percent of the population, whereas only 6 percent are French (*Freedom in the World 1998*: 114). It is important to note, however, that many rights and privileges, such as the right to vote, are reserved to Andorran citizens only. Since the majority of the population is made up of Spaniards, Andorra is classified as a former Spanish colony.

As a consequence of the "republican" revolution in China in 1911, Mongolia managed, with the aid of czarist Russia, to proclaim itself as independent. However, as early as 1915, the Chinese managed to restore control over the territory. Having recovered from the First World War and the communist revolution, the new Soviet government came to the aid of the Mongolians in 1921, helping Mongolian nationalists to overthrow Chinese rule. Although in practice not subjected to Chinese rule after that year, Mongolia did not gain formal independence from China until 1946. The problem of establishing the colonial heritage of Mongolia is accentuated by the fact that, until the fall of the Soviet Union, it was heavily dependent on Moscow, both politically and economically. I have, however, with some doubt, chosen to regard Mongolia as a country without a colonial past. The reason for this is the fact that the ties to China were only formal; in practice Mongolia was more dependent on the Soviet Union after 1921.

Vanuatu was a joint condominium between Britain and France until it gained its independence in 1980. The two countries did indeed carry the idea of joint government to its extreme. The administration was divided into the British national service, the French national service and the joint departments. The system was complicated by the fact that the indigenous population was permitted neither French nor British citizenship. Accordingly, a rather complex system developed with "two official languages, two police forces, three public services, three courts of law, three currencies, three national budgets, two resident commissioners in Port Vila (the capital) and two district commissioners in each of the four districts" (*Regional Surveys of the World: The Far East and Australasia 1997*: 841, parenthesis in original). Although Vanuatu was formally under the influence of both Britain and France, it is, however, fair to say that the British legacy is much stronger than the French (van Trease 1995).

The colonial legacy of Yemen is also difficult to assess. North Yemen received its independence in 1918 as a consequence of the fall of the Ottoman Empire, and was consequently never under colonial rule as defined in this study. South Yemen, on the other hand, came under British rule in 1839, largely due to the strategic position of its capital Aden. The importance of the location of Aden grew tremendously with the opening of the Suez Canal in 1869 (Olson 1991: 2). It was not until 1967 that South Yemen finally gained its independence. The political structure of the two countries was very different indeed. North Yemen was an Islamic country, economically dependent on Saudi Arabia, whereas South Yemen quickly became a socialist state with economic ties to Moscow (*Regional Surveys of the World: the Middle East and North Africa 1997*: 1065). The break-down of socialism in Europe opened the way for unification between the two states. In 1990, North and South Yemen were united into one single country, Yemen. The relations between the two parts remained tense, and finally a civil war erupted in 1994. It ended after a few months when north-ern troops managed to capture Aden. The question is whether to regard Yemen as a country with a colonial past under British rule (the history of South Yemen) or as a country without a history as a colony (North Yemen). Here, I choose to regard Yemen as a country without a colonial past. For one thing, the position of North Yemen was always stronger due to the poor economy of South Yemen. In addition, the political, economic and military position of North Yemen was accentuated with its victory in the civil war of 1994.

Another operationalization difficulty is how to treat colonies of colonies; that is, countries that have been under the rule of a country, which, in turn, has been under the rule of another country. Luckily, there are only a few such cases. Nauru and Papua New Guinea both have a colo-nial past under Australian rule. Samoa was administered by New Zealand as a United Nations trust territory until it gained independence in 1962. Namibia was under South African rule until it gained independence in 1990. Since Australia, New Zealand and South Africa are former British colonies, I treat Namibia, Nauru, Samoa and Papua New Guinea as coun-tries with a British colonial heritage.

State longevity

Although there are a few exceptions, the general trend is that more and more countries abolish or restrict the use of the death penalty. Over the last few decades, the abolitionist movement has really started to gather momentum. Unlike the situation a few decades ago, today a territory with ambitions of independence that intends to incorporate the death penalty into its penal code is likely to face severe criticism and condemnation from many states and international organizations. The fact that the popularity of the death penalty has decreased allows us to link state longevity to its use. The assumption is that, in countries that have received independence at a later stage in history, capital punishment should be applied to a lesser extent than in countries that have been independent for a long time. Essentially, I expect that countries with a long history of independence have not been subject to pressure from other countries when constructing their penal code. Younger state formations, on the other hand, have not been able to turn a deaf ear to the international community when choosing whether or not to allow the use of the death penalty.

A simple and useful measure of state longevity is the number of years an entity has existed as an independent state. The problem, of course, is in determining at what point in time the entities have gained the status of independent states. In international law, an entity is regarded as a state if it exhibits:

1   a population,
2   a territory and
3   a government capable of maintaining foreign relations.
                                    (See, for instance, Akehurst 1997: 75–80)

Max Weber, again, claimed that "a compulsory political organization with continuous operations will be called a 'state' insofar as its administrative staff successfully upholds the claim to the monopoly of the legitimate use of physical force in the enforcement of its order" (cited in Lane and Ersson 1994: 30).

Although these criteria appear to be reasonable, it goes without saying that it is a difficult task to find out when these criteria have been met in all the countries in the world. Instead, it is necessary, at least to some extent, to use self-definition as a point of departure when establishing the year of state formation. In other words, the year the entity formally organized itself as a state is crucial. Derbyshire and Derbyshire (1999) provide information on dates of state formation for the countries of the world. One problem with this source is that it does not specifically state how the year of state formation has been determined. It appears, however, as if recognition by other states has not been required. On the other hand, it is equally evident that a simple declaration of independence is not a sufficient criterion of state formation. The United States of America is considered an independent state as from 1776, the year of its formal declaration of independence. On the other hand, the declaration of independence of Turkish Cyprus in 1985 has not made the authors consider it an independent state. The rule of thumb seems, nevertheless, to have been to use self-definition as a point of departure. To some extent, of course, there is an element of uncertainty imbedded in this kind of operationalization since every country has an opportunity to choose the date of independence. However, as long as this rule is not absolute (as the example of Turkish Cyprus illustrates) this does not constitute a real threat to the validity of the study.

There are a few countries for which the year of state formation requires further consideration. As stated earlier, it is cumbersome to establish the date of independence for Mongolia. The proclamation of independence dates back to 1911, and was a direct consequence of the "republican revolution" in China. In 1921, Chinese rule was overthrown with the aid of the Soviet government and Mongolia was granted autonomy. It was not until 1946, however, that Mongolia receive formal independence from China. During this period China had very little influence on Mongolia. Instead, Mongolia was heavily dependent on the Soviet Union, and in many respects it is fair to say that Mongolia did not receive formal independence until the fall of the Soviet Empire. However, since most of the countries to some extent are dependent on other, more powerful, countries, too rigorous criteria of independence should not be applied. If this was the case, we would soon end up struggling with endless deliberations of different aspects of independence. With this in mind, I choose to regard 1921 as the year of independence for Mongolia.

Canada's path toward independence has been long and curved. Changes have occurred gradually, and it is indeed difficult to establish the year of independence. In 1867, the British North America Act came into effect. Canada was granted a constitution "similar in principle to that of the United Kingdom". Britain retained control over external affairs. The British Judicial Committee of the Privy Council constituted the final court of appeal. In 1931, the Statute of Westminster was passed by the British Parliament. With this statute, Canada was totally independent except in two respects: the power to amend certain parts of the constitution was still confined to the British Parliament and the final court of appeal was still situated in London. In 1949, the Supreme Court of Canada replaced the Privy Council as the final court of appeal. However, it was not until 1982 that Canada got the right to amend its constitution. It is evident that Canada could hardly be regarded as an independent state in 1867. It is equally evident that Canada, in effect, had been acting as an independent state for quite a while prior to 1982. Therefore, the year of independence should fall in between these two points in time. One important period of time covers the two world wars. The participation of Canadians in the First World War gave it a stronger position in its relation to the mother country. The same held true in respect to the Second World War, the end of which, of course, constitutes a crucial landmark in British imperialism. As a compromise I choose to regard 1931 as the year of independence for Canada (Derbyshire and Derbyshire 1989; Olson 1991: 109–112). An equal pattern applies to Australia, New Zealand and South Africa. For these countries, as well, I regard the Statute of Westminster of 1931 as the crucial landmark. The year each of the former colonies has chosen to act under the authority of the Statute of Westminster consequently constitutes the year of independence for these countries.

History of slavery

The issue of slavery was uncontroversial for an extremely long time. Throughout history, forced labor has been used more or less across the whole world. In ancient Greece, Aristotle was a fierce advocate of slavery. According to the philosopher, slavery was an optimal way of distributing the work. Those who had been blessed with a great mind could concentrate on ruling and those who were physically strong were natural slaves (Aristotle 1991: 12–14). In fact, the legitimacy of slavery was not really questioned until the Age of Enlightenment in the writings of Montesquieu and Rousseau (see Sawyer 1986: 6).

There are a few good arguments that support the assumption of a causal relation between a history of slavery and the use of the death penalty. The fundamental feature of slavery is, of course, the repudiation of the view that all people have the right to personal freedom. From here it is easy to draw the parallel that slavery, by necessity, implies disrespect of human life. Although this is true in many cases, it should nevertheless be stressed that the way slaves have been treated differs from society to society and from slave owner to slave owner. However, it is fair to say that slavery in most cases gave rise to what today would be classified as severe breaches of fundamental human rights. Corporal punishment was the common form of punishment and also served the function of humiliating the slaves. In many societies where slavery was applied, the slave owner had the right to punish the slaves severely. This held true especially for the European form of slavery, where the slave owner held absolute property rights. Within the African context and under Islam, slaves were treated with more respect (Rodriguez 1999: 198).

Now, it is reasonable to assume that in societies where slavery was considered to be both natural and legitimate, the respect for the human life was quite different than in societies where slavery was met with repulsion and consequently forbidden. Opponents of the death penalty often claim that proponents of the death penalty in general have a low opinion of human beings. The argument is, of course, difficult to refute since defendants of the death penalty advocate the killing of human beings. Proponents of the death penalty, on their part, argue that they, in fact, have a much greater respect for human life than their opponents; namely for the respect of the lives of the victims of the criminals sentenced to death. Be that as it may, it is reasonable to assume that, in societies where the human body and soul traditionally have been regarded with awe, the threshold for killing criminals is higher than in societies where, for instance, corporal punishment has been commonplace. One manifest indicator of a neglect of respect for the dignity of humanity is slavery. Consequently, it is natural to assume that the threshold for making use of the death penalty is lower in countries with a history of slavery than in countries where slavery has been forbidden.

Today, most people tend to associate slavery with the African slave trade, which started in the early sixteenth century, reached its peak in the eighteenth century and finally died out in the nineteenth century. However, contrary to common belief, slavery has not yet been abolished all over the world, although it is true that no state formally allows the use of slaves. As one observer notes: "the old traditional theory that slavery was good both for society and the individual slave has given way to an Orwellian double-think process: all states forbid it and many practise it" (Sawyer 1986: 7).

Still, if it is an overstatement to say that slavery has been abolished all over the world, to suggest that slavery is widely practised is even more erroneous. For a long time, the use of slaves was vindicated by most religions. However, a few Protestant denominations (such as the Quakers and the Methodists) fiercely opposed slavery at a relatively early stage. In Islamic countries, slavery remained legitimate until 1964 until it was finally condemned at the sixth Moslem world conference. One year later, the Catholic Church finally dissociated itself from slavery (Sawyer 1986: 6–7).

We cannot, however, only consider the formal abolition of slavery when determining whether a country has a history of slavery or not. Although slavery is commonly associated with the European colonial powers, the real picture is quite different. The roots of slavery date farther back in time, especially in Africa. When the Europeans arrived, they found a well-working system of slave trade and slavery. The existence of these structures facilitated the rise and development of the African slave trade (Rodriguez 1997: 13). If the colonial powers were not responsible for introducing slavery, they can, on the other hand, be credited for its abolition. By the late eighteenth century, voices of protest were raised in many parts of Europe. As time went on, these protests grew stronger and stronger. Proponents of slavery suffered a major setback in 1833, when the British parliament enacted the Emancipation Act, which put an end to slavery in all British colonial possessions (Rodriguez 1999: 84). In the following decades, France (1848), the Netherlands (1863) and Spain (1886) followed the British example. The legitimacy of slavery was further undermined when the American Civil War ended in victory for the abolitionist northern states.

The aforesaid seems to suggest that slavery was abolished in virtually every corner of the world well before the turn of the century. This, however, is very far from the truth. First, it should be stressed that the colonial period was still just beginning. Most parts of Africa remained unexplored, and the European powers were actually only now starting the "race for Africa". In other words, slavery existed in many non-colonized parts of the world. Second, in many colonies the implementation of the rules that outlawed slavery moved slowly. For example, in Zanzibar the legal status of slavery was not abolished until 1897 (Rodriguez 1999: 641). Third, and this is crucial, the actions taken against slavery often did not encompass indigenous slavery; that is, slave–master relations where both parts belonged to the native population. In many parts of the colonies, the colonial powers took a passive attitude toward this form of slavery (see Rodriguez 1999: 109).

Slavery is supposed to effect attitudes toward the death penalty because it evolves a notion of disrespect for the human being. Therefore, the assumption is that, if slavery exists, this is because slavery is accepted in the culture of the specific country. It cannot be stressed enough that what is important is the culture of the specific country in itself and not the culture of the former colonial power. Therefore, simply focusing on formal dates of abolition, which merely reflect a changing attitude toward slavery in Europe, cannot be used as such for their former European colonies as well. Instead, we must try to find out when slavery was abolished de facto in the countries of the world. Needless to say, this is not an easy task since countries are generally eager to defuse their experiences with slavery. When assessing the history of slavery, I have mostly made use of the work of Rodriguez (1997, 1999). Although this work provides detailed accounts of the history of slavery in the world, it fails to come up with a systematic compilation of the dates of the abolition of slavery for each country. With regard to the bulk of countries, a careful reading of the sources nevertheless makes it possible to determine whether or not slavery was used after the relevant date or not.

This discussion gives me reason to include a history of slavery among the independent variables. However, slavery cannot be treated in the same manner as the other independent variables. The operationalization of slavery is extremely difficult. Slavery is by now abolished in all countries of the world (although persistent reports indicate that forms of chattel slavery still exist in Mauritania and Sudan). This means that we have to go quite far back in history when looking for evidence of slavery. Reliable information of numbers of slaves is, of course, impossible to find, which means that we are compelled to apply a dichotomous scale of measurement. Countries with a history of slavery are given the value 1 and countries with no such history are given the value 0. We then have to find a relevant point in time when slavery will be measured. As mentioned earlier, slavery is now abolished in the whole world and has been so for quite a while (the last country to officially abolish slavery was Mauritania in 1980).

It is impossible to go very far back in time. On the one hand, slavery has existed in most societies, which means that if we go very far back in time there will be no variation in the variable. On the other hand, the point in time must be relevant for the present situation. In other words, the farther back in time we go, the less relevance a history of slavery has with regard to the death penalty. After giving this question a lot of thought I have chosen to use the year 1880 as a cut-off point. At this point in time, a great number of countries had already abolished slavery, but the phenomenon was anything but extinct. In addition, it could be argued that a time period between the observation on the independent variable and the dependent variable should not be stretched to a period that exceeds much more than approximately 100 years. Thus, countries where slavery was applied at or after that date are considered to be former slave countries whereas countries where slavery was abolished prior to that year are regarded as states without a history of slavery.

This strategy is, however, not totally satisfactory. It should immediately be stressed that information about the existence of slavery is scarce and often unreliable. Thus, even a meticulous examination of the sources leaves me with many missing cases. Furthermore, the extent of slavery is not accounted for. Thus, a country where forms of slavery have existed in a few remote areas is given the same value on the independent variable as a country where slavery has been common, and, perhaps, sanctioned by the government. The measure also fails to account for cases where slavery was abolished before 1880, but where a large part of the population is made up of descendants of former slaves. In such societies (such as the Caribbean countries), it is reasonable to expect that the history of slavery still has an impact on attitudes toward the death penalty. It should also be stressed that a history of slavery is related to a number of other independent variables. Generally, various forms of slavery have existed in Africa and the Middle East, but not in Europe and Latin America. The history of slavery is strongly related to low degrees of democracy, Islam and low levels of socioeconomic development. Bearing these shortcomings in mind, I now proceed with the empirical analyses of the relation between historical explanations and the death penalty.

Empirical evidence

Since colonial background is a multi-categorical variable, I use a comparison of means tests to assess the relation between colonial background and the death penalty. Table 2.22 presents the arithmetic means of the death penalty for 12 categories of countries.[2]

Table 2.22 Colonial heritage and capital punishment in 1985 and 2000 (arithmetic means)

Colonial heritage	1985	2000
None	1.37 (65)	0.85 (64)
British	2.03 (65)	1.85 (65)
French	2.30 (25)	1.94 (25)
Portuguese	1.94 (5)	0.00 (5)
Belgian	2.60 (3)	2.73 (3)
Japanese	2.40 (2)	2.80 (2)
Dutch	2.30 (2)	2.20 (2)
American (USA)	2.20 (1)	0.63 (4)
Spanish	2.30 (1)	1.20 (2)
Ethiopian	–	2.00 (1)
Soviet	–	1.54 (15)
Yugoslavian	–	0.25 (4)
Eta squared	0.164	0.269
Sig.	0.000	0.000
N	169	192

Note
N in parentheses.

As the results show, there are some differences in the use of the death penalty between countries with different colonial heritages. For what it is worth, the between-group variance is higher in 2000 than in 1985. If we concentrate on the first three categories, i.e. those categories with a sufficient number of cases to allow generalizations, one very interesting result strikes out: countries without any colonial past tend to be markedly more restrictive toward the use of capital punishment than countries with a British or French colonial past. At the same time, former British and French colonies make use of the death penalty to an equal extent. Concerning the other categories, conclusions can hardly be drawn due to the limited number of cases. Nevertheless, it is worth noting that none of the former Portuguese colonies make use of the death penalty in 2000.

We then turn to the association between state longevity, slavery and the death penalty. Results are given in Tables 2.23 and 2.24 and they show that

Table 2.23 Associations between state longevity, slavery and capital punishment in 1985 (bivariate regressions)

	B	Beta	T-value	R^2	N
State longevity (log)	−0.198	−0.278	−3.447**	0.077	169
Slavery	1.144	0.580	8.267**	0.336	137

Notes
**Significance at the $p < 0.01$ level.
*Significance at the $p < 0.05$ level.

Table 2.24 Associations between state longevity, slavery and capital punishment in 2000 (bivariate regressions)

	B	*Beta*	*T-value*	R^2	N
State longevity (log)	−0.126	−0.132	−1.834	0.017	192
Slavery	1.322	0.552	8.220**	0.305	156

Notes
**Significance at the $p < 0.01$ level.
*Significance at the $p < 0.05$ level.

there is no link between state longevity and the death penalty in 2000. In 1985, there was a weak, but statistically significant, association between state longevity and the death penalty. It is, perhaps, interesting to note that the results indicate that younger countries use the death penalty to a higher extent than older state formations. In other words, the association points in the opposite direction than the assumed one. A different picture emerges when we relate a history of slavery to the death penalty. The association is not only statistically significant but also very strong. Countries that have abolished slavery after 1879 have a more positive attitude to the use of capital punishment than states where slavery was abolished prior to 1880.

Concerning state longevity, some additional reflections are needed. A closer examination of the cases reveals that the bulk of the countries which have received independence at a later stage in history are in Africa, most of which gained independence in the 1960s. Now, it is plausible that the international pressure to reject the death penalty was not as strong at that period of time. Instead, it is possible that the year of independence does not affect the outcome of the dependent variable until very late in time. I therefore redefine the independent variable. Instead of using a continuous variable I choose to dichotomize it, operating with two categories. The variable can then be used as a dummy variable in a regression analysis. Countries that gained independence prior to 1990 are given the value 0 whereas countries that gained independence later than 1989 are given the value 1.

Results are shown in Table 2.25, and they clearly show that the modifi-

Table 2.25 Association between state longevity-dichotomy and capital punishment in 2000 (bivariate regression)

	B	*Beta*	*T-value*	R^2	N
State longevity (dummy)	−0.416	−0.129	−1.788	0.017	192

Notes
**Significance at the $p < 0.01$ level.
*Significance at the $p < 0.05$ level.

cation of the independent variable does not alter the earlier conclusion that state longevity is an irrelevant explanatory factor for capital punishment. Despite the fact that the abolitionist movement has grown stronger during the last decade, a substantial number of the countries that have received their independence during the 1990s have chosen to make use of the death penalty.

3 Contextual patterns

Global patterns

Multivariate analyses

So far, I have concentrated on identifying bivariate relations between the independent and the dependent variables. Along the way, many significant associations between various independent variables and the dependent variable have been detected. However, it is hazardous to draw any far-reaching conclusions on the determinants of the death penalty on the basis of these bivariate analyses. Many of the independent variables dealt with so far can be expected to be interrelated and I shall therefore proceed by assessing the relative impact of the independent variables studied so far. This is done by means of multiple regression analyses. Since I have made use of a substantial number of explanatory variables, it is necessary to reduce the number of independent variables in order to avoid making the regression models unstable. Another reason for cutting down the number of independent variables is the expectation already put forward that quite a few of the variables interact.

First it is reasonable to exclude from further analysis all independent variables that in the bivariate analyses have been found not to interact with the dependent variable. The criterion for inclusion is that Pearson's r equals or exceeds $(-)0.30$ (for the multi-categorical independent variables, that Eta squared equals or exceeds 0.09) and that $p < 0.01$). This leaves us with the following list of crucial independent variables: dominating religion (1985, 2000), GDP/cap (1985, 2000), infant mortality (1985, 2000), urbanization (1985), literacy (1985), human development index (1985, 2000), number of offenses (1985), corruption (1985, 2000), degree of democracy (1985, 2000), form of government (1985, 2000), colonial heritage (1985, 2000), leadership duration (1985, 2000), regime stability (1985) and slavery (1985, 2000).

Most of these variables are quantitative, which means that they are suitable for multiple regression analyses. Religion, form of government and colonial heritage are qualitative. Consequently they need to be modified before their relative explanatory power can be assessed. The form of government, however, will not be subject to further analysis. The findings showed that democracies made use of the death penalty to a significantly lesser extent than other categories. However, between the other categories there were no significant differences as regards the use of capital punishment. This dimension is consequently already captured by the measure of degree of democracy. As regards religion, we noted that Christian countries (in particular Catholic and Protestant ones), were restrictive in their use of capital punishment whereas Muslim and Buddhist countries made extensive use of the death penalty. In order to assess the relative impact of religion on the death penalty, I create four dummy variables: one where Christian countries are given the value 1 and all other countries 0, labeled "Christianity", another where Muslim countries are given the value 1 and all other countries 0, labeled "Islam", yet another where Buddhist countries are given the value 1 and all other countries 0, labeled "Buddhism" and, finally, one variable labeled "other religion" where countries with other religions than the three mentioned above are given the value 1 and all other countries the value 0. The Christianity-dummy is used as a reference category and will consequently not be included in the regression analyses.

The variable denoting colonial background will also be dichotomized. In the bivariate analysis, there was an interesting finding suggesting that countries without a colonial past applied the death penalty to a lesser extent than other countries. Consequently, I create a dummy variable where countries with a colonial past are given the value 1 and countries without a colonial past the value 0.

Before conducting the multiple regressions we still have to check for multicollinearity among the independent variables. In order to cope with the issue of multicollinearity I have, as a rule, adopted the following strategy: when the internal correlation between two or more independent variables exceeds $(-)0.70$, the variables are not included in the same regression analysis; instead they are introduced in separate regression analyses. A different strategy applies for variables that are considered to express more or less the same phenomenon, such as population size and area. In these cases I include the independent variable that was more strongly related to the dependent variable in the bivariate analyses.

For the year 2000, the following correlations exceed $(-)0.70$: HDI and GDP/cap (0.741), HDI and infant mortality (-0.901), GDP/cap and level of corruption (0.861). The level of corruption will be excluded from the regression analyses, not only due to its connection to other independent variables but also due to its high number of missing cases. HDI, GDP/cap and infant mortality are all measures of socioeconomic development. Since HDI was more strongly related to the death penalty than the two other measures it is included in the regression analysis. A similar picture emerges when studying the variable interactions for 1985. HDI is strongly associated with the degree of democracy, level of corruption and the other measures of socioeconomic development, such as GDP/cap, literacy and infant mortality. The inclusion of HDI strongly reduces the number of cases since we lack information on HDI for the year 1985. Therefore, instead of operating with HDI for the year 1985, I include infant mortality as an indicator of socioeconomic development. Among the four original measures of socioeconomic development, infant mortality was the one most strongly linked to the death penalty. Since GDP/cap, infant mortality, urbanization and literacy are also interlinked, infant mortality is the only measure of socioeconomic development that is included in the regression analysis. Furthermore, I disregard corruption due to the limited number of observations.

The most serious problem of multicollinearity however, is, caused by the variable slavery. As we shall see, a history of slavery goes hand-in-hand with Islam. In addition, slavery is negatively related to Christianity and with the degree of democracy (for 1985 the correlation coefficient yields the value 0.664, whereas the corresponding value for 2000 is somewhat lower, 0.614). What makes these associations problematic is the fact that each of these independent variables was found to possess a considerable amount of explanatory power in the bivariate analyses. Consequently it is not an easy task to determine which of the variables are the most important. Some caution is advised when interpreting the results of the multivariate analyses.

We are thereby ready to turn to the multivariate analyses of the variable interactions. The results for 1985 are given in Table 3.1. The number of variables is very high in relation to the number of cases. In addition, the problem of multicollinearity is not eliminated. An examination of the variance inflation factors (VIF) indicates that slavery is particularly problematic since it is linked to many of the other independent variables. Slavery cannot be included in the same regression as religion and degree of democracy. Therefore, I run two separate regressions, one where slavery is excluded and another where degree of democracy and religion are excluded but slavery is included. The results show that the degree of democracy is the most important factor for explaining the variation in the death penalty at this point of time. Colonial heritage and Buddhism are also linked to the death penalty. The directions of the associations are in conformity with our earlier findings. In other words, countries with a high degree of democracy have a restrictive attitude toward the use of the death penalty whereas countries without a colonial past make use of the

Table 3.1 Dominating religion, infant mortality, number of offenses, degree of democracy, leadership duration, regime stability, colonial heritage and history of slavery as determinants of capital punishment in 1985 (multiple regressions)

Independent variables	Regression 1	Regression 2
Islam	0.261	Not included in model
	0.115	
	1.173	
Buddhism	0.904	Not included in model
	0.165	
	2.023*	
Other religion	0.380	Not included in model
	0.080	
	1.004	
Infant mortality	−0.001	0.001
	−0.026	0.034
	−0.225	0.261
Number of offenses (log)	−0.115	−0.142
	−0.129	−0.160
	−1.324	−1.305
Degree of democracy	0.091	Not included in model
	0.360	
	3.049**	
Leadership duration	0.008	0.027
	0.057	0.166
	0.644	1.729
Regime stability	−0.011	−0.013
	−0.162	−0.173
	−1.797	−1.639
Colonial heritage	0.516	0.447
	0.250	0.214
	2.811**	1.909
History of slavery	Not included in model	0.582
		0.275
		1.939
Multiple R	0.760	0.699
R^2	0.578	0.489
Adjusted R^2	0.527	0.442
F-sig.	0.000	0.000
N	84	72

Notes
In each column, the regression coefficients are listed first, followed by the standardized regression coefficients and the T-values.
**Significance at the $p < 0.01$ level.
*Significance the $p < 0.05$ level.

death penalty to a significantly lesser extent than countries that have been subject to foreign rule. Finally, countries with a Buddhist majority have a more positive view of the death penalty than Christian countries.

Another important issue we have to deal with is the fact that the regression analyses suffer from a serious shortcoming in that the number of cases is quite limited. The inclusion of all relevant independent variables in a multiple regression analysis reduces the number of countries to 72. In order to confirm the results obtained, I further exclude infant mortality and number of offenses, both of which failed to reach a $p < 0.10$ level of statistical significance in both regression analyses. Results are given in Table 3.2, and they confirm the importance of degree of democracy and colonial heritage. However, slavery now appears as a strong determinant of the death penalty. Furthermore, the explanatory power of Buddhism is

Table 3.2 Dominating religion, degree of democracy, leadership duration, regime stability, colonial heritage and history of slavery as determinants of capital punishment in 1985 (multiple regressions)

Independent variables	Regression 1	Regression 2
Islam	0.384	Not included in model
	0.177	
	2.604*	
Buddhism	0.290	Not included in model
	0.076	
	1.216	
Other religion	0.532	Not included in model
	0.165	
	2.727**	
Degree of democracy	0.091	Not included in model
	0.393	
	5.372**	
Leadership duration	0.014	0.028
	0.100	0.182
	1.571	2.528*
Regime stability	−0.008	−0.009
	−0.121	−0.128
	−1.924	−1.751
Colonial heritage	0.363	0.364
	0.185	0.184
	2.999**	2.383*
History of slavery	Not included in model	0.822
		0.416
		4.919**
Multiple R	0.698	0.639
R^2	0.487	0.408
Adjusted R^2	0.464	0.389
F-sig.	0.000	0.000
N	164	132

Notes
In each column, the regression coefficients are listed first, followed by the standardized regression coefficients and the T-values.
**Significance at the $p < 0.01$ level.
*Significance the $p < 0.05$ level.

reduced and, instead, Islam and, especially, a religion other than the three biggest ones emerge as relevant explanatory variables.

Let me thereafter turn to the situation in 2000. This time, all relevant variables can, initially at least, be included in the same regression (an examination of VIF-values indicates that the highest value, 2.690 is obtained for slavery). The results, shown in Table 3.3, suggest that colonial heritage outweighs all other variables. However, it is evident that the internal association between religion, democracy and slavery makes it difficult to interpret the results. In addition, the inclusion of slavery reduces the number of cases to 137. The inclusion of religion and slavery in the same regression appears to be particularly problematic. It is therefore necessary to run additional analyses where religion and slavery are not included in the same regressions. Since HDI turned out to be unimportant and there are a number of missing cases for this variable, I also exclude it from the regression. Results are shown in Table 3.4 and they show that, when slavery is excluded from the regression, democracy and Islam (and, to a lesser extent, Buddhism) affect the death penalty. Furthermore, when excluding religion, we find that slavery stands out as a relevant determinant of the death penalty. Finally, we note that colonial heritage is positively related to the death penalty in all regressions, which means that former colonies make use of the death penalty to a higher extent than countries without a colonial past.

One question is still left open and it concerns the impact of corruption on the death penalty. Since values for corruption were not available for a

Table 3.3 Dominating religion, human development index, degree of democracy, leadership duration, colonial heritage and history of slavery as determinants of capital punishment in 2000 (multiple regression)

Independent variables	B	Beta	T-value
Islam	0.465	0.179	1.709
Buddhism	0.087	0.014	0.180
Other religion	0.280	0.064	0.841
HDI	0.871	0.127	1.409
Degree of democracy	0.072	0.244	2.360*
Leadership duration	0.003	0.013	0.160
Colonial heritage	0.636	0.264	3.646**
History of slavery	0.587	0.248	2.269*

Notes
Multiple R = 0.674.
$R^2 = 0.454$.
Adjusted $R^2 = 0.433$.
N = 137.
**Significance at the $p < 0.01$ level.
*Significance at the $p < 0.05$ level.

Table 3.4 Religion, degree of democracy, leadership duration, colonial heritage and history of slavery as determinants of capital punishment in 2000 (multiple regressions)

Independent variables	Regression 1	Regression 2
Islam	0.582	Not included in model
	0.222	
	2.904**	
Buddhism	0.703	Not included in model
	0.142	
	2.254*	
Other religion	0.441	Not included in model
	0.106	
	1.763	
Degree of democracy	0.089	0.082
	0.306	0.280
	3.902**	3.491**
Leadership duration	0.020	0.016
	0.099	0.072
	1.526	1.030
Colonial heritage	0.452	0.532
	0.183	0.220
	3.009**	3.362**
History of slavery	Not included in model	0.686
		0.288
		3.502**
Multiple R	0.632	0.643
R^2	0.388	0.414
Adjusted R^2	0.368	0.398
F-sig.	0.000	0.000
N	190	154

Notes
In each column, the regression coefficients are listed first, followed by the standardized regression coefficients and the T-values.
**Significance at the $p < 0.01$ level.
*Significance the $p < 0.05$ level.

substantial number of cases, the variable was not included in the multiple regressions. In order to check for the impact of corruption, I included the level of corruption along with the degree of democracy in one regression for 1985 and in another for 2000. The results were indisputable to say the least. In 1985, the beta for the degree of democracy was 0.720 (sig. 0.000) and for the level of corruption −0.029 (sig. 0.804). The corresponding values for 2000 were 0.592 (sig. 0.000) and −0.001 (sig. 0.994). Thus, the level of corruption does not contain explanatory power on its own.

Overall, we note a high level of conformity in the explanatory power of the independent variables in the two points of time. The degree of democracy, slavery and the colonial heritage have a strong impact on the death penalty both in 1985 and in 2000. Religion is also important. When Christianity is used as a point of reference, Islam in particular is a conducive factor for the death penalty. However, before any definitive conclusions can be reached, we still have to try to assess the relative weight of slavery, democracy and religion. As already mentioned, slavery was not only difficult to operationalize, it also aggravated the problem of multicollinearity. Furthermore, since there were many missing cases for the variable, the inclusion of slavery in multiple regression analyses substantially reduced the number of cases. Nevertheless, the statistical analyses suggest that a history of slavery is an important determinant of the death penalty. As has already been stated, the difficulty in assessing the impact of slavery is that it is strongly associated with both the degree of democracy and religion. It is quite possible that each of these variables carries explanatory power, but it is equally possible that only one or two of the variables are important determinants of the death penalty. Furthermore, we cannot overlook the possibility that combinations of these variables are more important than any of the variables independently. In order to assess the impact of each of these independent variables, further tests are required. I therefore proceed with comparisons of means tests in cross-tabulations where Christianity, form of government and a history of slavery are kept constant. Results are given in Tables 3.5 and 3.6.

As can be seen in Tables 3.5 and 3.6, most of the cases are concentrated in two categories, which, of course, reflects the strong association between the three independent variables. However, the cases that fall within the other cells allow us to reach some conclusions of the relative weight of democracy, Christianity and slavery with regard to the death penalty. The results suggest that each of the three variables is important for explaining variations in the death penalty. Both in 1985 and in 2000, none of the

Table 3.5 Form of government, slavery, Christianity and capital punishment in 1985 (arithmetic means and median values)

	Stable democracies		Unstable democracies		Non-democracies	
	Slavery		*Slavery*		*Slavery*	
	Yes	*No*	*Yes*	*No*	*Yes*	*No*
Yes	1.0000 (1.0000) 1	0.9574 (1.0000) 47	2.4000 (2.4000) 2	1.2889 (1.0000) 9	2.4444 (2.3000) 9	2.0571 (2.3000) 14
Christianity						
No	1.8667 (2.3000) 3	2.3500 (2.3500) 2	2.4333 (2.4000) 9	No cases	2.4488 (2.4000) 41	No cases

Table 3.6 Form of government, slavery, Christianity and capital punishment in 2000 (arithmetic means and median values)

	Stable democracies		Unstable democracies		Non-democracies	
	Slavery		Slavery		Slavery	
	Yes	No	Yes	No	Yes	No
Yes	1.3500 (1.3500) 4	0.6556 (0.0000) 63	1.4500 (1.6500) 4	0.8429 (0.2500) 14	2.1600 (2.6000) 5	1.2000 (1.0000) 4
Christianity						
No	2.2500 (2.5000) 8	1.3500 (1.3500) 2	1.8867 (2.0000) 12	1.0000 (1.0000) 1	2.3818 (2.6000) 33	1.9500 (2.5000) 6

variables constitutes a sufficient explanatory factor of the death penalty by itself. In both points in time, the most restrictive attitude toward the death penalty is found in stable democracies, without a history of slavery, and where Christianity is the dominant religion. Correspondingly, non-democracies, with a history of slavery where the dominant religion is another than Christianity have a favorable attitude toward the death penalty. However, positive attitudes toward the death penalty can also be found in democracies with a history of slavery and with a dominant religion other than Christianity. Finally, Christian countries can have a positive view of the death penalty if the country has a history of slavery and/or the form of government is not democratic.

In Tables 3.7 and 3.8 similar cross-tabulations are carried out, where the Christianity-dichotomy is substituted by the Islam-dichotomy. The results

Table 3.7 Form of government, slavery, Islam and capital punishment in 1985 (arithmetic means and median values)

	Stable democracies		Unstable democracies		Non-democracies	
	Slavery		Slavery		Slavery	
	Yes	No	Yes	No	Yes	No
Yes	No cases	No cases	2.4167 (2.3500) 6	No cases	2.4600 (2.4000) 30	No cases
Islam						
No	1.6500 (1.6500) 4	1.0143 (1.0000) 49	2.4400 (2.5000) 5	1.2889 (1.0000) 9	2.4300 (2.3000) 20	2.0571 (2.3000) 14

Table 3.8 Form of government, slavery, Islam and capital punishment in 2000 (arithmetic means and median values)

	Stable democracies		Unstable democracies		Non-democracies	
	Slavery		Slavery		Slavery	
	Yes	No	Yes	No	Yes	No
Islam						
Yes	2.0000 (2.0000) 1	No cases	2.2667 (2.0000) 9	1.0000 (1.0000) 1	2.4462 (2.6000) 26	1.9500 (2.5000) 6
No	1.9455 (2.5000) 11	0.6769 (0.0000) 65	1.1143 (1.0000) 7	0.8429 (0.2500) 14	2.1500 (2.6000) 12	1.2000 (1.0000) 4

are generally in concordance with those obtained in the tables where the Christianity-dichotomy was used. However, the high number of empty cells – a consequence of the fact that Islamic countries have a history of slavery and generally authoritarian forms of government – makes it extremely difficult to come up with generalizations of the effects of the independent variables. This is especially the case concerning 1985 data. Nevertheless, at both points in time the most restrictive attitude toward the death penalty was found in stable democracies, without a history of slavery with a religion other than Islam. Similarly, on both occasions, the most positive attitude toward the death penalty was found in non-democracies, with a history of slavery where Islam was the dominant religion.

The relatively small differences in the death penalty index between Islamic states and other states is perhaps confusing. We should, however, be aware of the fact that Islamic countries are compared to countries with a Christian, Buddhist or "other" religion, whereas the Christian countries were compared to countries with an Islamic, Buddhist or "other" religion. Since Buddhist countries also have high levels of death penalty usage, differences between Islam and all other religions are not, and, indeed cannot be, very high. This, of course, raises the question of the importance of Buddhism. Unfortunately, the number of countries with a Buddhist majority is too small to allow similar cross-tabulations to be conducted. Table 2.6 showed that far more Islamic countries had abolished the death penalty than Buddhist ones (of course the number of Islamic countries was much higher than the number of Buddhist countries). Here, it is still important to note that the multiple regression analyses suggested that the impact of Islam was somewhat stronger than that of Buddhism, when Christianity was used as a reference point. Be that as it may, the evidence nevertheless confirms the earlier finding that

Christianity in particular seems to be conducive to a negative view of the death penalty. The results of the multivariate analyses can thus be expressed in the following way: both in 1985 and 2000, degree of democracy, colonial heritage, a history of slavery and religion constitute the determinants of the death penalty.

Discussion

I shall proceed by discussing the results obtained in the empirical study. Although the multivariate patterns are quite similar in the two points of time, some differences do exist. On both occasions, the degree of democracy constitutes a powerful determinant of the death penalty. The importance of the colonialism-dummy is also stable across time. As concerns religion, the analyses indicated that the difference between Christianity and Islam is important for explaining the use of the death penalty. In Christian countries the death penalty is applied to a lesser extent than in other countries. The association between Islam and the death penalty points in the opposite direction, that is Muslim countries make use of the death penalty to a higher extent than other countries. The bivariate analyses pointed to a strong association between Buddhism and the death penalty. Buddhist countries tended to have a quite favorable attitude toward the death penalty. However, based on the regression analyses it seems correct to draw the conclusion that the difference between Christianity and Islam is more relevant than the one between Christianity and Buddhism for explaining the use of the death penalty.

The link between Christianity and the death penalty cannot be a reflection of a strong inherent acceptance or repudiation of capital punishment in the Christian religions. As we have seen, the attitude toward the death penalty taken in the Bible is ambivalent, to say the least. It is reasonable to expect that the effects of Islam overshadow those of Christianity. This is so because in Muslim countries politics and religion are interlinked. As long as the Koran stipulates that the death penalty should be applied, it is very difficult indeed to abolish it. In other words, it is perhaps fair to say that religion is more important in Islamic countries than in countries where other religions dominate. The same argument applies to Buddhism, but to a lesser extent. As noted earlier, in Buddhism the attitude toward the death penalty is explicitly negative. However, since Buddhism, in contrast to Islam, is not an all-embracing religion, we cannot expect the same rigidity in relation to the use of the death penalty. In its position to the death penalty, Christianity falls between these two religions.

It should nevertheless be clearly stated that the explanatory power of Islam is difficult to assess. There is only one stable democracy where Islam is the dominant religion, Mali. Not all unstable or non-democracies are populated by Muslims, but with the exception of Mali, all Muslim countries fall within these two categories. Thus, Islam as a dominant religion varies almost exclusively among countries that are unstable democracies or non-democracies and thus are already likely to make use of the death penalty. Furthermore, Islam and a history of slavery go hand-in-hand. Regardless of these problems of keeping the three variables constant, the cross-tabulations provided one irrefutable finding: with the exception of one category, made up of the single case of Bosnia-Herzegovina in 2000, all categories where Islam was the dominant religion had high average values on the death penalty. The bivariate analyses also clearly showed that, in the core area of Islam, the death penalty was very popular. All countries with a Muslim majority that had a more restrictive attitude toward the death penalty where geographically located outside this area. Thus, an important qualification to the impact of Islam on the death penalty must be made. Countries with a Muslim majority do not *necessarily* have a favorable attitude toward the death penalty. However, these exceptions can be found only in countries situated outside the core area of Islam.

The most interesting finding is probably the negative relation between a lack of a colonial heritage and the death penalty. Countries that have not been subject to foreign rule have chosen a restrictive policy with regard to the use of the death penalty. As I indicated earlier, there are two theoretical bases to depart from when linking a lack of colonial heritage to a restrictive attitude toward the death penalty. On the one hand, the assumption of a relation between a lack of colonial heritage and a restrictive attitude toward the death penalty departed from the view that former colonies have incorporated the death penalty statutes of their former mother countries into their own legislation. Thus, the use of capital punishment would have been built into the legal frameworks of the former colonies by means of diffusion. As we have seen, there is some evidence in the literature to support this line of reasoning. When countries were colonized, capital punishment was used by all the major colonial powers. Within the African context, it has been argued, capital punishment was sparsely applied prior to the arrival of the Europeans (see Schabas 1997b: 33–35).

The other plausible explanation follows the same line of reasoning that applied to the discussion on the link between a history of slavery and the death penalty. The essence of colonialism implies to a higher or a lesser extent the subjugation of the inhabitants of the colony. In order to keep the native population under control, the use of force and severe punishments constitute useful tools. When people feel they are oppressed, the natural reaction is, of course, to take up the fight against the intruders. The struggle for independence has meant bloodshed, and loss of life in many cases. In the wake of such events, people tend to grow accustomed to corporal punishments and also consider such punishments to be legitimate. In contrast, in societies marked by a long uninterrupted period of independence, violence and corporal punishments are met with repulsion.

It is not an easy task to conclude which, if any, of the two theoretical bases is more relevant for explaining the association between colonial heritage and the death penalty. A tentative answer can nevertheless be obtained by comparing colonial heritage with the variable conflict intensity. If conflicts are more frequent in former colonies than in other countries, the argument that inhabitants of former colonies are more accustomed to violence wins support. If this is not the case, the argument of diffusion seems more plausible. A comparison of means tests reveals that the level of conflict is not higher in former colonies than in countries which have not been subject to foreign rule. For the year 2000, the average level of conflict was the same, 2.58, in both categories of countries. In 1985, the average level of conflict in former colonies was 2.27, whereas the corresponding value for countries without a colonial past was only slightly higher, 2.47. Thus, based on the evidence, it appears as if diffusion is more important than violence as an explanation of the use of the death penalty in former colonies.

Overall, we find that the independent variables explain a slightly higher share of the variation in the dependent variable in 1985 than in 2000. The adjusted R-squares are generally higher in Tables 3.1 and 3.2 than in Tables 3.3 and 3.4. This is probably a reflection of the increasing role of diffusion. As stated earlier, the Western European countries in particular have taken a firm stand against the death penalty during the last decade. The desire to take part in European integration has led to the abolition of the death penalty in many of the former Soviet republics. Consequently we now find a number of anomalies: countries that have abolished the death penalty despite the fact that they are, for instance, non-democratic or have a Muslim majority. Perhaps it is not too venturesome to suggest that generalizations of the determinants of the death penalty will be less and less deterministic as time goes on.

The death penalty in democracies and non-democracies

As we have seen, the degree of democracy is a very strong determinant of the death penalty both in 1985 and 2000. However, since there is some degree of variation in the dependent variable within democracies and autocracies respectively, it is reasonable to assess the determinants of the death penalty within the respective categories as well. A useful strategy is to keep the degree of democracy constant by splitting up the population in democracies and non-democracies. We can then determine if those independent variables, other than the degree of democracy, that were found to contain a high amount of explanatory power in the total population, affect the dependent variable in these two categories to the same extent as before. To begin with, I need to split up the population into relevant subcategories within which further studies can be undertaken. The question is how rigorous should the criteria be when identifying countries with a democratic form of government? Earlier, I used the following categorization: democracies, unstable democracies and authoritarian systems. The issue, of course, is what to do with the middle category, that of unstable democracies. Should these countries be included among the democracies or among the authoritarian systems? Neither alternative is very appealing. Therefore I choose a simple strategy and exclude all countries falling within this middle category. Fortunately, the number of countries classified as unstable democracies is not high enough to render statistical analyses impossible.

Within the respective category, I initially undertake bivariate correlation analyses between all independent variables that have been used in the study at the global level and the death penalty. Since the two contexts are very different from the previous one, which encompassed the whole world, it is certainly fruitful to conduct bivariate analyses with all independent variables that have been used in the study. In other words, although a variable turned out to be unimportant for explaining variations in the death penalty at the global level, it is still possible that effects of variations in the same variable are important within one particular context. The drawback is that the sample is much smaller when we are focusing on either stable democracies or authoritarian states. Bivariate analyses where all variables are included are likely to yield a number of statistically significant results. However, many of these associations are likely to be effects of multicollinearity, and in some cases at least it will be extremely difficult to distinguish the "real" associations from the "false" ones. At the same time it is obvious that we cannot disregard potentially important explanations of the death penalty simply because their inclusion makes the statistical models unstable. Therefore, I choose a middle road and start by running bivariate analyses between independent and dependent variables. However, if and when the results of these bivariate analyses suggest that a surprisingly high number of independent variables are related to the dependent variable, and that many of these associations are likely to be effects of multicollinearity, I shall reduce the number of independent variables by trying to include only those variables that, from a theoretical point of view, are likely to be relevant.

I begin the empirical part by focusing on the category consisting of democracies. For the situation in 1985, the results reveal that six independent variables are linked to the death penalty (the criterion being that Pearson's $r \geq (-)0.30$, or for the multi-categorical variables that Eta squared ≥ 0.09, and $p < 0.01$), namely insularity, index of ethnic fragmentation, index of ethnic–religious fragmentation, dominating religion, the colonial-dummy and state longevity. The impact of Islam and Buddhism cannot be assessed due to lack of variation. Instead, the regression measures the impact of a religion other than Islam or Buddhism in relation to Christianity. The association between IERF and the death penalty is marginally stronger than the one between IEF and the dependent variable (0.391 compared to 0.373) and I therefore include IERF in the regression analysis. The check for multicollinearity reveals that the colonial-dummy and state longevity are highly interrelated (-0.828). Since the colonial-dummy has proven to be more important than state longevity in the previous analyses, and is more strongly connected to the dependent variable in bivariate analysis (0.470 against -0.355), I exclude state longevity from the regression analysis. We can thereby proceed with the multiple regression analyses. Results are given in Table 3.9 and they reveal that none of the independent variables stands out as an important determinant of the death penalty.

Turning to the situation in 2000, bivariate analyses show that the following variables are linked to capital punishment when applying the same criteria as above: index of ethnic–religious fragmentation, dominating religion, income inequality, human development index, corruption, EU trade, colonial heritage and slavery. The incorporation of corruption among the variables reduces the number of cases, since there are many missing values for the level of corruption. In addition, the inclusion of the level of corruption, income inequality and HDI creates a problem of multicollinearity. HDI and income inequality are both measures of socio-economic development and I choose to incorporate only HDI since this

Table 3.9 Insularity, index of ethnic–religious fragmentation, dominating religion and colonial heritage as determinants of capital punishment in stable democracies in 1985 (multiple regression)

Independent variables	B	Beta	T-value
Insularity	0.385	0.193	1.241
IERF	0.511	0.194	1.416
Other religion	0.774	0.223	1.830
Colonial heritage	0.391	0.198	1.117

Notes
Multiple R = 0.556.
$R^2 = 0.309$.
Adjusted $R^2 = 0.255$.
F-sig. = 0.001.
$N = 57$.
**Significance at the $p < 0.01$ level.
*Significance at the $p < 0.05$ level.

measure was more strongly associated with the death penalty in bivariate analyses within the category of stable democracies (−0.398 compared to 0.391). I also disregard corruption, due to the large number of missing cases. Since only one Islamic country, Mali, is classified as a stable democracy, religion includes only the Buddhist- and the "other religion"-dummies.

The result is given in Table 3.10. The first regression is conducted among all democratic countries and EU trade is consequently not included among the explanatory variables. In the second regression, I have included EU trade and therefore left out all EU member states. The results of the first regression suggest that the colonial heritage is the most

Table 3.10 Index of ethnic–religious fragmentation, dominating religion, human development index, EU trade, colonial heritage and history of slavery as determinants of capital punishment in stable democracies in 2000 (multiple regressions)

Independent variables	Regression 1	Regression 2
IERF	0.110	−0.318
	0.042	−0.115
	0.320	−0.814
Buddhism	2.070	1.342
	0.227	0.163
	1.999	1.315
Other religion	0.551	0.568
	0.153	0.172
	1.232	1.315
HDI	−1.575	−0.962
	−0.172	−0.103
	−1.235	−0.726
EU trade	Not included in model	−0.014
		−0.484
		−4.182**
Colonial heritage	0.750	0.728
	0.347	0.320
	2.700**	2.383*
History of slavery	0.003	0.117
	0.001	0.042
	0.007	0.264
Multiple R	0.574	0.663
R^2	0.330	0.439
Adjusted R^2	0.266	0.354
F-sig.	0.000	0.000
N	70	54

Notes
In each column, the regression coefficients are listed first, followed by the standardized regression coefficients and the T-values.
**Significance at the $p < 0.01$ level.
*Significance at the $p < 0.05$ level.

important determinant of the death penalty among democratic countries. However, when EU trade is included among the independent variables, the explanatory power of EU trade stands out as the most important explanatory variable.

The finding which shows that EU trade is a very important determinant of the death penalty is surprising since the dependency factor was expected to be important, particularly among authoritarian countries. Now, it is possible that this finding only reflects the fact that European countries have a more negative attitude toward the death penalty than countries situated in other continents. Of course, we expect those democracies that are situated in Europe to trade more with the countries of the EU than democracies in America or Asia. It is therefore too early to draw any conclusions from the impact of EU trade on the death penalty. In order to eliminate the impact of European democracies I once again re-ran the regression where EU trade was included among the explanatory variables, this time, however, excluding all European democracies. Furthermore, I exclude IERF, religion, HDI and slavery from the regression since the variables did not possess any explanatory value in regression 2. The results are shown in Table 3.11 and they show that the explanatory power of EU trade is reduced when the European democracies are excluded. We also note that colonial heritage no longer possesses any explanatory value.

It is evident that the statistical analyses cannot provide irrefutable evidence of which variables are most important for explaining the death penalty in democracies. Additional analyses are needed. However, for the moment I shall let the matter rest and, instead, proceed by paying attention to the other side of the coin; that is, trying to establish which factors constitute the determinants of the death penalty among non-democratic countries. The analysis will follow the same pattern that applied within the

Table 3.11 EU trade and colonial heritage as determinants of the death penalty in stable non-European democracies in 2000 (multiple regression)

	B	Beta	T-value
EU trade	−0.010	−0.297	−1.886
Colonial heritage	0.372	0.160	1.016

Notes
Multiple R = 0.290.
$R^2 - 0.084$.
Adjusted $R^2 = 0.039$.
F-sig. = 0.165.
$N = 44$.
**Significance at the $p < 0.01$ level.
*Significance at the $p < 0.05$ level.

category of democratic countries. First, I run bivariate analyses between the independent variables and the dependent variable. Having done that, I proceed with checking for multicollinearity among all independent variables that were related to the death penalty.

With regard to the situation in 1985, we find that population size, area, insularity, religion, conflict intensity and regime stability are associated with the death penalty. The association between slavery and the death penalty is above the 0.30 threshold (0.313), but not significant since there are a number of missing cases. However, I choose to include slavery in the regression. Population size is once again incorporated in the regression model and area and insularity are left out. Since slavery and religion are interrelated, they are included in separate regressions. With regard to the year 2000, the results reveal that population size, area, infant mortality and slavery (with the same qualification as in 1985) are statistically linked to the death penalty. Again I choose to include population size and not area in the regression.

Tables 3.12 and 3.13 show the results of the multiple regression analyses for the two points in time. First, we note that slavery is important in 1985. In this respect, the results are in concordance with previous findings. Also in 1985, the explanatory power of Islam seems to be lower than that of slavery. However, in other respects the results of the regressions are rather surprising. For one thing, we note that population size suddenly appears to be the strongest determinant of the death penalty in 1985. The most confusing finding, however, is the strong negative association between infant mortality and the death penalty in 2000. The result suggests that authoritarian countries with a high socioeconomic standard make more frequent use of the death penalty than authoritarian countries with a low socioeconomic standard.

One plausible explanation is that the regression models are unstable. A closer look at the cases reveals that there is indeed good grounds for dismissing the findings in Tables 3.12 and 3.13. The odd findings are probably due to the fact that very few authoritarian countries have abolished the death penalty, either completely or for ordinary crimes. This, of course, makes it difficult to come up with generalizations based on statistical analyses. For instance, the association between infant mortality and the death penalty is almost exclusively explained by those six countries that have abolished the death penalty.[1] All of these have a comparably high level of infant mortality. Now, since there is so little variation on the dependent variable in this category (only seven countries have abolished the death penalty, no less than 56 countries make use of it) the regression models necessarily become unstable. For 1985, the distribution is even more distorted. Only four countries had abolished the death penalty completely (one of which was the extremely small Vatican State, which, of

Table 3.12 Population size, religion, conflict intensity, regime stability and history of slavery as determinants of capital punishment in non-democratic countries in 1985 (multiple regressions)

Independent variables	Regression 1	Regression 2
Population (log)	0.152	0.189
	0.559	0.716
	4.648**	5.710**
Islam	0.195	Not included in model
	0.176	
	1.831	
Buddhism	−0.007	Not included in model
	−0.004	
	−0.038	
Other religion	0.192	Not included in model
	0.113	
	1.202	
Conflict intensity	0.001	−0.114
	0.002	−0.287
	0.018	−2.347*
Regime stability	−0.004	−0.001
	−0.079	−0.020
	−0.805	−0.182
History of slavery	Not included in model	0.433
		0.348
		3.423**
Multiple R	0.639	0.691
R^2	0.408	0.478
Adjusted R^2	0.363	0.442
F-sig.	0.000	0.000
N	86	63

Notes
In each column, the regression coefficients are listed first, followed by the standardized regression coefficients and the T-values.
**Significance at the $p < 0.01$ level.
*Significance at the $p < 0.05$ level.

course, contributes heavily to the strong association between population size and the death penalty), one country had only abolished it for ordinary crimes, and 83 countries applied it.

A better strategy for explaining variations in the death penalty in authoritarian countries is to take a closer look at the deviant cases; that is, the few countries that are non-democratic but have abolished the death penalty partly or completely. At the same time it is, of course, of interest to take a closer look at the other side of the coin as well; that is, the democratic countries that apply the death penalty. As we remember, in this category as well, the statistical analyses failed to come up with unassailable results. I begin the analysis of the deviant cases by identifying the demo-

Table 3.13 Population size, infant mortality and history of slavery as determinants of capital punishment in non-democratic countries in 2000 (multiple regression)

Independent variables	B	Beta	T-value
Population (log)	0.094	0.172	1.239
Infant mortality	−0.009	−0.390	−2.853**
History of slavery	0.430	0.200	1.456

Notes
Multiple R = 0.466.
R^2 = 0.217.
Adjusted R^2 = 0.163.
F-sig. = 0.014.
N = 47.
**Significance at the $p < 0.01$ level.
*Significance at the $p < 0.05$ level.

cracies that apply the death penalty. These countries are listed in Table 3.14.

On examination, it transpires that many of the countries are located in the Americas. One is especially struck by the fact that the death penalty is very popular among the Caribbean democracies. The use of the death penalty in the Caribbean in general and in Jamaica in particular is often motivated by high levels of violent crime (Hood 1996: 45). The death penalty is used as a means of deterrence. From a comparative perspective, the crime rates in many Caribbean countries are indeed higher than in the Americas in general. However, this holds true only for total offenses and not for murders. In 2000, the average number of total offenses per 100,000 inhabitants was 4,596 in the Caribbean and 2,892 in the rest of America (T-sig. 0.317), whereas the corresponding numbers for murders were 12.0 for the Caribbean countries and 16.0 for the other countries in the Americas (T-sig. 0.514). For 1985, the average number of offenses in the Caribbean reaches the level of 2,896, whereas the value for the rest of the Americas is roughly the same, 3,100 (T-sig. 0.901). Corresponding numbers for murders are not available. Thus, although the crime rate might help to explain the popularity of the death penalty in the Caribbean, it hardly stands out as the exclusive determinant in the region.

The Caribbean exception should be viewed from a completely new angle. One plausible explanation immediately stands out when we consider the history of the Caribbean nations, namely slavery. The Caribbean countries are to a very large extent populated by adherents of emancipated slaves. In this respect, the countries stand in sharp contrast to the other nations on the American continent. In most of the Americas, the bulk of the population's ancestors saw the new continent in terms of freedom and new opportunities, not a life in chains. Slaves, of course, grow

Table 3.14 Democratic countries with capital punishment at two points in time

Democracies with capital punishment in 1985	Democracies with capital punishment in 2000
Antigua & Barbuda	Bahamas
Bahamas	Barbados*
Barbados	Belize*
Belgium*	Benin*
Belize	Botswana
Bolivia*	Chile*
Botswana	Dominica*
Dominica	Ghana
Greece*	Grenada*
Grenada	Guyana
India	India
Ireland*	Jamaica*
Jamaica	Japan
Japan	Korea (South)
Liechtenstein*	Mali*
Mauritius	Mongolia
Nauru*	Nauru*
St. Kitts & Nevis	Papua New Guinea*
St. Lucia	Philippines
St. Vincent & Grenadines	Samoa (Western)*
Trinidad & Tobago	St. Kitts & Nevis
USA	St. Lucia
	St. Vincent & Grenadines
	Suriname
	Taiwan
	Thailand
	Trinidad & Tobago
	USA

Note
*Countries where no executions have occurred in ten years or more.

accustomed not only to hard labor, but also to hard punishments and the ever-presence of death. Therefore, it should come as no surprise that in societies where a large majority of the population is made up of ex-slaves, corporal punishment is widely applied and human lives are not greatly valued. The importance of a history of slavery wins support when we compare the island states in the Pacific with the Caribbean countries. Although the two categories of countries are geographically far from each other, they are quite similar in many respects. In both regions the countries are small island states. Both categories are made up of countries with exceptionally high levels of democracy. In both categories the countries have a British colonial heritage. The level of development is approximately the same in the two regions. Yet, whereas the death penalty is extremely popular in the Caribbean countries, it is rarely applied in the

Pacific. One plausible explanation for the differing attitude between the two categories of countries toward the death penalty is their differing experience with slavery. The Caribbean countries were populated by emancipated slaves at the same time as the native population, the Carib Indians, was becoming extinct. The native population in the British colonies in the Pacific, however, was never put in chains.

The Caribbean countries were not classified as countries with a history of slavery since they had abolished slavery prior to 1879. As mentioned earlier (page 86), there are features of slavery that my independent variable labeled "history of slavery" fails to capture. Slavery thus appears to be a more relevant explanatory factor than the statistical analyses suggest. On the other hand, we should be careful not to exaggerate the importance of slavery. Although it provides a reasonable explanation for the use of the death penalty in the Caribbean, the number of countries predominantly populated by adherents of ex-slaves is, after all, quite low. Another plausible explanation is that the Caribbean is a region which historically is associated with violent crime. With the arrival of Columbus, many places in the Caribbean became dreaded centers of pirates. It was the geographical center for the Atlantic slave trade and the Caribbean countries are, to a very large extent, populated by ancestors of African slaves. Today, despite high levels of democracy, some of the Caribbean countries are havens for various kinds of money-launderers, and the unapproachable archipelago constitutes an important geographical link in the drug-traffic from South America to North America and Europe.[2]

Another striking feature is the absence of European democracies that make use of capital punishment in 2000. Fifteen years earlier, a number of Western European democracies still had death penalty statutes, although these had not been applied for many years. The unpopularity of the death penalty among European democracies in particular can be linked to the discussion of the role of diffusion. Diffusion plays an important role in explaining the death penalty, especially for the European continent. In 1996, the Council of Europe adopted Protocol No. 6 to the Convention for the Protection of Human Rights and Fundamental Freedoms. In order to qualify as members of the Council of Europe, countries were required to abandon the death penalty, at least for ordinary crimes. The Eastern European countries, eager to take part in European integration, have consequently been more or less forced to abolish the death penalty. It would indeed be interesting to know whether or not the former Eastern European countries would have abolished the death penalty to such an extent had this requirement not existed. It is not unreasonable to expect that the link between democracy and the absence of capital punishment would be considerably weaker without this requirement. (The impact of the

European Union's forceful stand against the death penalty on the former Eastern European countries will be discussed later, see pages 137–138).

Finally, it is reasonable to assume that stable democracies are more likely to have rejected the death penalty than newly democratized countries. The democracies that have partly or completely abolished the death penalty have a somewhat higher degree of democracy than the democracies that make use of the death penalty. In 1985, the average degree of democracy for the democratic countries that upheld capital punishment statutes was 3.59 and the corresponding value for the remainder of the democratic states was 3.11 (T-sig. 0.136). In 2000, the average degree of democracy for the democracies that made use of the death penalty was 3.57, whereas the corresponding value for the other democracies was 2.88 (T-sig. 0.003). These results seem to suggest that countries that turn from an autocratic form of government to a democratic one tend to make use of the death penalty for some time after the transition to democracy before eventually joining the abolitionist movement. In this respect, Ghana, Mali and Suriname are illustrative. These three countries did not qualify as democracies until the year 2000. If the empirical material had been collected one year earlier, the countries would not constitute anomalies.

In addition to the extreme cases of democracies that still apply the death penalty, we find countries that are anomalies in the opposite direction; that is, they are non-democratic but have restricted the use of, or, alternatively, completely abolished the death penalty. From a theoretical point of view, these latter cases are at least as interesting as the former ones. Table 3.15 lists the authoritarian countries that have abolished the death penalty completely or partly.

Table 3.15 Authoritarian abolitionist countries at two periods in time

Authoritarian countries that had abolished the death penalty in 1985	*Authoritarian countries that had abolished the death penalty in 2000*
Cape Verde	Angola
Nicaragua	Azerbaijan
Panama	Cambodia
Vatican State	Haiti
	Ivory Coast
	Turkmenistan
	Vatican State
Authoritarian countries abolitionist for ordinary crimes only in 1985	*Authoritarian countries abolitionist for ordinary crimes only in 2000*
Seychelles	

Table 3.15 reveals that no geographical pattern emerges. Europe, Asia, Africa and Latin America are all represented. There are nevertheless some characteristics that are common for the countries included in Table 3.15. If we start by looking at the extreme exceptions, i.e. authoritarian countries that have abolished the death penalty completely (with the exception of the Vatican State), we immediately become aware of a striking difference between the situation in 1985 and the one in 2000. For 2000, the exceptions are countries where the people have recently lived through breaking points in their modern history. In order to pinpoint the reasons underlying the decisions not to make use of the death penalty in these countries, it is necessary to discuss the deviant cases in detail.

Angola gained its independence in 1975 after a bitter struggle against the Portuguese government. During the Cold War, Angola was one of the many battlegrounds where the interests of the USA and the Soviet Union clashed. The consequence was a long and brutal civil war where the socialist government was supported by the Soviet Union and Cuba, and the rebel National Union for Total Independence (UNITA) was backed by the USA and South Africa. With the end of the Cold War, it finally became possible for the United Nations to make a tenacious effort to reach a peace agreement. As a result of the UN involvement, a peace treaty was signed in May 1991 in Bicesse, Portugal. The ruling Popular Movement for the Liberation of Angola (MPLA) was subject to tremendous external as well as internal demands for reforms. Consequently, fundamental changes were undertaken, including a new electoral law, a movement in the direction of a market economy and with reforms enhancing the civil liberties of the citizens (Tvedten 1993: 110). General elections were held in September 1992, and international observers generally regarded them as "free and fair". The elections were won with a safe margin by MPLA. However, the democratic experiment in Angola was not to be long-lived. A little more than a month after the elections, fighting recurred, and in early 1993 the elected institutions "worked only on paper" (Tvedten 1993: 116).

The fate of the death penalty in Angola is very closely linked to the end of the civil war and the reforms undertaken in that period. In the MPLA draft constitution of the republic of Angola, article XIII states that:

> The role of the state is to respect and protect human life, which constitutes a fundamental right to the individual. No law of Angola may prescribe death as a competent sentence. No Court or Tribunal shall have the power to impose a sentence of death upon any person. No executions shall take place in Angola.
>
> (Blaustein and Flanz, 1992–1997)

Angola thus abolished the death penalty for all crimes in 1992 as an effect of the end of the civil war. The Angolan exception, as well as the negative stands toward the death penalty taken by Mozambique and Namibia, "has been interpreted as a respone to the repression that these states endured under decades of oppressive white rule" (Schabas 1997b: 35). This view, however, is contradicted by another plausible explanation which argues that the unpopularity of the death penalty in Angola, Mozambique and Namibia is explained by their past as former Portuguese colonies. Portugal, it is suggested, "has been one of the world's most resolutely abolitionist states and ... its former colonies did not have the death penalty, at least for common crimes, while under colonial rule" (Schabas 1997b: 56–57).

Along with the other countries formerly part of the Soviet Union, Azerbaijan became independent in 1991. Ever since, these former republics of the Soviet Union have taken quite different approaches toward capital punishment. Azerbaijan chose to join the abolitionist movement and capital punishment was consequently abolished for all crimes in 1998.[3] It should be stressed that, regarding the death penalty, Azerbaijan is highly deviant, as it is also a Muslim state. Thus, the case of Azerbaijan contradicts two strong generalizations that have been made in the course of the study: that authoritarian states and Islamic states make use of the death penalty.

The political situation in Azerbaijan had been highly unstable prior to the dissolution of the Soviet Union due to the conflict in Nagorno-Karabakh, a region in Azerbaijan with a predominantly Armenian population. After the fall of the Soviet Union, the conflict over Nagorno-Karabakh continued, and spoiled relations between Azerbaijan and Armenia. Finally, a cease-fire was reached in May 1994. Contrary to many other former Soviet republics, Azerbaijan has not yet embarked on the road to democratization. The constitution of 1995 gives the president far-reaching powers. Presidential elections were held in October 1998, where the president, Heydar Aliyev was re-elected with a vote share of 76.1 percent. The elections were criticized by international observers as "flawed and undemocratic" ("Election Watch", *Journal of Democracy* 1999, 10, 1: 173). Earlier, in January 1998, President Aliyev had proposed that the death penalty be completely abolished. The following month the bill was adopted by parliament by an overwhelming majority. Although Aliyev claimed his decision was based on humanitarian grounds, observers argued that the real reason was a desire to join the Council of Europe (Halperin 1998).

If Azerbaijan's position as an abolitionist state is explained by a desire to take part in European integration, the same does not apply for Turkmenistan. Turkmenistan abolished the death penalty in 1999. To date it is the only post-communist country that has abolished the death penalty without being subject to European pressure (at least not to the same extent as the countries that have applied for membership to the Council of Europe). Turkmenistan has not applied for membership in the Council of Europe.

When it comes to Cambodia, it is indeed easy to agree with Jeldres (1993: 104) who states that "[f]ew societies have been as badly devastated by war, foreign occupation, and state repression as Cambodia". In 1975, the violent Marxist organization Khmer Rouge overthrew the government. Even though widespread terror was not unfamiliar to the Cambodians, few could foresee the cruelties committed by the Khmer Rouge in the following years. At least one million Cambodians lost their lives during the Khmer Rouge terror until Vietnamese forces finally invaded the country in 1979.

Violence did not come to an end with the Vietnamese intervention, however. Threatened by Vietnam, the countries of the Association of Southeast Asian Nations (ASEAN), along with the USA and China, gave their support to opposition forces. In 1982, a coalition called the Coalition Government of Democratic Kampuchea (CDGK) was created. The alliance was made up of Khmer Rouge along with two non-communist groups: The National Army of Independent Cambodia and the Khmer People's National Liberation Front. In the 1980s, the Hun Sen regime in Phnom Pehn, backed by Vietnam, had to confront the powerful resistance of the unholy alliance of CDGK. The political stalemate finally came to an end when, in 1989, Vietnam announced that it was pulling out of Cambodia. In October 1991, the parties signed agreements on a settlement of the conflict. A broad coalition comprising representatives of all parties was established. This body, called the Supreme National Council of Cambodia (SNC), was to exercise full authority during a transitional period. Along with SNC, the UN was heavily involved in the peace process, with the creation of the United Nations Transitional Authority in Cambodia (UNTAC) which was to work in close cooperation with the SNC (Jeldres 1993: 105).

Under the auspices of the UN, elections to a Constituent Assembly were held in 1993. The most successful political group was the royalist United National Front for an Independent, Neutral, Peaceful, and Co-operative Cambodia (FUNCINPEC). A coalition government was established where Prince Ranariddh and Hun Sen acted as co-premiers. The struggle for power continued between the two leaders and, in 1997, a coup gave Hun Sen all of the power. After international pressure, elections were held in 1998, but "[i]nternational observers gave conflicting reports on the fairness of the elections" ("Election Watch", *Journal of Democracy* 1998, vol. 9, No. 4: 176).

Cambodia abolished the death penalty for all crimes in 1989, at the end of the civil war. At that point, the Hun Sen regime was under severe pressure. As a means of appealing to a larger part of the population, a number of political, economic and agricultural reforms were undertaken between 1988 and 1989. One of those was to change the name of the country from the People's Republic of Kampuchea to the State of Cambodia (*Regional Surveys of the World: The Far East and Australasia 1997*: 178). The abolition of the death penalty can thus probably be seen primarily as an attempt by the Hun Sen Regime to widen its support base.

In 1957, François Duvalier was elected President of Haiti. Ethnicity played a major role in Haiti during the first decade of Duvalier's government. Duvalier sought to enhance the position of the black population in relation to the mulattos, which had previously held political power. Violence soon erupted and many people were killed or left the country. In 1964, Duvalier, through an amendment of the Constitution, made himself president for life. In 1971, Duvalier died and was succeeded by his son Jean-Claude. For a long time, the USA, eager to prevent ties between Haiti and Cuba from becoming too close, had supported the regimes of the Duvaliers. In 1984, discontent with Duvalier was widespread and riots broke out. By this time, the position of the USA had changed, and the US government openly demanded political reforms. In 1986, Duvalier was forced to flee the country and was substituted by General Henri Namphy, who enjoyed the support of the US government.

Political reforms were promised and a new constitution was adopted in 1987, paving the way for a democratic form of government. However, opposition from groups loyal to Duvalier was fierce. After a turbulent period, during which Namphy was overthrown and substituted by General Prosper Avril, presidential elections were finally held in 1990. The elections were won by Jean-Bertrand Aristide, who, however, soon lost the support of the groups that previously had supported him. In September 1991, Aristide was overthrown in a military coup, but subsequently reinstalled as president in September 1994 after heavy pressure from the USA. In 1996, Aristide left office and was substituted by René Préval, who had won by a landslide in the presidential elections in December 1995 (*Regional Surveys of the World: South America, Central America and the Caribbean 1997*). Ever since, the political system of Haiti has been turbulent and the country has not yet gained the status of a democracy.

The fate of the death penalty in Haiti is closely tied to the historical events described above. The death penalty was abolished in the constitution of 1987. Article 20 bluntly states: "[t]he death penalty is abolished in all cases". It should nevertheless be stated that, although the death penalty was allowed prior to 1987, death sentences had not been carried out for a long time in Haiti. The last execution took place in 1972 (Hood 1996: 214). The constitution was adopted in 1987, after the overthrow of Jean-Claude

Duvalier. The same constitution frames a democratic country. Legislative power is vested in a two-chamber parliament, elected by universal suffrage. Executive power is conferred to the president and the government headed by the prime minister. The government is responsible before parliament. Thus, Haiti is a good example of a country which forbids the use of the death penalty in the aftermath of turbulent periods, where initial steps toward democratization are taken. Therefore, even though Haiti constitutes an anomaly in the sense that it is a non-democratic country which forbids the use of the death penalty, the abolition of the death penalty occurred at a stage in a process which aimed at introducing a democratic form of government. In other words, one could argue, democracy explains why the death penalty is forbidden in non-democratic Haiti.

Ever since gaining independence from France in 1960, the Ivory Coast has been an authoritarian state. Elections have been held at regular intervals, but until 1990 only one party was allowed to participate. However, elections after 1990 have not met the standard of "free and fair". For 33 years, the Ivory Coast was ruled by Felix Houphouët-Boigny. After his death in 1993, he was succeeded by Henri Konan Bédié, who, in his turn, was overthrown in 1999 by General Robert Guëi (*Freedom in the World 2000–2001*: 158).

The death penalty was abolished in 2000, when a new constitution was adopted. However, in the Ivory Coast, executions had not occurred for many decades. This is probably best explained by the fact that long-time president Felix Houphouët-Boigny was opposed to the death penalty. However, this negative view of capital punishment was not shared by all politicians in the Ivory Coast. In 1995, parliament extended the range of crimes for which death sentences could be laid down. The law, which was never ratified by President Bédié, also stipulated that executions be public (Amnesty International, September 2000, ACT 53/03/00). What is remarkable in the case of the Ivory Coast is the fact that the death penalty was abolished in connection with a military coup. The constitution, framed by the military government led by General Guëi, and adopted in a referendum in July 2000, outlawed the death penalty. However, the abolition of the death penalty did not go hand-in-hand with an increase in human rights. Amnesty International (September 2000, AFR 31/003/2000), for instance, has noted that "[the] practice of summary executions has dramatically increased since the coup of December 1999". The situation in the Ivory Coast is still highly unstable. In October 2000, Guëi lost the presidential elections to Laurent Gbagbo and was subsequently forced to leave the office.

Many of the cases thus show remarkable similarities in the respect that they all have experienced violent conflicts prior to the abolition of the death penalty. For Angola, Cambodia, the Ivory Coast and Haiti, the abolition of the death penalty coincides with the end of internal struggles. Thus, when trying to reach an agreement that would stabilize the political situation, the different parties have had to come up with solutions to overcome the bleeding wounds from the civil wars. In such a situation the abolition of very cruel punishments comes naturally. Another factor also seems to be at least as important. One striking feature for Angola and Cambodia is the active role the United Nations played in the peace processes. It is probably not an overstatement to say that UN involvement in the Angolan peace process has been decisive for the abolition of the death penalty from the penal code of the country. The situation in Cambodia is a little bit different. The death penalty was abolished slightly before the UN gained an active role in the peace process, as a first step in the process of liberalization started by the Hun Sen regime in 1988.

Although there are some similarities with other countries studied here, notably the occurrence of an armed conflict, overall the case of Azerbaijan is different. In Azerbaijan, the death penalty was abolished as a first step in the process of becoming a member of the Council of Europe. Thus, it is evident that pressure from an international organization played a crucial role in the abolition of the death penalty in Azerbaijan as well. In January 2001, Azerbaijan gained the status of a member of the Council of Europe along with Armenia, where the death penalty was abolished for ordinary crimes in 2003. The conclusions that can be drawn from the studies of the non-democratic countries that have abolished the death penalty completely is that special circumstances explain the negative stand against capital punishment in each country. Nevertheless, it is evident that some common characteristics can be found; that is, a violent modern history combined with the active involvement of international organizations in the shaping of the political landscape and constitutional framework. Thus, it seems fair to say that diffusion seems to be the key word when explaining the anomalies in 2000.

Let me now turn to the deviant cases in 1985. At this point of time, Cape Verde, Nicaragua and Panama had abolished the death penalty completely, despite the fact that they were non-democratic. In addition, the Seychelles had abolished the death penalty for ordinary crimes. A former Portuguese colony, Cape Verde gained the status of an independent state in 1975, and adopted a constitution in 1980. At that time, the ambition was to unite Cape Verde and Guinea-Bissau. However, these plans were given up following the coup in Guinea-Bissau in 1980. Until 1991, Cape Verde was a single-party state, ruled by the African Party for the Independence of Cape Verde (PAICV). During this period, Cape Verdeans lived under quite favorable socioeconomic conditions, at least in comparison to other states in the region (Medhanie 1993: 63). In comparison to many other countries, the transition to democracy was smooth, and was not preceded by "much pressure from the street" (Anckar and Anckar 1995: 225). In 1990, PAICV decided that multiparty elections were to be held (Blaustein and Flanz, 1993–1994). Following elections in 1991, Cape Verde became the first single-party state in sub-Saharan Africa where a change in power took place as a consequence of free elections (Cahen 1991). In these elections, PAICV lost the power to the Movement for Democracy (MpD), which was also victorious in the 1995 elections.

Cape Verde abolished the death penalty for all crimes in 1981, one year after the adoption of the constitution. Prior to that, the death penalty had not been in active use for a very long period – the last execution took place in 1835 (Hood 1996: 241). The unpopularity of the death penalty in Cape Verde is probably best explained by the Portuguese colonial heritage. As mentioned earlier, in the Portuguese colonies, the death penalty was never applied for ordinary crimes.

As a consequence of a revolt, caused by objections in the Colombian Congress to the canal concession treaty with the United States, Panama received its independence in 1903. Because of the important strategic location of Panama and the US-administered Canal Zone, Panama has been strongly influenced by the United States during its whole period as an independent state. The marked US presence in Panama and discontent with the treaty caused protests from the Panamanians. In 1977, the United States and Panama agreed to abolish the Canal Zone and the Panama Canal Company was replaced by the Panama Canal Commission (*Regional Surveys of the World: South America, Central America and the Caribbean 1997*: 517).

The reasons for Panama's position as an abolitionist country cannot be sought in its history. Panama received its independence in 1903, and the death penalty was immediately abolished. It is important to note that the country from which Panama seceded, Colombia, abolished the death penalty seven years later. A distinguishing quality for Latin America is that, whereas the death penalty in many parts of the region was abolished at a very early stage in history, military governments have had no difficulties in reinstating it in times of political instability (Hood 1996: 43–44). Panama, however, does not fit into this pattern. Along with Colombia, Costa Rica, Ecuador, Uruguay and Venezuela, Panama belongs to the group of Latin American countries that abolished the death penalty for all crimes in the late nineteenth or early twentieth century and have remained abolitionist after that, irrespective of whether a democratic or a military regime has been in power. Thus, the strong abolitionist tradition seems to be the best explanation for Panama's position as a deviant case in 1985.

For a long time, Nicaragua was ruled by the Somoza family. This period began in 1936, when the Commander of the National Guard, Anastasio Somoza, seized power in a coup. Somoza's two sons, Luis and Anastasio, followed in the footsteps of their father. This meant concentrating power in the hands of the family and increasing its ownership within the economic and agriculture fields (*Regional Surveys of the World: South America, Central America and the Caribbean 1997*: 494). Popular dissatisfaction with the Somoza rule allowed the Marxist guerrillas, the Sandinistas (named after General Augusto César Sandino), to widen its base of support among the population. In the forefront of the non-Marxist opposition was a party coalition led by Pedro Joaquín Chamorro. In the 1970s, internal and external dissatisfaction with the Somoza regime grew stronger and, in 1978, culminated in the assassination of Chamorro. In 1979, Somoza was overthrown in "one of the most broadly-based and popular insurrections in the history of Latin America" (*Regional Surveys of the World: South America, Central America and the Caribbean 1997*: 495).

Power was conferred to the earlier-established Junta of National Reconstruction, which was made up of representatives of the Sandinistas and their allies. In the beginning, the new government had widespread support. The property of the Somoza family was expropriated and social, political and economic reforms initiated. As the Sandinastas became more radical, and sympathetic to the Soviet Union, opposition against the Sandinista regime grew stronger, and in 1981, former members of the National Guard, loyal to Somoza, began fighting the regime. The guerilla groupings, called Contras, received massive support from the Reagan administration. Along with military aid to the Contras, the US government put an embargo on trade with Nicaragua in 1985. The economic sanctions, combined with the costs of fighting the Contras, had devastating consequences for the Nicaraguan economy. In 1989, President Daniel Ortega announced that elections would be held in 1990. The elections were observed by 2,578 accredited foreign observers from 278 organizations (Pastor 1990: 18), and they resulted in a comfortable victory for the candidate of the opposition, Violeta Chamorro, widow of Pedro Joaquín Chamorro. The elections ended the era of the Sandinastas in Nicaragua. The Sandinistas suffered another loss in the 1996 presidential and parliamentary elections when Daniel Ortega was again defeated in the presidential race.

Like many other Latin American countries, Nicaragua had a restrictive policy concerning the use of the death penalty. The last execution occurred in 1930 (Hood 1996: 242). The death penalty was abolished for all crimes in 1979 by the Sandinistas immediately after they came to power (Hood 1996: 40–41). Thus, Nicaragua fits nicely into the pattern found in 2000, where capital punishment is abolished in the aftermath of a bloody internal conflict.

The Seychelles gained independence from Britain in 1976. The country was initially governed by a coalition comprising the Seychelles Democratic Party (SDP) and the socialist Seychelles People's United Party

(SPUP). However, in 1977, the SPUP and its leader, Albert René, usurped power in a *coup d'état*. In 1979, a new constitution was proclaimed, whereby a one-party state was established. During the 1980s the Seychelles was a one-party socialist state. However, in 1992 and 1993 a process of democratization occurred (*Europa World Yearbook* 2003: 3650–3651). A new constitution was approved in a referendum in 1993 and, ever since, the Seychelles can be classified as an unstable democracy. What is remarkable is the fact that René's rule has survived the transition from a socialist state to a democracy and he has been able to hold on to power ever since 1977.

Death penalty trends in the Seychelles go hand-in-hand with the changes in the form of government described above. The death penalty was abolished for ordinary crimes in the constitution of 1979, which was introduced after René's coup in 1977. The total abolition of the death penalty was related to the transition toward a democratic form of government. In the new democratic constitution of 1993, the death penalty was abolished for all crimes. Thus, in the Seychelles, the death penalty is linked to major upheavals in society.

The discussion of the anomalies seems to suggest that, although non-democratic countries are likely to make use of the death penalty, this is not a rule without exceptions. A past experience with violent internal conflicts appears to constitute a conducive factor to the abolition of the death penalty, particularly if international organizations have been involved in the peace process. In addition, as the case of Azerbaijan clearly illustrates, non-democratic countries might abandon capital punishment as a consequence of international pressure. For a few other cases, it is more difficult to point at direct reasons for the choice to not make use of capital punishment. Although tradition is a concept difficult to capture, it is obviously very important for explaining the anomalies in Latin America.

Regional patterns

So far, all the analyses have been conducted at the global level. The aim has been to identify universal explanations for the death penalty. As a result of these analyses, a number of explanatory factors have been established. At the same time, we know, based on the evidence in Chapter 1 (pages 18–20), that there are significant regional variations with regard to the use of the death penalty. It is not unreasonable to expect that different factors explain the use of the death penalty in different regions. I shall therefore continue the study by conducting statistical analyses within regional settings. In the overview of the use of the death penalty in Chapter 1 (pages 18–20), the countries of the world were confined to six regions, namely Africa south of the Sahara, America, Asia, Europe, North

Africa, and the Middle East and Oceania. As we recall, the use of the death penalty varied a lot across these regions. Nevertheless, some variation does exist within the regions as well, and it is of foremost importance that we establish if different independent variables explain the variation in the dependent variable in different regional settings.

Both for theoretical and methodological purposes it is now necessary to operate with a looser definition of region. On the one hand, there is a substantial risk that the theoretical conclusions reached by studying small regions are quite vague and self-evident. It is fair to expect that countries that are geographically close to each other are similar in many respects, as well as in regard to many of the variables used in the study. This, of course, has the implication that the independent variables do not vary enough to allow us to reach any far-reaching conclusions of the determinants of the death penalty. The region of North Africa and the Middle East is especially problematic, as all countries but one (Israel) are non-democratic and Islamic. Furthermore, from a methodological point of view, it is desirable that the number of countries in each region is large enough to allow us to apply the same statistical methods that we have used so far in the study.

These arguments, of course, have to be weighed against the obvious advantage of operating with small regions, namely that the regions are distinct to the extent that it is reasonable to expect that different factors might explain the death penalty in those regions. After weighing these arguments against each other, I have chosen to alter the earlier-adopted regional partition in two respects. First, the problematic region North Africa and the Middle East is no longer used as such. Instead, North Africa is combined with sub-Saharan Africa to make the region of Africa, and the rest of the countries in the Middle East are now included in the category of Asian countries. Second, the region of Oceania is merged with the region of Asia into a regional setting called Asia and the Pacific. The aforesaid means that the determinants of the death penalty will be assessed in the following four regional settings: Africa, America, Asia and the Pacific, and Europe.

The analysis will be conducted in the same way as the studies within the separate categories democracies and autocracies. In other words, for each region, I run bivariate correlations between all the independent variables and the dependent variable. After a check for multicollinearity, those independent variables that were statistically linked to the dependent variable will be included in a multiple regression analysis.

Africa

I begin by assessing the situation in Africa. In 1985, six variables were statistically linked to the death penalty (the criterion being that Pearson's

$r \geq (-)0.30$, or for the multi-categorical variables, that Eta squared ≥ 0.09, and $p < 0.01$), namely population size, area, insularity, religion, conflict intensity and regime stability. It is worth noting that the degree of democracy is unimportant in this region. The three variables that denote physical characteristics – population, area and insularity – are interlinked and I choose to include insularity only because it is more strongly associated with the dependent variable than population size or area. Beside these relations, no other problems of multicollinearity exist (no other association between the independent variables exceeds $(-)0.50$). Since no African country is Buddhist, the Buddhism-dummy is excluded from the regression analysis, the results of which are shown in Table 3.16.

In 1985, the results indicate that only insularity is statistically linked with the death penalty. In Africa, island states are more restrictive with the use of the death penalty than mainland states. None of the other independent variables are linked with the death penalty. However, the fact that so few countries had abolished the death penalty in Africa in 1985 is likely to affect the reliability of the statistical analysis. The only abolitionist country was Cape Verde, and only the Seychelles had abolished it for ordinary crimes only. Needless to say, the results from the statistical analyses rest on a very fragile basis.

In 2000, however, the situation was different. The abolitionist movement had now reached the African continent. Bivariate analyses show that the following variables are statistically linked to the dependent variable: population size, area, insularity, religion, trade dependency (log), conflict intensity, degree of democracy and regime stability. Of the three physical variables, population size is more strongly linked to the death penalty than

Table 3.16 Insularity, dominating religion, conflict intensity and regime stability as determinants of capital punishment in Africa in 1985 (multiple regression)

Independent variables	B	Beta	T-value
Insularity (log)	−0.714	−0.495	−4.058**
Islam	−0.016	−0.017	−1.425
Other religion	0.232	0.206	1.701
Conflict intensity	0.069	0.214	1.664
Regime stability	−0.009	−0.171	−1.425

Notes
Multiple R = 0.699.
$R^2 = 0.489$.
Adjusted $R^2 = 0.432$.
F-sig. = 0.000.
$N = 51$.
**Significance at the $p < 0.01$ level.
*Significance at the $p < 0.05$ level.

area and insularity and is consequently included in the regression analysis. A check for multicollinearity among the remaining independent variables reveals that no association between the relevant independent variables exceeds $(-)0.70$. The result of the regression analysis is given in Table 3.17 and it shows that the degree of democracy and, to a lesser extent, regime stability affect the death penalty in Africa. The directions of the associations are in accordance with my assumptions. The death penalty is used frequently in countries where regime stability is low, whereas democracies refrain from using the death penalty.

The Americas

Let me then turn to the American continent. In 1985, the number of independent variables related to the death penalty is substantial. In order to avoid insurmountable problems of multicollinearity the threshold for inclusion is raised to Pearson's $r \geq (-)0.50$ or, for the multi-categorical variables, that Eta squared ≥ 0.25, and $p < 0.01$). The following three independent variables are related to the death penalty: index of religious fragmentation, colonial heritage and state longevity. Within the American context we encounter severe problems of multicollinearity. The highest internal correlation is between state longevity and colonial heritage (-0.922). I exclude state longevity, partly because previous analyses have shown that the variable is unimportant, and partly because the bivariate association between the colonial-dummy and the death penalty is stronger

Table 3.17 Population size, dominating religion, trade dependency, conflict intensity, degree of democracy and regime stability as determinants of capital punishment in Africa in 2000 (multiple regression)

Independent variables	B	Beta	T-value
Population (log)	0.141	0.225	1.362
Islam	0.174	0.087	0.659
Other religion	0.141	0.058	0.436
Trade dependency (log)	0.062	0.050	0.331
Conflict intensity	−0.026	−0.033	−0.205
Degree of democracy	0.120	0.380	2.859**
Regime stability	−0.041	−0.312	−2.365*

Notes
Multiple R = 0.671.
$R^2 = 0.451$.
Adjusted $R^2 = 0.365$.
F-sig. = 0.000.
$N = 53$.
**Significance at the $p < 0.01$ level.
*Significance at the $p < 0.05$ level.

than the one between state longevity and the death penalty (0.597 compared to −0.561). The evidence, shown in Table 3.18, suggests that the most important explanatory factor for the death penalty in the Americas in 1985 is the index of religious fragmentation.

Before reflecting on the underlying meaning of the result of this regression, I shall proceed with a corresponding analysis of the situation in 2000. Bivariate correlation analyses reveal that, when the same criteria as in 1985 are applied, the following independent variables are eligible for inclusion: index of religious fragmentation, state longevity and trade dependency.

There is a very serious problem of multicollinearity. State longevity is strongly related to trade dependency (−0.913) and I therefore only include state longevity in the regression, since this measure was more strongly related to the death penalty (−0.647 compared to −0.604). Results are shown in Table 3.19 and they are in general in concordance with the results for 1985 in the sense that IRF possesses explanatory power. However, it appears as if state longevity is even more strongly related to the death penalty. Younger state formations apply the death penalty to a higher extent than older ones.

The analyses conducted so far leaves many questions open. How are we to interpret the empirical findings within the American continent? The general finding of the analyses is that IRF and state longevity are more important than the other variables. This is indeed a peculiar finding. However, there is reason to believe that variations in the death penalty in the American context is not captured with statistical tools. The associations found are to a very large extent explained by the difference between the Caribbean countries and the rest of the Americas. These islands are exceptional in many ways in the region, and it is evident that, since the similarities concur, it is difficult to reach conclusions as to which

Table 3.18 Index of religious fragmentation and colonial heritage as determinants of capital punishment in the Americas in 1985 (multiple regression)

Independent variables	B	Beta	T-value
IRF	1.864	0.405	2.402*
Colonial heritage	0.680	0.342	2.029

Notes
Multiple R = 0.675.
$R^2 = 0.455$.
Adjusted $R^2 = 0.421$.
F-sig. = 0.000.
$N = 35$.
**Significance at the $p < 0.01$ level.
*Significance at the $p < 0.05$ level.

Table 3.19 Index of religious fragmentation and state longevity as determinants of capital punishment in the Americas in 2000 (multiple regression)

Independent variables	B	Beta	T-value
IRF	1.951	0.392	2.755*
State longevity (log)	−0.499	−0.441	−3.093**

Notes
Multiple R = 0.728.
$R^2 = 0.530$.
Adjusted $R^2 = 0.500$.
F-sig. = 0.000.
$N = 35$.
**Significance at the $p < 0.01$ level.
*Significance at the $p < 0.05$ level.

of the characteristics are important for explaining the death penalty and which merely reflect multicollinearity. The countries in the Caribbean are small, island states. They are, in general, young state formations and many of them have a British colonial heritage and consequently a different language and different culture than the Latin American countries.

The index of religious fragmentation captures the distinction between the Caribbean and the rest of the American countries extremely well. This is why this variable, which has turned out to be irrelevant for the death penalty in other settings, suddenly becomes important within the American context. Whereas the Latin American countries are predominantly Catholic, many of the English-speaking Caribbean countries accommodate both Catholic and Protestant groups. In addition, the importance of religious fragmentation is accentuated with the case of the USA, which also accommodates a wide variety of religions. Religion was not included among the independent variables in the American context since all countries are Christian. However, if we compare Protestant countries with Catholic ones, religion suddenly appears to be extremely important in the Americas. The mean value on the death penalty index for the nine Protestant countries is 2.33, whereas the corresponding value for the 26 Catholic countries is 0.92, rendering an Eta squared value of 0.35. This, of course is strange, given that, at the global level, the difference in the attitude toward the death penalty between Protestant and Catholic countries was much smaller. Again, this difference is explained by the fact that Protestantism is concentrated in the English-speaking Caribbean countries and North America. The Caribbean countries are also young state formations, which explains why state longevity, which has not been related to the death penalty in the previous analyses, all of a sudden stands out in the American setting.

The overall conclusion that can be drawn from these statistical exercises is that differences in the use of the death penalty in the Americas are almost exclusively captured by the differences between the Caribbean countries and the other countries. This leads us to another finding that is specific for the continent. In a global perspective, the degree of democracy goes hand-in-hand with the use of the death penalty. In the Americas, however, this association does not exist. It is remarkable that, although statistically insignificant, the correlation coefficient between democracy and capital punishment in 2000 is negative in the American context (-0.225), meaning that the death penalty is used more frequently the higher the degree of democracy. This, of course, is due to the fact that the death penalty is widely applied in the Caribbean countries and in the USA, despite the fact that these countries all exhibit high levels of democracy according to the Freedom House scales. Similarly, many Latin American countries have been forerunners in the abolitionist movement, although the democratic tradition in the region is short and unstable.

The reasons for the popularity of the death penalty in the Caribbean have already been accounted for in pages 109–111 and I shall not repeat myself here. The discussion in this chapter therefore leads me to draw the inevitable conclusion that variations in the death penalty within the American context is explained by cultural differences between the Caribbean and Latin American countries.

Asia and the Pacific

In relation to Asia and the Pacific, we find that a great number of variables are related to the dependent variable. Since many of the variables are strongly interrelated, the threshold of inclusion in the regression is once again that Pearson's $r \geq (-)0.50$ (or, for the multi-categorical variables, that Eta squared ≥ 0.25) and $p < 0.01$. The following variables are related to the death penalty in 1985: population size, dominating religion, number of offenses (log), conflict intensity, degree of democracy, regime stability and slavery. The association between the number of offenses and the death penalty is strong (Pearson's r -0.670, sig. 0.000), but based on only twenty-six countries.

Once again, we have to deal with multicollinearity. Slavery is highly related to religion (negatively to Christianity and positively to Islam). In addition, slavery is highly related to conflict intensity (0.724). The introduction of slavery also reduces the number of cases due to there being many missing cases. In order to reduce the number of variables, I ran internal regressions where the death penalty was regressed on two independent variables only (every possible combination of religion, degree of democracy, slavery and conflict intensity). In one respect, the result of these analyses was irrefutable; the explanatory power of conflict intensity was always decisively weaker than that of the other variable. Therefore, conflict intensity is excluded from further analyses. I proceed by running separate regressions for slavery and religion. The results of these are shown in Table 3.20 and they show that population size is the most important determinant of the death penalty. For what it is worth, it appears as if Islam is more important than democracy. Slavery possesses no independent explanatory power. However, once again, conclusions are hard to reach due to the high level of interrelatedness between Islam, slavery and democracy.

However, one important question is left open. The bivariate correlations showed that there was a strong association between the level of crime and the death penalty, although it was based on a limited number of

Table 3.20 Population size, dominating religion, degree of democracy, regime stability and history of slavery as determinants of capital punishment in Asia and the Pacific in 1985

Independent variables	Regression 1	Regression 2
Population (log)	0.138	0.132
	0.463	0.450
	3.810**	3.148**
Islam	0.706	Not included in model
	0.432	
	2.700*	
Buddhism	0.311	Not included in model
	0.167	
	1.053	
Other religion	−0.118	Not included in model
	−0.046	
	−0.316	
Degree of democracy	0.046	0.088
	0.203	0.383
	1.392	2.726*
Regime stability	0.022	0.008
	0.230	0.091
	2.041	0.776
History of slavery	Not included in model	0.308
		0.150
		0.912
Multiple R	0.824	0.801
R^2	0.679	0.641
Adjusted R^2	0.628	0.593
F-sig.	0.000	0.000
N	45	35

Notes
In each column, the regression coefficients are listed first, followed by the standardized regression coefficients and the T-values.
**Significance at the $p < 0.01$ level.
*Significance at the $p < 0.05$ level.

cases. Anyway, it is interesting to see if this relation persists when control-ling for other variables. However, the limited number of cases in combina-tion with high VIF-values do not allow me to include religion, democracy and slavery in any combinations. I therefore run three separate regres-sions, where the explanatory power of the number of offenses is compared to those of population size, the degree of democracy, religion and slavery. Results are shown in Table 3.21, but they should be interpreted with some

Table 3.21 Population size, dominating religion, number of offenses, degree of democracy and history of slavery as determinants of capital punishment in Asia and the Pacific in 1985

Independent variables	Regression 1	Regression 2	Regression 3
Population (log)	0.139	0.160	0.086
	0.392	0.452	0.229
	2.697*	3.472**	1.474
Islam	1.145	Not included in model	Not included in model
	0.693		
	4.451**		
Buddhism	1.216	Not included in model	Not included in model
	0.470		
	3.673**		
Other religion	0.330	Not included in model	Not included in model
	0.128		
	0.961		
Number of offenses (log)	−0.164	−0.053	−0.174
	−0.227	−0.073	−0.257
	−1.542	−0.454	−1.336
Degree of democracy	Not included in model	0.168	Not included in model
		0.709	
		4.766**	
History of slavery	Not included in model	Not included in model	1.147
			0.530
			2.994**
Multiple R	0.872	0.862	0.804
R²	0.760	0.743	0.647
Adjusted R²	0.700	0.708	0.588
F-sig.	0.000	0.000	0.000
N	26	26	22

Notes
In each column, the regression coefficients are listed first, followed by the standardized regression coefficients and the T-values.
**Significance at the $p < 0.01$ level.
*Significance at the $p < 0.05$ level.

caution since the number of cases is limited. The results reveal that, in all regressions, the number of offenses fails to explain the variation of the death penalty. The beta and the T-value for slavery in regression 3 are much lower than the betas and the T-values for Islam and degree of democracy in regressions 1 and 2, which confirms the earlier finding that slavery does not possess explanatory value in Asia and the Pacific.

Turning to the situation in 2000, we discover that population size, dominating religion, conflict intensity, level of corruption and degree of democracy are linked to the death penalty. The association between corruption and the death penalty is based on only 20 cases, therefore corruption is not included in the regressions. VIF-values show that some problems of multicollinearity still remain. The VIF-value for the Islam-dummy is very high indeed when included in the same regression analysis with the other independent variables. Its connection with democracy is particularly problematic, and religion and degree of democracy are therefore included in separate regressions. Table 3.22 gives the results of the regression analyses, and they show that Islam (as opposed to Christianity) is the strongest determinant of the death penalty in Asia and the Pacific. Buddhism (as opposed to Christianity) is also conducive to a favorable attitude toward the death penalty. The degree of democracy is also related to the death penalty, but this finding rests on a shaky ground, due to the interrelatedness between democracy and religion (democracy is positively connected to Christianity and negatively to Islam). Finally, there is a clear association between population size and the death penalty. Larger states have a more positive attitude toward the death penalty than small ones.

The most important deviation in Asia and the Pacific from the results obtained at the global level concerns population size, which turned out to carry some explanatory weight within the region. Why is it then that this factor seems to stand out within this particular context? I believe that the importance of size can be attributed to the extreme heterogeneity of the countries in this region.

On the one hand, we have the two most populous countries of the world, China and India, along with a number of other extremely populous countries, such as Indonesia and Japan. In the other end of the continuum we find (with the exception of the Vatican) the smallest states of the world, Tuvalu and Nauru, along with a number of Pacific island states. Although population size has been used in its logarithmized version, it is quite possible that these large differences in terms of size have a great impact on the results. To a large extent, the small island states of the Pacific are abolitionist, whereas the large countries in Asia and the Pacific make extensive use of the death penalty. However, at the global level, and in other contexts, especially in the American one, we have discovered that

Table 3.22 Population size, dominating religion, conflict intensity and degree of democracy as determinants of capital punishment in Asia and the Pacific in 2000

Independent variables	Regression 1	Regression 2
Population (log)	0.172	0.150
	0.430	0.375
	2.898**	2.643*
Islam (dummy)	1.252	Not included in model
	0.582	
	3.645**	
Buddhism (dummy)	0.847	Not included in model
	0.316	
	2.296*	
Other religion (dummy)	0.099	Not included in model
	0.027	
	0.200	
Conflict intensity	−0.044	0.063
	−0.068	0.096
	−0.428	0.603
Degree of democracy	Not included in model	0.086
		0.335
		2.687*
Multiple R	0.719	0.651
R^2	0.517	0.423
Adjusted R^2	0.469	0.390
F-sig.	0.000	0.000
N	56	56

Notes
In each column, the regression coefficients are listed first, followed by the standardized regression coefficients and the T-values.
**Significance at the $p < 0.01$ level.
*Significance at the $p < 0.05$ level.

smallness does not necessarily go hand-in-hand with a negative view of the death penalty and that a large size does not automatically lead to a favorable attitude to the death penalty.

The association between smallness and the death penalty in Asia and the Pacific is effectively captured by regional differences. The analysis conducted in Chapter 1 (pages 18–20) showed that the countries in Oceania, which are generally extremely small, have a restrictive attitude toward the death penalty. For Asia, values on the dependent variable were much higher. We must therefore ask ourselves if there is something special in the Pacific context that predestines the negative attitude to the death penalty. First, it is worth noting that values on the dependent variable do not vary much between the countries in the Pacific. No country in the region has carried out executions in the last ten years. However, death penalty statutes are in force in Nauru, Samoa,[4] and Tonga, whereas Fiji is abolitionist only for ordinary crimes. As with the case concerning the countries in the Middle East, the homogeneity on the dependent variable is matched by homogeneity on crucial independent variables. In none of the countries in the area is Islam the dominating religion. Instead, in all of the countries, Christianity is the dominating religion. The fact that a Christian religion coincides with a high degree of democracy in the Pacific countries is a powerful explanation for the negative attitude toward the death penalty in the region. On the other hand, none of the countries lack a colonial heritage. From a global perspective, it appears as if the Pacific countries are anomalies since they combine a colonial heritage with a restrictive attitude against the death penalty. The fact that size contains explanatory power in this particular setting is, however, not surprising given the theoretical assumption that population size should be a significant factor particularly in very small settings. The Pacific island states are not only extremely small, but also isolated. Perhaps this feeling of smallness and loneliness explain why the countries are unfavorably disposed to the ultimate form of punishment.

Europe

Within the European context, the analyses of the situation in 1985 reveals that, in the population consisting of all European countries, an extensive number of variables are related to the death penalty. Consequently, the threshold of inclusion in the regression analysis is once again that Pearson's $r \geq (-)0.50$ (for the multi-categorical variables, that Eta squared ≥ 0.25) and that $p < 0.01$. The following variables meet these criteria: GDP/cap, human development index, number of offenses, level of corruption, EC trade and degree of democracy. When measuring the effect of EC trade, only non-EC members were included in the bivariate correlation analysis. This means that, for each period in time, separate statistical analyses must be conducted for the whole population of European countries and for countries outside the European Community. As it turns out, within the population of non-EC members, the index of religious fragmentation is also linked to the death penalty and consequently included in the regression conducted among non-EC members.

First, I disregard the level of corruption, since it is highly associated with both the GDP/cap as well as the degree of democracy. Among the two socioeconomic variables, I include GDP/cap since there are a lot of missing values for HDI in 1985. The number of offenses is left out from the multiple regression since data is only available for 25 countries. No internal correlation exceeds $(-)0.70$ when all European countries are included (and the EC trade variable is consequently excluded). However, in bivariate analyses of variable interactions for the countries not part of the European Community in 1985, we face some problems of multi-collinearity. The degree of democracy and EC trade are highly inter-related (-0.845) and are therefore not included in the same regressions. In relation to the number of offenses, there are a number of missing cases. I therefore include this variable in a separate regression.

The results, shown in Table 3.23, indicate that the degree of democracy is the most important determinant of the death penalty in Europe in 1985. When EC trade is included in the multiple regression analysis instead of the degree of democracy, GDP/cap is statistically strongly related to the death penalty. However, when we include the degree of democracy in the regression, GDP/cap no longer contains any explanatory power. We can also note that the explanatory value of degree of democracy in regression 1 is higher than that of EC trade in regression 2. Thus, the degree of democracy seems to be more important than EC trade for explaining vari-

Table 3.23 Index of religious fragmentation, GDP/cap, EC trade and degree of democracy as determinants of capital punishment in Europe in 1985 (multiple regressions)

Independent variables	All European countries	Non-EC countries in Europe, regression 1	Non-EC countries in Europe, regression 2
IRF	Not included in model	0.634	0.834
		0.115	0.155
		0.806	1.200
GDP/cap (log)	-0.313	-0.342	-0.697
	-0.229	-0.259	-0.532
	-1.653	-1.632	$-4.139**$
EC trade	Not included in model	Not included in model	-0.014
			-0.457
			$-3.144**$
Degree of democracy	0.149	0.145	Not included in model
	0.630	0.617	
	4.549**	3.386**	
Multiple R	0.784	0.872	0.914
R^2	0.615	0.761	0.835
Adjusted R^2	0.589	0.718	0.796
F-sig.	0.000	0.000	0.000
N	33	21	17

Notes
In each column, the regression coefficients are listed first, followed by the standardized regression coefficients and the T-values.
**Significance at the $p < 0.01$ level.
*Significance at the $p < 0.05$ level.

ations in the death penalty in Europe in 1985. The negative association between EC trade and the death penalty probably reflects the fact that the mostly abolitionist, western European non-EC members trade more with the EC than the Eastern European countries.

The number of offenses was excluded due to the high number of missing cases. In order to test how powerful a determinant this variable is, I shall, in addition, undertake separate regression analyses where the number of offenses is included along with the degree of democracy and EC trade. Results are shown in Table 3.24, and they indicate that the level of crime does have explanatory power on its own. The level of crime is higher in countries with a restrictive view of the death penalty. However, the number of cases is too small to allow us to draw this conclusion with certainty.

For 2000, bivariate analyses show that, for the whole population of European countries, dominating religion, number of offenses, level of corruption and degree of democracy interact with the death penalty. However, again, some serious problems of multicollinearity exist. The level of corruption is strongly related to the number of offenses (0.796) and to the degree of democracy (−0.752). In terms of corruption, there are a few missing cases. In addition, the internal correlation between the

Table 3.24 Number of offenses, EC trade and degree of democracy as determinants of capital punishment in Europe in 1985 (multiple regressions)

Independent variables	All European countries	Non-EC countries in Europe, regression 1	Non-EC countries in Europe, regression 2
Number of offenses (log)	−0.398 −0.416 −2.575*	−0.389 −0.421 −3.768**	−0.490 −0.546 −2.969*
EC trade	Not included in model	Not included in model	−0.019 −0.526 −2.860*
Degree of democracy	0.141 0.464 2.869**	0.203 0.677 6.059**	Not included in model
Multiple R	0.775	0.950	0.869
R^2	0.601	0.903	0.756
Adjusted R^2	0.565	0.884	0.695
F-sig.	0.000	0.000	0.004
N	25	13	11

Notes
In each column, the regression coefficients are listed first, followed by the standardized regression coefficients and the T-values.
**Significance at the $p < 0.01$ level.
*Significance at the $p < 0.05$ level.

degree of democracy and the death penalty is stronger than the one between corruption and the death penalty (0.673 compared to −0.514). This enables me to not include corruption in the multiple regression. For the population of countries that are not members of the EU, the findings show that the association between EU trade and the death penalty does not reach the required threshold of (−)0.50 (Pearson's $r = -0.355$, T-sig. 0.059). Therefore there is no need to conduct separate analyses within this category of countries. Results of the regressions are shown in Table 3.25. This time, the results are easily interpreted. Once again, the degree of democracy is the most important determinant of the death penalty, whereas Islam and level of crime are irrelevant. It is, however, evident that the use of the death penalty in Europe follows the dividing line between Western and the Eastern European countries. While Western European countries are highly restrictive in the use of the death penalty, the abolitionist movement has not yet been victorious in the former Eastern bloc.

Conclusions

At the global level, the study showed that the death penalty is primarily sensitive to variations in degree of democracy, a history of slavery and religion. In addition, the lack of a colonial heritage was a conducive factor for a restrictive attitude toward the death penalty. However, contrary to the findings at the global level, a striking feature in the regional analyses was the unimportance of colonial heritage.

Overall, the analyses conducted within the regional contexts suffered from serious problems of multicollinearity. The problem was accentuated by the limited number of cases available in each region. In general, few

Table 3.25 Dominating religion, number of offenses and degree of democracy as determinants of capital punishment in Europe in 2000 (multiple regression)

Independent variables	B	Beta	T-value
Islam	−0.654	−0.206	−1.601
Number of offenses (log)	−0.057	−0.078	−0.501
Degree of democracy	0.217	0.760	4.723**

Notes
Multiple R = 0.729.
$R^2 = 0.532$.
Adjusted $R^2 = 0.497$.
F sig. = 0.000.
$N = 44$.
**Significance at the $p < 0.01$ level.
*Significance at the $p < 0.05$ level.

independent variables were statistically linked to the death penalty. This reflects the fact that many of the variables that were found to be important at the global level coincided with the regional settings. For instance, whereas Europe and the Americas are highly democratized, stable democracies are few in number in Africa. Also, when comparing the results obtained at the regional level with the results obtained at the global level, we noted that religion was unimportant in every region except Asia and the Pacific. This, of course, is mostly due to the fact that religions tend to be geographically concentrated and, consequently, there was very little variance in this independent variable in many regions. In the Middle East, Islam is the dominant religion in every country except in Israel, but in the Americas we do not find a country with a Muslim majority. So, evidently we cannot, for instance, expect Islam to be a major explanatory factor of the death penalty in the Americas, where no country has a Muslim majority. The findings have suggested that Christian countries are more abolitionist than countries where other religions are in a dominant position. However, at the same time, we must be careful not to exaggerate the importance of Christianity. The Christian countries are largely confined to Europe and the Americas, where, of course, the religion goes hand-in-hand with high levels of democracy and a history without slavery. In this respect it is interesting to note that the religion-dummies did not have explanatory value in Africa. In other words, Christianity did not reduce values on the death penalty in a context where its independent explanatory power was easiest to assess.

Although the operationalization of the slavery variable was difficult, the evidence suggested that a history of slavery was important for explaining the death penalty at the global level. At the regional level, slavery turned out to be unimportant. In the Americas, evidence suggested that there was a connection between the level of religious fragmentation and the death penalty, but this association was explained by the difference between, on the one hand, the USA and the Caribbean countries, and the Latin American countries on the other. Due to the dominant position of the Roman Catholic religion, the Spanish-speaking countries (as well as Portuguese Brazil) showed a low level of religious fragmentation. In contrast, although small, the Caribbean countries often include sizeable Protestant and Catholic groups, yielding higher levels of fragmentation.

At the regional level, population size was connected to the death penalty in Asia and the Pacific. As mentioned earlier, this is natural since the region incorporates both the largest countries in the world in terms of population (China and India) and the smallest ones (the states in the Pacific). The largest countries (China, India and Indonesia) make use of the death penalty, whereas the smaller ones tend to be abolitionist. The link between population size and the death penalty is interesting particularly since it cannot be attributed to a link between size and crime rates. In other words, the handy explanation that larger countries resort to the death penalty in order to cope with high crime rates does not hold.

The evidence also suggested that regime stability carried some explanatory weight within the African context. Indeed, it is precisely in this context that I expected it to be of importance. In non-democratic settings, where no established rules of transformations in power exist and political leaders grab the power by means of *coup d'états*, and are ousted from it in the same way, the death penalty constitutes an effective means to maintain control of the society.

The level of crime was associated with the death penalty in Europe. Abolitionist countries had a higher level of crime than countries which made use of the death penalty. The association was statistically significant only in 1985. A closer examination reveals that the negative association between level of crime and the death penalty is explained by the East–West dichotomy. Statistical figures indicate that the number of offenses was much higher in the stable European democracies than in the unstable or authoritarian countries. The stable democracies in Europe had a mean crime rate of 4,749.9 whereas the corresponding value for the unstable democracies or authoritarian countries was 1,485.7 (T-sig. 0.011).

Evidently, variations in Europe are explained by the division between East and West. Although the concept of diffusion is difficult to assess empirically, it is evident that it is particularly important in the European setting. The spread of the abolitionist movement in Eastern Europe and, in particular, in the former republics of the Soviet Union is more or less completely explained by a desire to move closer politically to the Western European countries and, eventually, fully participate in European integration. Of course, it is not easy to form an opinion of the extent to which countries have given in to the pressure put on them by Western European countries. Rick Fawn (2001) claims that the post-communist countries have had five options with regard to the requirement of the Council of Europe to abolish the death penalty. The first option is "abolition of the government's own accord". Countries that have abolished the death penalty prior to the adoption of Protocol No. 6 belong to this category. Among the former Eastern European states, Croatia, the Czech Republic, the former East Germany, Hungary, Macedonia, Poland, Slovakia, Slovenia and Romania fall within this category. Fawn labels the second option "abolitionist with western influence once it was made a criterion". This category "includes states that have undergone noticeable change in their statutory positions on the death penalty, and which can be attributed to international influence or pressure" (Fawn 2001: 73). This category includes Albania, Bulgaria, Estonia, Latvia, Lithuania and Moldova. Although the last five countries were accepted as members prior to the adoption of Protocol 6, all of them were subject to "varying degrees of pressures from outside" before the abolition of the death penalty (Fawn 2001: 73).

The third option is called "unfulfilled or belated abolition", and includes Belarus, Ukraine and Russia. Ukraine and Russia were both admitted to the Council of Europe (Ukraine in 1995 and Russia in 1996). Both have conducted executions after their admittance to the Council of Europe and the status of the death penalty in the respective countries remains unclear (Fawn 2001: 74). Belarus, again, is not a member of the Council of Europe and continues to carry out executions. Fawn labels the fourth option "influenced by and emulating 'Europe'". The category comprises countries that have applied for membership after the adoption of Protocol 6. In the countries falling within this category (Armenia, Azerbaijan and Georgia) "we see not only measures to ensure compliance with the Council of Europe but also statements by leaders that abolition is an act to make their countries more 'European'" (Fawn 2001: 74). The final category is made up of countries "largely outside European influence". The category is made up of five former Soviet Republics that are neither located in Europe nor applicants to the Council of Europe, namely Kazakhstan, Kyrgyzstan, Tajikistan, Turkmenistan and Uzbekistan. While Kazakhstan, Kyrgyzstan, Tajikistan and Uzbekistan continue to make use of the death penalty, Turkmenistan abolished it in 1999. The case of Turkmenistan is interesting as it is the only post-communist country that has abolished the death penalty without being subject to European pressure (at least not to the same extent as the countries that have applied for membership to the Council of Europe).

Concerning the year 1985, the explanatory power of diffusion in Europe is probably weaker, but it is reasonable to assume that it plays an important role within the West European context. The pressure put on the former Eastern European countries by their Western European counterparts no doubt explains why the death penalty has been abolished so quickly in Eastern Europe. In other parts of the world, where the impact of the Western European countries is weaker, diffusion plays a subordinate role. The demands to abolish the death penalty raised by, for instance the United Nations, are counteracted by the powerful examples of China, USA and Japan, all of which make use of capital punishment.

4 The death penalty in the USA

The USA as a case study

So far, the study has been conducted at an international level, and all countries in the world have constituted units of analysis. When conducting empirical research, the choice of units of analysis often constitutes a stumbling-block for many social scientists. A common mistake is to choose as objects of research countries that are geographically, culturally or mentally close to the researcher. Instead of allowing the research problem to guide the choice of units of analysis, the units of analysis are chosen prior to formulating the research problem. A familiar problem in comparative research is that we have a lot of potential explanatory factors to control for, at the same time as we are operating with a limited number of units of analysis. As a "solution" to this problem, Arend Lijphart (1971: 686–690) has suggested that we should:

1   *increase the number of cases as much as possible*;
2   *reduce the "property space" of the analysis*, i.e. combine variables that express the same phenomenon;
3   *focus the comparative analysis on "comparable" cases*, i.e. variables ought to be dissimilar concerning the phenomenon we want to study and similar in those respects that we want to keep constant, and
4   *focus the comparative analysis on the "key" variables*, i.e. variables that are theoretically motivated.

In the preceding chapters, the number of cases has been as large as possible. All independent countries in the world have been included in the study. Admittedly, the inclusion of a large number of countries also has its drawbacks. The more countries that are included, the greater the risk that the operationalization of the variables becomes difficult (see Peters 1998: 19–21, 93–94). One has to make sure that concepts have the same meaning in different parts of the world. If this is not the case, there is a high risk of what Sartori (1970: 1034; 1991: 249) calls "concept-stretching". For example, take the level of ethnic fragmentation. In a European context, Belgium is considered a linguistically heterogeneous country with a population divided between Flemish and French parts, accompanied by a small German enclave. However, in an African context, such a linguistic constellation is by no means exceptional. The same holds true in other parts of the world as well. Thus, in Papua New Guinea, there are approximately 700 languages (*World in Figures* 1987: 283). This shortcoming can be partly remedied by using indices with a high travel capacity, meaning that they have the same meaning in virtually every context (see Sartori 1991: 245–246). In this study, the operationalizations of the variables have been made with such considerations in mind. However, we cannot totally reject the possibility that shortcomings of the kind dealt with above appeared within the empirical analyses. I shall therefore conclude this study by applying a strategy which gives the results a higher degree of validity. This strategy makes it possible to keep constant factors that are thought to be country-specific.

The analysis at the inter-state level has revealed that one of the most powerful determinants of the death penalty is the degree of democracy. However, as Table 3.14 shows (page 110), the rule that democracies restrain from using capital punishment is not without exceptions. There are a substantial number of democratic countries that apply the death penalty. Earlier, I tried to establish the causes of variations in the death penalty within the category of democracies. The ambition was thus to explain the use of the death penalty in cases where an important determinant of capital punishment was kept constant. Regression analyses, however, showed that most of the factors were irrelevant for explaining the death penalty among democracies. It is no doubt evident that additional studies of the causes of the death penalty in democratic settings are needed.

In this respect the USA constitutes the ideal test case. The country is a stable democracy where the death penalty is allowed and applied extensively. It is therefore an anomaly that has received much attention in the literature on capital punishment. By using the USA as a test case, I hope to identify those factors that overshadow the form of government, thus facilitating the use of the death penalty in such a "hostile" setting. What is important from a scientific point of view is that we find a great deal of variation in terms of the use of the death penalty between the different states in the USA. Although capital punishment is allowed under federal law, this does not mean that each state has an obligation to allow its use. The USA is a unique case in that the choice of making use of, or to disallow the use of, the death penalty is left to the states. This is important with regard to an ability to conduct empirical research. For methodological purposes it is desirable that one can keep constant many factors that might influence the relation between the independent and the dependent variables. The different states can thus be used as units of analysis and their role is similar to the role of the countries in the analysis at the international level.

Case studies are frequent in political science. This is regrettable, since many of the questions for which answers are sought through the use of case studies could be better answered by using comparative or statistical methods. In internationally renowned "comparative" journals, we run across far too many studies where the single purpose is to merely describe a political phenomenon in a particular country. These studies tend to leave the reader with the impression that the author, for one reason or another, has a general interest in the country in question and this interest has guided the choice of the object of research. It cannot be too strongly emphasized that the opposite should be the case; the theoretical problem must always guide the choice of units of analysis. The position of the French president is different from the position of presidents on the American continent; however, an article that merely describes the powers of the French president has very little scientific value (see Sartori 1991: 243). The crucial point is, of course, that we ought to have the ambition to arrive at generalizations. Now, it is self-evident that generalizations are impossible to arrive at by only observing one case, or as Lijphart (1971: 691) puts it: "[a] single case can constitute neither the basis for a valid generalization nor the ground for disproving an established generalization". Still, the mass production of case studies continues. The aforesaid should not be interpreted as if case studies are always of no value. There is, in fact, ample scope for case studies in political science. This implies, however, that certain criteria are met.

Lijphart (1971: 691–693) distinguishes between six ideal types of case studies: atheoretical case studies, interpretative case studies, hypothesis-generating case studies, theory-confirming case studies, theory-infirming case studies and deviant case studies. Atheoretical and interpretative case studies contain the lowest amount of scientific value. While the former are totally descriptive, the latter emerge from existing theories. However, in such studies "a generalization is applied to a specific case with the aim of throwing light on the cases rather than of improving the case in any way" (Lijphart 1971: 692). Hypothesis-generating case studies are used in inductive studies: "Their objective is to develop theoretical generalizations in areas where no theory exists yet" (Lijphart 1971: 692). Theory-confirming and theory-infirming case studies are actually two sides of the same coin. In both cases, the case study is used in order to test law-like generalizations. If the generalization is confirmed, the case study is theory-confirming; if the generalization is not verified, the case study is theory-infirming. One must, however, bear in mind that the study of only one case is unlikely to either totally confirm or totally reject an existing theory. As Sartori (1991: 252) puts it: "[case-studies] cannot confirm a generalization (one confirmation adds confidence, but cannot add up to a confirming test), and they can only disconfirm a regularity to a limited degree". In deviant case studies, cases that do not fit into a general pattern form the object of research. Such in-depth analyses are conducted in order to discover additional variables, which explain why the deviant case is deviant, and thus expand the theory.

In the present study, the case of the USA only partly fits into Lijphart's six categories. It is not a typical hypothesis-generating case study. The study conducted at the international level has given us, if not a perfect theory of the prerequisites of the death penalty, at least fragments of a theory. However, it is probably too early to state that we turn from an inductive approach to a deductive one. The possibility still exists that some important variables have been neglected. Furthermore, since we do not have a real theory from which to depart, the study is neither theory-confirming nor theory-infirming. The USA as a test case perhaps fits best into the category of deviant case analysis. One of the strongest associations found in the analysis conducted at the international level was the one between the form of government and the death penalty. The USA is indeed a highly deviant case from this pattern in that it is a country with a long and uninterrupted history of a democratic form of government. It is also worth pointing out that the democratic system has never been threatened in the USA. Still, capital punishment is widely used there and the trend seems to be the opposite from what applies globally; the use of death penalties is becoming more frequent.

However, the motive for the use of the USA as a test case goes beyond that of a thorough investigation of a deviant case. Generally, a study of a deviant case can, under the best circumstances, expand the theory by pointing at relevant variables that have previously been omitted. The core issue here is that the study of the USA is not a study of *one* deviant case, but instead a study of 50 cases situated within a deviant context.[1] Since each of the states has the right to pass legislation on capital punishment, they can be treated in the same manner as the countries of the world were treated in the study conducted at the international level. Focusing the study on one single country has one big advantage. Since we are operating with cases that possess many common characteristics, a large number of crucial contesting variables are controlled for. When making generalizations based on detected relations between the variables, we consequently stand on a rather firmer ground. However, we should be aware of the fact that this strategy has it drawbacks as well. Since the cases are situated within a fairly homogenous context, there is little variation in many of the independent variables, at least compared to the variations that existed at the analysis at the international level. This, of course, has the implication that the results are difficult to compare between the two levels of analysis.

Having said that, I turn to the case of the USA. I first give a brief history of the death penalty in the USA. After that, I operationalize the dependent variable. This will be done in a slightly different manner than at the international level. Thereafter I continue with the empirical part of the study, where associations between the independent and dependent variables are measured. In general, the presentation will follow the same pattern as the study at the international level. A number of variables used at the international level are excluded, either because they are irrelevant or (more or less) constant within the USA.

Mapping the death penalty in the USA

A historical overview

In the USA, the death penalty has been allowed in two separate periods of time. When the first European settlers landed in the American continent, they brought the death penalty with them from their native countries. The birth of the death penalty in America was thus a consequence of diffusion from one continent to another. The first recorded execution in what was to become the USA took place in 1608, when Captain George Kendall was executed for espionage (Bohm 1999: 1). In different colonies, different laws were adapted. This meant that, from the very beginning, there was a great variation between the colonies in their attitude toward capital punishment. The Puritans and the Quakers, for instance, had a very opposite view of the legitimacy of the death penalty. While the former group applied the death penalty for a variety of crimes, the latter went as far as forbidding the death penalty between the years 1646 and 1691 (Bedau 1982: 7; Vila and Morris 1997: 8–9).

The death penalty was widely applied in the colonies. The total number of legal executions carried out from 1608 to date is estimated to lie between 20,000 and 22,500 (Espy, cited in Bohm 1999: 2). The abolitionist movement eventually grew stronger in the nineteenth century, especially between the years 1825 and 1850 (Bohm 1999: 4). In 1846, the state of Michigan became the first English-speaking jurisdiction in the world to abolish the death penalty for all crimes except treason. Rhode Island abolished the death penalty for all crimes in 1852 and Wisconsin did the same in 1853 (Bohm 1999: 5). The process of abolitionism was interrupted by the Civil War (1861–1865) and not until 1887 did Maine follow the example set by Michigan.[2] The abolitionist movement temporarily grew stronger and, by 1917, six other states had abolished the death penalty completely (Kansas, Minnesota, Missouri, Oregon, South Dakota and Washington). However, in the early twentieth century, largely as a consequence of the prohibition and the depression, the death penalty again gained popularity and was reinstated in many states. Between 1918 and 1957 no state abolished the death penalty (Bohm 1999: 6–7).

Although the death penalty was not formally abolished, states started to restrict the number of executions after the Second World War. By the early 1960s, most states had stopped carrying out executions. In 1967, a moratorium was imposed and, in 1972, the Supreme Court in *Furman* v. *Georgia*, *Jackson* v. *Georgia* and *Branch* v. *Texas* finally ruled that the death penalty statutes were unconstitutional (Hood 1996: 47). It is important to emphasize that the Court never ruled that the death penalty in itself was unconstitutional. Only the fact that the statutes of the states in question gave the jury complete discretion as to whether to impose the death penalty or not in capital cases was seen to be in conflict with the constitution (Bohm 1999: 23–24).

However, after the bulk of the states that had applied the death penalty prior to 1972 had redrafted their constitutions, the Supreme Court in the cases of *Gregg* v. *Georgia, Proffitt* v. *Florida* and *Jurek* v. *Texas* ruled that the death penalty statutes of the different states were in accordance with the constitution (Hood 1996: 47).

After 1976, capital punishment has become more and more widely applied in the USA. Table 4.1 lists the number of executions for each year. Figures are from the Death Penalty Information Center (www.deathpenaltyinfo.org). In the years following the Supreme Court decision to reinstate the death penalty, the punishment was sparsely used. There were only a handful of executions each year. In the mid-1980s, there was a sharp increase in the number of executions. The next leap took place in 1995, when the number of executions rose to 56. This trend seems to continue: in 1999 a total of 98 executions were carried out, whereas the corresponding number for 2000 was 85. Although the number of executions has decreased somewhat in the last two-to-three years, the figures are still very high in a long-time perspective. It is perhaps interesting to note that there has not been a sharp increase in the number of states that make use of the death penalty. In the first years following the *Furman* v. *Georgia* case, quite a few states re-enacted the death penalty in their legislation. However, since 1979, the number of states making use of the death penalty has grown by only four. It should nevertheless be noted that there have been attempts to reintroduce capital punishment in several states that have remained abolitionist (Hood 1996: 47–48).

Table 4.1 Development of the death penalty in the USA since 1972

Year	Number of executions	Number of states with capital punishment	Number of states without capital punishment
1972	–	1	49
1973	–	12	38
1974	–	21	29
1975	–	27	23
1976	0	28	22
1977	1	31	19
1978	0	32	18
1979	2	34	16
1980	0	34	16
1981	1	34	16
1982	2	35	15
1983	5	35	15
1984	21	35	15
1985	18	35	15
1986	18	35	15
1987	25	35	15
1988	11	35	15
1989	16	35	15
1990	23	35	15
1991	14	36	14
1992	31	36	14
1993	38	36	14
1994	31	37	13
1995	56	38	12
1996	45	38	12
1997	74	38	12
1998	68	38	12
1999	98	38	12
2000	85	38	12
2001	66	38	12
2002	71	38	12
Total	820	38	12

Operationalization of the dependent variable

As stated earlier, the death penalty has effectively been allowed since 1976. In the present study I shall not consider cases prior to the *Furman* v. *Georgia* case. Since the time period is relatively short, and since the number of executions that took place in the first ten years after the Supreme Court decision in *Gregg* v. *Georgia* was relatively low, the study will be conducted at one point in time only. Data concerning the dependent variable reflect the situation on 31 December 2000.

The dependent variable will be structured in the same way as at the international level. Basically, when confronted with the issue of the death penalty, states have, in principle, the same options as independent countries. They can forbid the use of capital punishment under all circumstances; they can forbid the use of capital punishment except under special circumstances; they can allow the use of capital punishment but refrain from carrying out death sentences; and they can allow and apply the death penalty. However, when the states of the USA constitute the units of analysis, the category where capital punishment is only allowed under special circumstances is problematic. Although the legislation that regulates capital punishment varies a lot between the states, no state only applies the death penalty under special circumstances. This is not surprising since the term "special circumstances" usually refers to a state of war or, at least, a situation of severe unrest. Needless to say, these questions are not pertinent at the state level, since matters of war and peace are primarily the concern of the federal government. Therefore, the abolitionist for ordinary crimes only category will not be considered within this context.

Some minor alterations from the strategy applied at the international level will be made in relation to the category of states that do not allow the death penalty. There, I used the number of years that had elapsed since the last execution as a criterion for measuring variations in the attitude toward the death penalty within the category. Applying the same criterion within the US context does not work, since none of the abolitionist states have performed an execution since 1976. Instead, the number of years during which the death penalty has been applied will be used to measure variations in the attitude toward capital punishment among states that have abolished the death penalty. Again, a ten-degree scale is employed. The Supreme Court decision in the *Gregg* v. *Georgia* case was taken in 1976. Thus, the maximum period the death penalty can have been abolished is 24 years. Since I operate with a ten-level scale, it is necessary to convert the 24-level scale into a ten-level one. This is done by means of dividing 10 with 24, whereby the value 0.417 is obtained. Thus, beginning with the year 1977, each year a state has had death penalty statutes corresponds to 0.417 points. Since the scale ranges from 0 to 1, a state that has been abolitionist for the whole time period receives the value 0.000, a state that has been abolitionist for 23 years the value 0.0417, a state that has been abolitionist for 22 years the value 0.0834 and so on.

Currently, 38 states have statutes that allow the use of capital punishment. I shall again follow the same strategy that I applied at the inter-state level. The category consisting of countries that make use of the death penalty is split up into ten groups. Among the states that currently have death penalty statutes, there is a great deal of variation concerning the use of capital punishment. An examination of the data reveals that, in Texas, the death penalty is applied to a much higher extent than any other state.

Table 4.2 The death penalty in the USA since 1976

State	Death penalty status	Number of executions 1977–2000	Death penalty index
Alabama	Applied	23	1.7000
Alaska	Abolished	–	0.0000
Arizona	Applied	22	1.7000
Arkansas	Applied	23	1.7000
California	Applied	8	1.5000
Colorado	Applied	1	1.2000
Connecticut	Applied	0	1.0000
Delaware	Applied	11	1.6000
District of Columbia	Abolished	–	0.0000
Florida	Applied	50	1.9000
Georgia	Applied	23	1.7000
Hawaii	Abolished	–	0.0000
Idaho	Applied	1	1.2000
Illinois	Applied	12	1.6000
Indiana	Applied	7	1.5000
Iowa	Abolished	–	0.0000
Kansas	Applied	0	1.0000
Kentucky	Applied	2	1.3000
Louisiana	Applied	26	1.8000
Maine	Abolished	–	0.0000
Maryland	Applied	3	1.4000
Massachusetts	Abolished	–	0.2919
Michigan	Abolished	–	0.0000
Minnesota	Abolished	–	0.0000
Mississippi	Applied	4	1.5000
Missouri	Applied	46	1.9000
Montana	Applied	2	1.3000
Nebraska	Applied	3	1.4000
Nevada	Applied	8	1.6000
New Hampshire	Applied	0	1.0000
New Jersey	Applied	0	1.0000
New Mexico	Applied	0	1.0000
New York	Applied	0	1.0000
North Carolina	Applied	16	1.6000
North Dakota	Abolished	–	0.0000
Ohio	Applied	1	1.2000
Oklahoma	Applied	30	1.8000
Oregon	Applied	2	1.3000
Pennsylvania	Applied	3	1.4000
Rhode Island	Abolished	–	0.2919
South Carolina	Applied	25	1.8000
South Dakota	Applied	0	1.0000
Tennessee	Applied	1	1.2000
Texas	Applied	239	1.9000
Utah	Applied	6	1.5000
Vermont	Abolished	–	0.4170
Virginia	Applied	81	1.9000
Washington	Applied	3	1.4000
West Virginia	Abolished	–	0.0000
Wisconsin	Abolished	–	0.0000
Wyoming	Applied	1	1.3000

Note
In addition, the federal government and the military have separate death penalty systems. Since 1976 no execution has taken place under military statutes. The last execution under military statutes took place in 1961. The first two executions under federal law since 1963 took place in June 2001. Another execution occurred in March 2003.

In addition, large numbers of executions are carried out in Florida, Missouri and Virginia. Once again I relate the number of executions to the logarithmized size of the population of the states. The result is that Texas still stands out as the state with the highest number of executions in relation to its population, scoring the value 14.23. The next state in line is Virginia, with the value 5.15, followed by Florida (3.03) and Missouri (2.97). After these four states, there is a fairly long jump to the next state in line, Oklahoma, which scores the value 2.00. By applying the deciles of these figures, the states that make use of the death penalty are split up into ten categories. These states thus receive values on the dependent variable ranging from 1.00 to 1.9.[3]

The aforesaid means that, contrary to the international level, we now employ a scale ranging from 0 to 1.9. Table 4.2 lists the states, their value on the dependent variable as well as the number of executions that have taken place since 1976. The information is gathered from the Death Penalty Information Center (http://www.deathpenaltyinfo.org).

Physical factors

Size

The analysis of the determinants of the death penalty in the USA is structured in the same way as the analysis conducted at the international level. Consequently, I begin with studying the effects of physical variables. At the international level, four physical variables were used: population size, area, density and insularity. Since Hawaii is the only island-state in the USA, only the first three mentioned indicators are relevant in this context. The states differ a lot in terms of size. The largest state, California, has a population of 32,665,550, whereas the smallest one, Wyoming, encompasses only 480,907 individuals (figures are from 1998). Table 4.3 shows the results of the regression analysis where the death penalty is regressed on population size, area and density respectively.

Table 4.3 Association between size and capital punishment in the United States (bivariate regressions)

	B	*Beta*	*T-value*	R^2	N
Population (log)	0.255	0.404	3.088**	0.163	51
Area (log)	0.126	0.273	1.989	0.075	51
Density (log)	0.009	0.020	0.138	0.000	51

Notes
**Significance at the $p < 0.01$ level.
*Significance at the $p < 0.05$ level.

The results show that the trend that was manifest at the international level also applies within the United States. Large states make use of the death penalty to a higher extent than small states. In contrast to what was the case at the international level, the association between population size and the death penalty is markedly higher than that of area and capital punishment. The finding that density does not affect the outcome on the dependent variable is in agreement with the corresponding findings at the international level.

The cultural setting

The United States was built by immigrants. Although the earliest settlers were Europeans, immigrants nowadays come from virtually every corner of the world. During the last few decades immigration from Latin American countries has been pronounced. It is therefore justified to use the term "melting pot" when describing the ethnic heterogeneity of the population of the United States. At the same time, the level of ethnic fragmentation in the United States should not be exaggerated. The index of ethnic fragmentation for the USA is 0.3315, which is neither very high nor very low in a global perspective (Anckar, Eriksson and Leskinen 2002: 7–14). The theoretical considerations underlying the assumption that ethnic diversity is likely to create a favorable attitude toward the death penalty departed from an assumption that ethnic diversity was conducive to instability. The death penalty was seen as a tool for upholding order in societies marked by ethnic or religious divisions. Within the United States, this way of arguing is particularly important. We know that racial tensions have been frequent in the past, particularly between African-Americans and whites in the south. These tensions culminated, in the 1950s and 1960s, with the fight for civil rights, but even today tensions persist, as the example of the riots in Los Angeles in 1992 illustrates. Although tensions between blacks and whites have been particularly in focus, we should not neglect other ethnic divisions. The massive immigration of Chinese citizens in the late nineteenth century provoked expressions such as the "yellow danger", and led to the 1882 decision by Congress to close off immigration from China for a period of ten years (Hofstadter, Miller and Aaron 1959: 101). In recent years the immigration from Latin American countries, and from Mexico in particular, has raised the percentage of persons with Hispanic origin.

Ethnicity is treated in the same manner as in the analysis at the international level. For each state an index of ethnic fragmentation is calculated according to the same formula that was used at the international level. Since a strict definition of ethnic groups is unwarranted in the US context (see discussion on pages 31–32) I shall use a broad definition of

Table 4.4 Association between index of ethnic fragmentation and capital punishment in the United States (bivariate regression)

	B	Beta	T-value	R^2	N
IEF	1.432	0.293	2.144*	0.086	51

Notes
**Significance at the $p < 0.01$ level.
*Significance at the $p < 0.05$ level.

ethnicity. Consequently, when calculating the index of ethnic fragmentation, the following ethnic groups are considered: whites; blacks; Asian and Pacific; American Indian, Eskimo, and Aleuts; and Hispanic.

In addition to ethnicity I also considered religion in the analysis at the international level. In terms of religions, the United States is even more heterogeneous than in terms of ethnicity. The bulk of the population is Christian, but within this group there is a lot of variation. It should nevertheless be pointed out that the intensity of conflicts between the Christian denominations is very low indeed. However, the relation between Catholics and Protestants is not totally problem-free. One illustration of this is the election of the Catholic John F. Kennedy for president in 1960, where religion was made an issue in the campaign. It is therefore not impossible that religious divisions play a role in explaining the death penalty within the United States. Unfortunately, religious divisions cannot be accounted for in the USA, since data on religious affiliation are not reported in surveys. Table 4.4 returns the results of a regression analysis where capital punishment is regressed on ethnic fragmentation. The results indicate that the more ethnically divided the state, the more inclined it is to make use of capital punishment.

Socioeconomic development

At the international level, socioeconomic development was found in the bivariate analyses to interact with the death penalty. However, in the multivariate analyses, the associations between socioeconomic development and the death penalty vanished. As mentioned earlier, socioeconomic development encompasses not only purely economic measures, such as GNP/GDP, but also various indicators of social development, such as infant mortality and literacy. Within the American context it is reasonable to expect that indicators of social development are not related to the dependent variable to the same extent as they were at the international level. This is simply due to the fact that, in terms of these variables, there is not as much variation between the states of the USA as there was between the countries of the world. However, in terms of

Table 4.5 Association between socioeconomic development and capital punishment in the United States (bivariate regressions)

	B	Beta	T-value	R^2	N
GSP/cap (log)	0.549	0.196	1.399	0.038	51
Infant mortality	0.020	0.054	0.380	0.003	51

Notes
**Significance at the $p<0.01$ level.
*Significance at the $p<0.05$ level.

economic performance, the states do differ a lot. Consequently, I shall make use of two measures of socioeconomic development. The first is gross state product (in the logarithmized form), and the second is infant mortality.

Table 4.5 shows bivariate associations between the two measures of socioeconomic development and the death penalty. The results show that neither gross state product nor infant mortality is a powerful determinant of the death penalty.

Level of crime

At the international level, I made use of three variables which reflected various aspects of security: conflict intensity, level of corruption and level of crime. Within the USA, only the level of crime is relevant as a plausible explanatory variable. In terms of conflict intensity and corruption, there is very little variation among the units of analysis. At the international level, the evidence gave some support to the view that the use of the death penalty was associated with low crime rates. In Table 4.6, the death penalty is regressed on the level of crime. The results indicate that there is indeed an association between the level of crime and the death penalty. The results show that states with a favorable attitude toward the death penalty have a higher crime rate than states with a restrictive attitude. This is especially the case concerning murders. These results stand in sharp contrast to the finding obtained at the international level, which suggested that countries with a positive view of the death penalty had a lower level of crime than countries with a more negative attitude.

Political actors

State legislatures

In the USA, the power of the government is divided between the federal and the state levels. Each state has its own written constitution. The

Table 4.6 Association between level of crime and capital punishment in the United States (bivariate regressions)

	B	Beta	T-value	R^2	N
Number of murders	0.116	0.440	3.398**	0.194	50[1]
Number of offenses (log)	0.886	0.373	2.811**	0.139	51

Notes
1 I exclude the District of Columbia which has a murder rate of 46.4 per 100,000 inhabitants whereas the second highest value in the population is many times lower, 10.7 (in Louisiana).
**Significance at the $p < 0.01$ level.
*Significance at the $p < 0.05$ level.

principle of separation of powers, meaning that the legislative, executive and judicial branches are separated from each other, applies both at the federal and the state level. The chief executive at the state level is the popularly elected governor. Furthermore, we note that all states have their own popularly elected legislature. The judicial system at the state level is organized in a very similar way to the system of courts operating at three stages at the federal level. At the state level, these are called Trial Courts or District Courts at the lowest level, followed by Appellate or Appeals Courts, and at the highest level, Supreme Courts.

The American constitution gives the states considerable powers. Indeed, the states form the basic units of national politics in the USA. The framers of the American Constitution only specified the powers of the national government. This had the consequence that all remaining powers belonged to the states. This was later confirmed explicitly in the Tenth Amendment, which stated that all "powers not delegated to the United States by the Constitution, nor prohibited by it to the States, are reserved to the States respectively, or to the people" (Carr *et al.* 1963: 74–75). Despite the emphasis on the powers of the states, we have witnessed a growing trend of centralization, especially in the fields of finance and regulation in federal countries. This trend is perceptible in the USA as well as in other federal systems (Riker 1964; Paddison 1983: 107).

The structure and powers of the legislature differ from state to state. As mentioned earlier, the legislatures are bicameral, thus mirroring the structure of the legislature at the federal level. The only exception is the unicameral congress of Nebraska. It is reasonable to assume that differing political views affect the use of the death penalty within the United States. True, scholars generally agree that the American party system is an anomaly among the democracies in the world, as no major socialist party has been able to challenge the position of the Democratic and the Republican parties. Nevertheless, although the ideological differences between the parties are small and often virtually non-existent at the local level, differences can still be found in specific issues. Consequently, Republicans are generally more conservative and have a tougher attitude to crime. This is something that I expect to be reflected in attitudes toward the death penalty. The assumption is thus that in states where the bulk of the population vote Republican, the attitude toward capital punishment is more sympathetic and the use of the death penalty consequently more frequent.

In order to test this assumption, I have checked the political color of the 50 state legislatures. States where Republican Members of Congress are in the majority in the legislature are confined to one category and states where the Democrats constitute the majority to another. When classifying the states as either Democrat or Republican, I have for each state considered a time period ranging from (and including) the year 1972, the year of the US Supreme Court ruling in *Furman* v. *Georgia, Jackson* v. *Georgia* and *Branch* v. *Texas*, until 31 December 2000.

The operationalization is made in the following manner: for each state, I calculate the number of years the Republicans have been in control of the legislature. Thus a scale ranging from 0 (not a single year when the Republicans have been in control of the legislature) and 29 (Republicans have been in control throughout the whole time period) is obtained. Since the state legislatures with one exception are bicameral, the question arises of how to deal with divided legislatures, i.e. situations where one chamber is dominated by the Republicans and the other by the Democrats. In such cases, it seems appropriate to make the assumption that Republicans and Democrats are equally strong. Every year a state has a divided legislature, the state in question receives the value 0.5. Things get more complicated when Republicans and Democrats have an equal number of representatives in one of the chambers, but one of the parties is stronger in the other chamber. In such cases, the value 0.75 is given if the Republicans dominate the other chamber. If the other chamber is dominated by the Democrats, the state receives the value 0.25. In a few cases, neither Republicans nor Democrats have an absolute majority of the seats in the legislature due to the existence of third parties and independent candidates. These representatives have been disregarded. Thus, dominance of the legislature presupposes a plurality, and not a majority of the seats.

In addition to looking at the long-term dominance in the legislature, another dimension is also of importance. One could argue that the crucial issue is not whether Democrats or Republicans have made up the majority in the state legislature during the last three decades, but that the decisive factor is which party dominated the state legislature at the time of re-enactment. I therefore introduce a similar dichotomous variable reflecting the power structure in state legislatures at the time of the re-enactment of the death penalty statutes. For states that have no death penalty statutes,

I have chosen to consider the situation in 1973. States where Republicans were in a dominant position at that specific point in time receive the value 1, and states where Democrats had a dominant position the value 0.

The governor

With regard to the death penalty, the most interesting individual actor is no doubt the governor. The powers of the governors vary from state to state. In some states, the position of the chief executive is quite weak, meaning that they face short terms in office, are not allowed to stay in office for more than one term and have limited executive power. Strong governors typically have four-year terms, can succeed themselves in office (preferably for an unlimited period of time), have strong appointment and budgetary powers and do not depend heavily on other officials in the execution of the duties (see Grant 1991: 278).

Although the powers of the governors vary across the states, it is still fair to say that they generally play an important role in the execution of death sentences. In many states that apply capital punishment, the governor has been granted the power to pardon convicted felons. The powers of the governors to grant clemency vary a lot among the states that apply the death penalty. For instance, in Alabama, the governor has exclusive powers of granting clemency. In other states, for instance in Arizona and Texas, the powers of the governor are more restricted. The governor has the right to grant clemency or reprieve, but needs a favorable recommendation from the Board of Pardons and Paroles in order to do so (however, the governor does not have to follow the recommendation). There are also examples of states where the governor has very limited powers to intervene in the process of carrying out death sentences. This is the case, for instance, in Connecticut, where the power to grant clemency rests in the Board of Pardons and Paroles. The governor can only grant a reprieve. In yet other states, the governor has virtually no impact at all on the process of carrying out death sentences.

Following the same arguments that applied when studying state legislatures, it is reasonable to expect that the party affiliation of the governor affects the use of the death penalty. Again, I expect Democratic governors to have a more restricted attitude toward the death penalty than their Republican counterparts. Concerning the operationalization, I apply the same strategy as when studying the effects of the color of the state legislatures. This means that I use two indicators of governor characteristics. The first is the long-term party affiliation of the governor; that is, whether the states have been ruled by a Democratic or a Republican governor during the period following the Furman decision – from 1972 to 2000. I have used the number of years the states have been ruled by a Republican governor during this period of time. The scale thus ranges from 0 (no year with a Republican governor during the specified period) and 29 (the state has had Republican governors throughout the whole period). The second one takes into account the party affiliation of the governor at the time of re-enactment of the death penalty statutes (or, for states that have no death penalty statutes, in 1973). States in which the governor was a Republican at the time of re-enactment, or for states that have no death penalty statutes in 1973, are given the value 1, and states where a Democratic or an independent governor was in power during the same period of time receive the value 0.

Empirical evidence

Table 4.7 shows the results of regression analyses where the death penalty is separately regressed on the four independent variables. The results leave no room for interpretation. The color of the state legislature does not explain the use of the death penalty in the USA, and neither does long-term party affiliation of the governor. However, a different picture emerges when studying the effect of party affiliation of the governor at the time of re-enactment of the death penalty. This variable appears to be very important indeed for explaining the variation in the dependent variable.

Table 4.7 Associations between party dominance in state legislatures, party affiliation of governor and capital punishment in the United States (bivariate regressions)

	B	Beta	T-value	R^2	N
Long-term dominance in state legislature	−0.006	−0.095	−0.656	0.009	49[1]
Dominance in state legislature at time of re-enactment or 1973	0.067	0.047	0.325	0.002	49[1]
Long-term party affiliation of governor	−0.013	0.137	0.956	0.019	50
Party affiliation of governor at time of re-enactment or 1973	0.562	0.423	3.232**	0.179	50

Notes
1 The non-partisan legislature of Nebraska is excluded.
**Significance at the $p < 0.01$ level.
*Significance at the $p < 0.05$ level.

Historical explanations

The Civil War and the issue of slavery

Within the United States, we cannot overlook the possibility that historical events carry a great deal of explanatory value as regards the attitude toward, and the use of, the death penalty. Theoretically, a number of historical divisions could contribute to explaining variances in the attitudes toward the death penalty. One division probably carries much more weight than any other, namely the dividing line between north and south in the Civil War between 1861 and 1865. It has been said of the American Civil War that "[t]he conflict marked a bloody dividing line across American history, indicating a crucial stage in the transition from an agricultural, rural, religious, and personalized America to an industrial, urban, secular, and institutionalized America" (Rozwenc 1949: v). The single most important reason for the outbreak of the war was, of course, the issue of slavery, which had affected relations between the north and south ever since the declaration of independence. For quite some time, the question of slavery was dormant, in the sense that there was a balance between states where slavery was prohibited, so called "free states", and states where slavery was allowed, so called "slave states". Of the 22 states that made up the United States, 11 were free and 11 allowed slavery. In 1803, the USA purchased the wide territory of Louisiana from France. The status of slavery in this territory became an issue that infected relations between the free states in the north and the slave states in the south.

In 1818, the territory of Missouri, where slavery was allowed, applied for statehood. The admission of Missouri jeopardized the balance between free states and slave states. As a consequence of this, the admission of Missouri was postponed. In 1819, Maine, where slavery was forbidden, also applied for statehood. A compromise was then reached which provided for the inclusion of Missouri and Maine in the Union; Missouri as a slave state and Maine as a free state. Furthermore, and perhaps more importantly, the compromise stated that, in the territory of Louisiana, slavery would be forbidden north of 36°30′ (Missouri constituting an exception). This compromise was later to be known as "The Missouri Compromise". This compromise was nullified when Congress passed the so-called Kansas–Nebraska Act. By this decision, the question of slavery was left open to the territories to decide.

The immediate response to the Kansas–Nebraska Act was a race between northern and southern settlers into Kansas, and also violent confrontations between the groups. Eventually, the northern settlers outnumbered the southern settlers and Kansas was admitted to the Union as a free state. Nebraska, situated in the north, did not experience similar hostilities. The election of Abraham Lincoln, a fierce opponent of slavery, as President of the United States in 1860 made relations between the north and the south even more strained. In December 1860, South Carolina seceded from the Union. In 1861, Mississippi, Florida, Alabama, Georgia, Louisiana and Texas followed suit. A few months later, Virginia, Arkansas, Tennessee and North Carolina did the same (for a comprehensive description of occurrences that preceded the war see, for instance, Rhodes 1949).

After four long years, the war ended following southern General Robert E. Lee's defeat at Appomattox. The southern rebellion states were forced back into the Union and slavery was forbidden all over the United States. Although peace had been restored, the Civil War left many wounds open. The Civil War also brought about a general acceptance of violence as a means of solving conflicts. Indeed, it has been said that "[the civil war] left in its wake a callousness toward suffering and destruction, an acceptance of ruthlessness and deceit, and a legacy of hatred and mistrust that lived on for many years to come" (Hicks *et al.* 1971: 2).

With regard to the death penalty, the legacy of the Civil War is both interesting and problematic. As has been stressed in the preceding discussion, the issue of slavery has been seen as the most important explanation of the Civil War. In the analysis conducted at the country level, I dwelled upon the plausible association between slavery and capital punishment. These arguments apply to the American case as well. What makes the analysis within the USA problematic is the fact that the two independent variables – north–south affiliation in the Civil War and the legal status of slavery – coincide. The states that were part of the confederacy were all slave states. Fortunately, the multicollinearity is not perfect. Although all confederated states were slave states, not all of the slave states joined the confederacy. Four slave states were unionist: Delaware, Kentucky, Maryland and Missouri (see Hofstadter *et al.* 1959: 594).

Since the independent variables are nominal, strengths of associations between the variables are measured by means of the Eta squared technique. Results are shown in Tables 4.8 and 4.9, and they clearly show that there is a strong connection between, on the one hand, Civil War affiliation and the use of the death penalty and, on the other hand, experiences with slavery and the death penalty. As I presumed, former unionist states and abolitionist states (with regard to slavery) take a more negative stand toward the use of the death penalty than the former confederated states and states where slavery was allowed. As outlined earlier, the problem of multicollinearity is manifest in the analyses, and it is not evident which of the factors – Civil War adherence or experience with slavery – that carries more explanatory power. However, comparisons of means tests suggest that experience with slavery is more important than Civil War affiliation.

Despite the high level of multicollinearity between experience with slavery and Civil War status, the Eta squared is considerably higher in Table 4.9 than in Table 4.8. The four unionist slave states evidently strengthen the explanatory power of slavery in relation to Civil War adherence. The death penalty is allowed and has been applied in all four states (in Missouri to a higher extent than in the others).

Multivariate patterns in the USA

The study of bivariate associations in the American context is now completed. Following the strategy applied at the international level, I now turn to multivariate analyses of the relations between the independent and the dependent variables. So far, the analyses have shown that the following independent variables are related to the death penalty when the requirement is that Pearson's $r \geq (-)0.30$ (or for the multi-categorical variables that Eta squared ≥ 0.09) and $p < 0.01$): population size, number of murders, number of offenses, party affiliation of governor at the time of re-enactment of the death penalty, Civil War status and slavery. In addition, the association between IEF and the death penalty almost reached the threshold of 0.30 (the coefficient being 0.293) and I therefore include it in the regression analysis. Before studying the multivariate patterns, it is necessary to once again consider a few problems of multicollinearity. Civil

Table 4.8 Civil War status and capital punishment in the USA (arithmetic means and standard deviations)

Unionist ($N = 25$)	0.8280 (0.6511)
Confederate ($N = 11$)	1.7000 (0.2098)
No status as state ($N = 15$)	1.0933 (0.6088)
Eta squared	0.269
Sig.	0.001
N	51

Table 4.9 History of slavery and capital punishment in the USA (arithmetic means and standard deviations)

Abolitionist ($N = 21$)	0.6905 (0.6116)
Slave states ($N = 15$)	1.6600 (0.2261)
Western territories[1] ($N = 15$)	1.0933 (0.6088)
Eta squared	0.381
Sig.	0.000
N	51

Note
1 Including Alaska and Hawaii.

War status and experience with slavery were, of course, highly inter-related. The bivariate analyses showed that slavery was more important than Civil War status and I therefore make use of the former variable only. In order to test the impact of slavery in a multiple regression analysis, I treat it as an ordinal variable, where states where slavery was forbidden receive the value 0, and states that allowed slavery receive the value 2. All other states receive the value 1. In these states, the issue of slavery is not assumed to be as important as in the former unionist states or in the former confederated states. In the bivariate analyses, the murder rate turned out to be more strongly connected to the death penalty than the total crime rate and is consequently included in the regression analysis. Among the remaining variables, no internal associations exceed 0.60, and they are consequently all included in the regression analysis, the result of which is given in Table 4.10.

The results are easy to interpret. The most important determinant of the death penalty in the USA is a history of slavery. The states where slavery was allowed prior to the Civil War are the ones that make most frequent use of the death penalty. In addition to a history of slavery, population size carries substantial explanatory power. The inclination to make use of the death penalty grows as population size grows.

Discussion

How are we to grasp the findings of the empirical part of the study? At first glance we are left in disarray. The results show that the explanatory

Table 4.10 Population size, index of ethnic fragmentation, number of murders, history of slavery and party affiliation of governor as determinants of capital punishment in the United States (multiple regression)

Independent variables	B	Beta	T-value
Population (log)	0.228	0.359	3.038**
IEF	−0.846	−0.172	−1.080
Number of murders	0.026	0.099	0.679
History of slavery	0.459	0.597	4.568**
Party affiliation of governor at time of re-enactment	0.251	0.189	1.701

Notes
Multiple R = 0.741.
$R^2 = 0.549$.
Adjusted $R^2 = 0.498$.
F-sig. = 0.000.
$N = 50$.
**Significance at the $p < 0.01$ level.
*Significance at the $p < 0.05$ level.

power of the political variables is subordinate to population size and historical divisions. The only political variable that was related to the dependent variable in the bivariate analyses was party affiliation of the governor at the time of the re-enactment of the death penalty. However, this association no longer existed in the multivariate analyses. To a high extent the relative unimportance of the political variables can probably be explained by a lack of marked ideological divisions between the Republican and the Democratic parties. Indeed, the alternatives given to the voters in the USA have pertinently been described as "Tweedledum or Tweedledee" (Grant 1991: 203). In terms of the death penalty, the similarity between the Democrats and the Republicans are even more pronounced. As we recall, the assumption was that states where Democrats held a dominant position would take a more negative stand against the death penalty than states dominated by Republicans. At the same time, we should be aware of the fact that, traditionally, the real stronghold of the Democratic party has been in the southern states (although the situation has been changing for quite a while now, especially since the presidential elections in 1980 and 1984, where a large number of southern voters supported the Republican candidate, Ronald Reagan).

However, ideologically, these southern Democrats have been very conservative indeed. The reason for the dominance of the Democratic party in an area where a large part of the population has conservative values goes back to the divisions of the Civil War. Since the death penalty is quite popular in these states, it is actually not surprising that there are no links between party domination and the death penalty. The picture can be quite different if we exclude the southern states, dominated by conservative Democrats, and run the analyses among states where the differences between Republicans and Democrats are expected to be more profound. Table 4.11 returns results of bivariate regression analyses where the death penalty is regressed on the four political variables in all non-southern states.[4]

However, the results show that the exclusion of the southern states does not significantly alter earlier findings. Party affiliation of the governor at the time of re-enactment of the death penalty is still the only variable that falls above the level of statistical significance.

Since the party affiliation of the governor at the time of re-enactment is more strongly associated with the death penalty when excluding the southern states, it is necessary to incorporate the variable in a multivariate regression analysis encompassing the same states along with population size, IEF and crime level (slavery cannot be included since only two states in the population, namely Delaware and Maryland, are former slave states). This is done in Table 4.12 and the results show that, when excluding the states where southern Democrats are strong, party affiliation of

Table 4.11 Associations between party dominance in state legislatures, party affiliation of governor and capital punishment in 36 states in the United States (bivariate regressions)

	B	Beta	T-value	R^2	N
Long-term dominance in state legislature	0.013	0.199	1.164	0.039	35[1]
Dominance in state legislature at time of re-enactment or 1973	0.383	0.308	1.859	0.095	35[1]
Long-term party affiliation of governor	−0.005	−0.057	−0.335	0.003	36
Party affiliation of governor at time of re-enactment or 1973	0.630	0.513	3.486**	0.263	36

Notes
1 The non-partisan legislature of Nebraska is excluded.
**Significance at the $p < 0.01$ level.
*Significance at the $p < 0.05$ level.

Table 4.12 Population size, index of ethnic fragmentation, number of murders and party affiliation of governor at time of re-enactment of the death penalty as determinants of capital punishment in 36 states in the United States (multiple regression)

Independent variables	B	Beta	T-value
Population (log)	0.056	0.098	0.596
IEF	−0.049	−0.009	−0.048
Number of murders	0.037	0.149	0.755
Party affiliation of governor at time of re-enactment or 1973	0.556	0.453	2.797**

Notes
Multiple R = 0.546.
R^2 = 0.298.
Adjusted R^2 = 0.207.
F-sig. = 0.017.
$N = 36$.
**Significance at the $p < 0.01$ level.
*Significance at the $p < 0.05$ level.

governor suddenly emerges as a powerful determinant of the death penalty. Indeed, in this sub-population, population size is no longer statistically linked to the death penalty. Thus, we reach the conclusion that the political color of the governor seems to be of relevance for the use of the death penalty.

Within the US context, we also noted that socioeconomic indicators were irrelevant for explaining variations in the attitude toward the death penalty. On the one hand, it could be argued that this finding is perhaps not as much a reflection of a lack of a general link between socioeconomic development and the death penalty, but merely a consequence of the fact that there is not enough variation on the variable within America to allow a meaningful test of the relation. On the other hand, bearing in mind the results obtained at the global level, another explanation stands out. When the countries of the world constituted units of analysis we noted that socioeconomic indicators were associated with the death penalty in bivariate analyses. However, this was explained by the correlation between socioeconomic development and democracy. When controlling for the level of democracy, the indicators of development no longer possessed any explanatory value. Since the degree of democracy is constant within the American context, it is only natural that socioeconomic development fails to interact with the dependent variable in bivariate analyses.

Bivariate analyses showed that both ethnic heterogeneity and the crime level were related to the death penalty. However, these associations no longer persisted in multivariate analyses. In relation to the association between ethnic fragmentation and the death penalty, this is probably explained by collinearity between independent variables. The level of ethnic fragmentation is particularly high in the southern states, which accommodates a substantial number of African-Americans and/or Hispanics. In terms of degree of ethnic fragmentation, former slave states have a mean value of 0.35, whereas the corresponding value for the northern abolitionist states is 0.19. The link between the historical heritage and ethnic fragmentation probably explains the conflicting findings concerning the effect of ethnic heterogeneity on the death penalty. As we recall, bivariate patterns showed that ethnically fractionalized states were more positive toward the use of the death penalty than ethnically homogeneous ones. The multivariate analysis, however, suggested that the tendency was the opposite; that is, ethnic homogeneity corresponded with a positive attitude toward the death penalty, although it has to be stressed that the association did not surpass the level of statistical significance.

A similar argument can be raised in relation to the relative insignificance of the level of crime in the multivariate analysis, although bivariate analyses showed that there was a strong positive association, particularly between number of murders and the use of capital punishment. Again, we note that the level of crime is markedly different in former slave states and the northern abolitionist states. The mean number of offenses in the former category of states is 5,004, whereas the corresponding value for the latter category of states is significantly lower, 4,058 (T-sig. 0.027). For murders, the difference is even more clear: former slave states have an average murder rate of 6.80, whereas the corresponding value for the northern abolitionist states (excluding District of Columbia) is 4.03 (T-sig. 0.000). These findings of course nurture the belief that the historical dimension is decisive for explaining the variation in the death penalty within the USA.

We still have to consider the relevance of population size, which was strongly connected to the dependent variable in the total population (however, when excluding the southern states, where the Democrats have been dominating, population size was no longer connected to the death penalty). One possible explanation for population size's relation to the death penalty immediately stands out. This is the relation between size and the level of crime. One argument is that, in larger societies, the level of crime (in relation to population size) should be higher than in smaller societies. Dahl and Tufte (1973: 13–15) list several claims extracted from classical political theory concerning the characteristics of small societies. Some of these are presumably of relevance when we reflect over the association between population size and the death penalty. For instance, it has been argued that "smaller democracies are likely to generate loyalty to a single integrated community" and that "smaller democracies produce stronger pressures for conformity to collective norms" (Dahl and Tufte 1973: 14). Thus, in general it is reasonable to assume that the mechanisms of social control are tight in small societies, where "everybody knows each other". This, of course, has a preventive effect on crime. However, this line of reasoning receives no empirical support. The regression analyses clearly showed that population size was more important than the level of crime.

One could, of course, argue that the size of states in itself is irrelevant for explaining the death penalty. Instead, the dependent variable should be sensitive to variations in the distribution of the population. Consider two states of equal size. In one of the states, the bulk of the population lives in large cities, and in the other the population is evenly spread in small towns throughout the state. In the latter case, the same character-istics that applied for small societies should be present, whereas the oppos-ite should be true for the former case. In order to control for population distribution, I used the percentage of people living in cities with more than 100,000 inhabitants. The results, however, showed that this measure was not related to the death penalty at all. The correlation was a meager 0.022.

Instead, the explanation might very well be that the absolute number of crime is much higher in larger entities than in smaller ones. Since the overall level of crime is higher in larger states, there will, by necessity, be a higher number of capital crimes in larger states. When there are many capital cases, legislators and jurors have to confront the issue of the death penalty more often than their counterparts in small states. Perhaps there is a threshold effect. When murders are frequent and jurors and judges have to consider the death penalty on a regular basis, the threshold for implementing death sentences is lowered in the long run. In smaller states, with fewer capital crimes, the threshold for considering and implementing the death penalty is higher, since capital crimes occur rarely.

5 Determinants of the death penalty

Summary of findings

The death penalty is a highly controversial issue. The aim of this book has been to assess the determinants of capital punishment without taking a stand for or against the death penalty. The study has been conducted at several levels of analysis. The primary focus was on a global comparison, where all the countries of the world were included. In addition, separate analyses were carried out within democracies and non-democracies. Furthermore, variable interactions were measured in four regional settings. Finally, I used the states of the United States of America as units of analysis. Overall, the findings of the different analyses were quite consistent. Table 5.1 summarizes the results obtained in the different analyses.

The degree of democracy tends to carry explanatory power in a number of contexts. As has been pointed out on several occasions, it is linked to religion and a history of slavery, which means that it is difficult to assert the relative impact of the three variables. Based on cross-tabulations, however, I reached the conclusion that each of the three variables contains explanatory value on their own. The explanatory value of religion is probably most difficult to assess. The empirical evidence showed that Christianity is negatively associated with the death penalty and that Islam, and to a lesser extent Buddhism, goes hand-in-hand with a positive view of the death penalty. However, since Islam is strongly associated with degree of democracy and a history of slavery, the impact of Islam is probably stronger than the statistical analyses have revealed. With regard to the impact of Islam on the death penalty, it was also clearly shown that the farther we move from the core area of Islam, i.e. the Middle East, the higher the likelihood that we find exceptions from the rule that Islam and the death penalty go hand-in-hand.

Population size was related to the death penalty in Asia and the Pacific and also within the United States. The association was positive; that is, bigger units were more prone to make use of the death penalty than

Table 5.1 Determinants of the death penalty in eight settings

Context of analysis	Determinants of the death penalty	
	1985	*2000*
Global	Religion, degree of democracy, colonial heritage, history of slavery	Religion, degree of democracy, colonial heritage, history of slavery
Democracies	No clear pattern	No clear pattern
Non-democracies	Unique historical events, violent internal conflicts, external pressure	Unique historical events, violent internal conflicts, external pressure
Africa	(Insularity)	Degree of democracy, regime stability
America	Historical/cultural differences between the English-speaking Caribbean countries and other countries	Historical/cultural differences between the English-speaking Caribbean countries and other countries
Asia and Pacific	Population size, religion, (degree of democracy)	Population size, religion, (degree of democracy)
Europe	Degree of democracy, (EU trade), (level of crime), (external pressure)	Degree of democracy, external pressure
USA	–	History of slavery, population size, party affiliation of the governor at the time of re-enactment of the death penalty

Note
Parentheses indicate that the variables are associated with the death penalty but the strength of association is weak or the association is not theoretically unassailable.

smaller ones. It is not easy to come up with a comprehensive explanation for this. It could be that population size coincides with high levels of crime. The association between population size and the death penalty would therefore be a function of the association between population size and level of crime. However, the statistical analyses indicated that population size contained independent explanatory value on its own. Based on the discussion in Chapter 2 (p. 25), a plausible explanation for the relation between population size and the death penalty was the fact that, in small entities, intimacy and homogeneity raises the threshold for applying capital punishment. Another explanation could be that the absolute number of crimes committed is, by necessity, higher in larger entities. The threshold for applying the death penalty is consequently lowered in the long run as jurors and/or judges have to confront the issue of the death penalty on a regular basis.

The association between a lack of colonial heritage and a negative attitude toward the death penalty found at the global level is worth noting. Here, too, two plausible explanations stand out. On the one hand, it could be argued that diffusion plays a crucial role. Former colonies have simply incorporated the death penalty statutes of their former mother countries into their own legislation. The other explanation follows the same line of reasoning that applied to the discussion on the link between a history of slavery and the death penalty. The inhabitants of the colonies grew accustomed to the use of force and cruel punishments in the colonial era. Consequently, in these countries, various forms of corporal punishment were thought to be legitimate. Of these two explanations, diffusion is probably more important. It is also of interest to note that colonial heritage contained explanatory value exclusively at the global level. At the regional level, the association was not detected. This is to some extent probably due to the fact that almost all of the colonial powers were European. However, within Europe as well, there were a number of countries that had been in a subordinate position to another country

Aside from the form of government, the explanatory value of purely political variables was generally low. In Africa, a weak association between regime stability and the death penalty was noted. Countries with frequent regime changes were more prone to make use of the death penalty than countries where regime duration was longer. Within the USA, we found that states with a Republican governor at the time of re-enactment of the death penalty were more likely to make use of the death penalty than states with a Democratic governor.

The highly controversial issue of whether or not capital punishment has a deterrent effect was not answered within the framework of this study (indeed, this was never the ambition, since I have only been interested in causes, and not effects, of the death penalty). In one context, Europe in 1985, there was a relation between the level of crime and the death penalty. The finding suggested that the use of the death penalty went hand-in-hand with low levels of crime. This finding, however, was effectively captured by the demarcation line between Eastern and Western Europe.

Even though the explanatory power of democracy generally turned out to be very strong, it is important to remember that exceptions were found. All democracies have not abolished the death penalty, and all authoritarian countries do not make use of it. At the same time, it is evident that a democracy that makes use of the death penalty is a far more common phenomenon than a non-democracy that has forbidden its use. A closer look at these anomalies has shown that, whereas a number of explanations are relevant for understanding why some democracies apply the death penalty, unique historical events, often a bloody history in combination with heavy involvement by international organizations, explain the negative attitude toward the death penalty found in a few authoritarian countries.

Although, the importance of the different indicators have been discussed, it is evident that an assessment of the determinants of the death penalty is not complete without a more thorough analysis of the results obtained so far. It is also necessary to answer the question of what the future of the death penalty looks like in a global perspective. I shall therefore conclude this book by discussing three essential features of the death penalty: legitimacy, diffusion and trends.

Legitimacy, diffusion and trends

Legitimacy

The most controversial issue regarding the death penalty is its basis of legitimacy. At the beginning of the study I pointed out that I would, as far as possible, refrain from discussing the question since it was beyond the aim of this work. However, it is evident that an analysis of the empirical evidence that does not touch upon the issue of legitimacy is incomplete. The evidence has shown that a number of indicators are important for explaining variances in the death penalty. At the same time, variable interactions are far from deterministic. A number of anomalies have been found. We have, among other things, seen that not all democracies refrain from using the death penalty and that not all countries with a Muslim majority make use of capital punishment. Incorporating the concept of legitimacy into the discussion does not solve the whole puzzle, but it does give us some clue in understanding how these deviant cases can emerge and subsist.

At least from a European perspective, it is evident that international pressure to abolish the death penalty grows stronger all the time. The attitude toward capital punishment has sharpened, especially during the last two decades. The United Nations and the European Union in particular are forerunners in the abolitionist movement. Among (Western) European politicians, there is wide agreement on the negative attitude toward the death penalty. This, however, is the European view. When we travel across the Atlantic, quite another picture emerges. The attitude toward the death penalty is generally more favorable among politicians and it is probably fair to say that, for a serious contender for the US presidency, it would be political suicide to take a stand against the death penalty.

Apparently, then, there is a strong discrepancy between the attitude toward the death penalty in Europe and in the United States. However, a more careful consideration suggests that this is not necessarily the case. Attitudes toward the death penalty are regularly measured in opinion polls both in Europe and in America. Although Americans tend to have a more favorable attitude toward capital punishment than Europeans, it is clear that the wide consensus of complete deprecation of capital punishment by the governments of European countries is not always mirrored in the population at large. For instance, in a number of European countries, opinions polls show that a majority was in favor of the death penalty at the time of abolition and that support for the death penalty continues to be high (see Hood 2002: 233–236; Fawn 2001: 76–77; Death Penalty Information Center, available online: http://www.deathpenaltyinfo.org/article.php?scid=23&did=210).

It is telling that even in a country like Sweden, where capital punishment has not been a political issue for decades and where virtually every politician from right to left condemns the use of the death penalty, figures suggest that not less than 33 percent of the population is in favor of the death penalty. The figure of 33 percent becomes even more interesting when we compare it with the proportion of the population in favor of the beating of children as a method of discipline within the home, which is 9 percent (Rothstein 1995: 79). It is indeed remarkable that a substantial proportion of the population believes that the government should have the right to kill its citizens, but a much smaller proportion is ready to allow parents to smack their children. It is also evident that popular demands for the death penalty are sensitive to general modes of security and that general opinion varies, particularly in times when society is affected by heinous crimes (Mohrenschlager 1987: 513; Beristain 1987: 620–622).

It is thus evident that, as far as the attitude toward the death penalty is concerned, there is a gap between the elite and the masses (see Hood 2002: 234). However, it must be emphasized that this gap is probably deeper in democracies than in authoritarian societies. Although reliable results of opinion polls are difficult to come across for authoritarian countries, it is fair to assume that both rulers and the ruled share a positive view of the death penalty (at least as long as the punishment is not applied for political crimes). Consequently, a very interesting picture emerges. In one form of government, popular opinion should play a crucial role for the governing body, namely in democracies. Nevertheless, with regard to one policy area, the death penalty, this is not the case. With regard to this issue, the elite have turned a deaf ear to public demands (see Fawn 2001: 93). Why, then, do governments in democracies feel there is no need to respond to popular demands for the death penalty?

One plausible explanation, which is not very far-fetched, has to do with the different bases of legitimacy that democratic and authoritarian governments stand on. In a democracy, the ruling class knows it has come to power by means of popular elections. When the majority of the population constitutes your basis of support, you can allow yourself to go against popular demands as long as you are convinced you have a moral obligation to do so. After the fall of the Soviet Union, the legitimacy of non-democratic forms of government has been questioned. Nowadays, international pressure on authoritarian governments can sometimes be very hard indeed. In situations where authoritarian governments face the difficult task of legitimating their rule, it is difficult to see why they should confront the population in an issue which does not constitute a threat to its rule. Evidently, this line of reasoning probably performs better in explaining why democratic governments remain unperturbed by popular demands for capital punishment than why authoritarian governments uphold the death penalty. For many non-democratic governments, the ultimate reason for holding on to the death penalty is probably that this form of punishment is an effective tool for keeping a firm grip on the society.

The issue of legitimacy becomes very important indeed, however, for one category of non-democratic countries – the Islamic countries. In Islamic countries the legitimacy of the death penalty rests on a solid base. In purely Islamic societies, all aspects of life are regulated by the *Sharia*. Thus, there is no separation of the religious from the political sphere. As we have seen, the *Koran* is unequivocal with regard to the death penalty and capital punishment is prescribed for a number of crimes. In a strictly Islamic country, the hands of the governments are tied when the issue of capital punishment is raised. The death penalty is not only an option, it is an obligation. One could, of course, object to this line of reasoning and claim that the Old Testament also prescribes the death penalty for a number of crimes. The crucial difference between governments in Islamic countries and in Christian countries, however, is that the latter do not have to confront the *Sharia*.

This means that if decision-makers in Islamic countries were to abolish the death penalty, they would have to confront not only the majority of the population but also the fundamental values on which the whole Islamic society is built. Needless to say, this is an insurmountable task to any power-holder. The legitimacy of the death penalty is deeply rooted in Islamic tradition, and it is not venturesome to predict that, in this category of countries, the abolitionist movement has a very difficult task indeed. The combination of authoritarian rule and the positive attitude toward the death penalty in the *Koran* is of particular interest. On the one hand, power-holders are likely to regard the death penalty as a useful tool for keeping its grip on society. As long as tradition and religion supports this view, public opinion will not work against capital punishment. Thus, to put it bluntly, the future of the death penalty looks bright in Islamic countries.

I have argued in this chapter that the concept of legitimacy can help to explain differences in the attitudes of the political elite and the public in democratic societies. At the same time, we should not exaggerate the differences. Nevertheless, the total absence of the death penalty from the political agenda in Western Europe is remarkable, given the fact that a substantial part of the population has a favorable attitude toward it. Perhaps the ever-present term "political correctness" plays a crucial role. Articulating an interest is not easy since virtually all political parties refuse to lobby in favor of the death penalty. Thus, demands for its (re)installation are raised mainly by populist movements, ostracized by their political counterparts.

Diffusion

The role of legitimacy cannot be understood without reference to diffusion. As I have pointed out on numerous occasions, the international pressure to abolish the death penalty is now stronger than ever before. I have argued that the abolition of the death penalty in former Soviet republics is explained by the fierce negative stand toward capital punishment taken by Western European governments. In many Eastern European countries marked by economic instability and high rates of crime, public opinion favored (and still favors) the death penalty. However, even in these situations, where not only a substantial minority but a vast majority of the population were/are in favor of capital punishment, governments have chosen to abolish the death penalty.

I have argued that these decisions are explained by international pressure, mostly from Western Europe. However, legitimacy probably plays a role too. It is difficult to see how political leaders could reject the death penalty in countries where adherents of the punishment constituted a majority unless the leaders felt their decision had a strong basis of legitimacy. Under these circumstances, pressure from foreign countries alone is probably not a sufficient condition for the legal status of the death penalty. Consider for a moment the possibility that the situation was the opposite, and that a country expressed its desire to join or cooperate with an international organization. In the country in question, the death penalty would be forbidden and the general attitude toward the death penalty would be negative. However, as a condition for joining the organization, the country in question would be required to install the death penalty. The idea that the leaders of the country, in their eagerness to join the organization, would disregard public opinion and introduce the death penalty does indeed sound far-fetched. At least from a European perspective, it is evident that it is more legitimate to be against the death penalty than in favor of it.

What is particularly interesting is the fact that the empirical evidence shows that the trend in the United States is opposite to the one that can be discerned at the global level. In USA, the death penalty is nowadays more widely applied than ten or twenty years ago. I would argue that diffusion plays a crucial role in explaining these contrary trends between Europe and the USA. Within the European context, the role of diffusion is straightforward. The Eastern European countries are required to abolish the death penalty in order to take part in European integration and cooperation. Without exaggerating too much, one can say that the farther east we go from Brussels, the more positive the attitude of the governments toward the death penalty becomes. This is simply due to the fact that the farther east we go, the smaller the possibility of the countries joining the European Union within a foreseeable future. Countries situated on the outskirts of Europe do not feel obliged to adapt to the norms of the European Union.

Within the USA, another kind of diffusion is of relevance. Statistical analyses showed that there was a clear link between a history of slavery and a positive attitude toward the death penalty. The Supreme Court decision in 1972 (*Furman* v. *Georgia*), which effectively suspended the death penalty in the USA, was a devastating blow, particularly to the southern states were capital punishment was more widely applied and less controversial than in the north. With the Supreme Court decision in 1976 (*Gregg* v. *Georgia*), the new death penalty statutes of Florida, Georgia and Texas were held to be constitutional. Although it is perhaps an overstatement to say that the south won the "battle of the death penalty" in 1976, it is illustrative that the subsequent wave of death penalty statutes following the Gregg decision was, to a large extent, a southern phenomenon.

As we have seen, the north–south division is highly relevant when discussing the death penalty in the USA. During the whole of the twentieth century, the issue of the death penalty was highly controversial in the USA. To simplify the matter, we can stipulate that states in the north were restrictive toward the use of the death penalty, whereas the southern states were positive. It is easy to imagine that a general positive attitude toward the death penalty had been smoldering in the south for many decades prior to the Supreme Court decision in 1976. At least from a legal point of view, the legitimacy of the death penalty was no longer questioned after 1976. It can, of course, be argued that this line of reasoning overemphasizes the importance of one court ruling. The counterargument is that the 1976 decision was crucial for the general view of the legitimacy of the death penalty. Proponents of the death penalty found that they were – implicitly at least – backed by the highest judicial organ of the USA. For state legislators, the Supreme Court decision meant that the question of legitimacy, in principle at least, was turned upside down. When the death penalty statutes of the three Southern states were ruled to be constitutional, the issue was no longer controversial from a judicial point of view. Accordingly, state governments no longer had to defend the use of the death penalty. In fact, the snowball was already rolling. As a large number of states chose to reinstall the death penalty, it became harder and harder for state legislators in other states to defend its prohibition.

As I have argued, in Europe there is a discrepancy between the public attitude toward the death penalty and that of the political decision-makers. While ordinary citizens can have a quite favorable view of the death penalty, Western European governments no longer seriously consider its return. I have argued that Western European governments disregard popular demands for the death penalty on the ground of legitimacy. Their argument is basically that even though there is widespread support for the death penalty, capital punishment cannot be allowed because it is a cruel and inhuman form of punishment.

In America, political power-holders with a negative view of the death penalty do not have the same basis of legitimacy. The Supreme Court has explicitly stated that death penalty statutes are in accordance with the constitution. When popular support for the death penalty is high, it is not difficult to imagine that state governments in states where the death penalty is not allowed sometimes come under increasing pressure to defend their position. As the number of executions increase at a high rate in many states, it becomes harder to resist popular demands for the death penalty. This is particularly the case in a country with exceptionally high levels of violent crime. Accordingly, we find that diffusion explains death penalty patterns both in Europe and the USA. However, within these two settings, diffusion works in different directions. In Europe, diffusion works to *decrease* the use of the death penalty whereas, in the USA, diffusion probably helps to explain the *increasing* use of the death penalty.

Trends

As we now approach the end of the study, it is time to turn our eyes to the future. When discussing the future of the death penalty, two questions are of particular interest. The first one is merely academic, whereas the second one is of general interest. Although neither of these questions can be answered in its entirety, some tentative answers are nevertheless possible. From a scientific point of view, it is important to ask ourselves what consequences the results of the present study have for future research on the death penalty. On the one hand, we ask ourselves what the future of the death penalty looks like. Will it persist as a form of punishment in the future or has capital punishment outlived itself?

The results of the empirical analyses show that there was not much variation between the results obtained at the two different points in time. What, then, can we expect with regard to similar studies in the future? Will the same explaining indicators be important or will other factors carry more explanatory weight? I would say, in the future, a research design similar to the one applied in the framework of the present study is less likely to produce unequivocal results. I base this conclusion (or opinion, if you prefer) on the discussion about the importance of diffusion conducted above. This study was conducted at two points in time, 1985 and 2000. The biggest difference between the two points in time was that, during the latter period, diffusion had started to play an increasingly important role with regard to the death penalty.

The international pressure for the abolition of the death penalty is likely to reduce the strength of relationships between independent and dependent variables. The unpopularity of the death penalty in many countries and with international organizations heavily influences the choice of countries to abolish or retain capital punishment. Accordingly, we can assume that a growing number of countries, which would not consider abolishing the death penalty without international pressure, are likely to forbid the use of capital punishment in order to please abolitionist countries or organizations. It is easy to imagine that poor and less-developed countries are the most likely ones to give in to these demands. Socioeconomic development, again, is negatively related to authoritarianism and a history of slavery, both of which were strong determinants of the death penalty. Thus, in the future, we will probably witness a growing number of countries with an authoritarian form of government and a history of slavery where the death penalty is not applied. A growing number of non-democracies without capital punishment means, of course, that the overall strength of association between degree of democracy and a negative attitude toward the death penalty will be reduced.

Let us then turn to the second question. From a global point of view, it is an undeniable fact that the popularity of the death penalty is decreasing at a steady rate. Even though a majority of the independent countries still have death penalty statutes in their legislation, it is evident that the abolitionist movement is currently very strong. In 1985, only 29 countries had abolished the death penalty for all crimes. By the end of the year 2000, 73 countries were abolitionist for all crimes. The absolute number of countries that applied the death penalty had not decreased as much due to the fact that many states received their independence during the same time period. In 1985, 123 countries had death penalty statutes for ordinary crimes. In 2000, the corresponding number was 106. However, if we look at relative figures, the picture is clear. In 1985, 17.2 percent of the countries were abolitionist for all crimes, whereas 72.8 percent had death penalty statutes for ordinary crimes. In 2000, 38.0 percent were abolitionist for all crimes whereas 55.2 percent still had death penalty statutes for ordinary crimes.

Although this is not a rule without exceptions, the general trend is obvious: more and more countries abolish the death penalty or put a moratorium on executions. At the same time, we should be aware of the fact that there are countries which contradict this rule. Thus, the process could well be described as "two steps forward and one step backward". In other words, the number of countries where capital punishment is allowed does not necessarily decrease every year. From one year to another it is even possible that the number increases. However, if we compare average figures for the last five years with average figures for, say, the last ten or fifteen years, the decrease in the use of capital punishment becomes clear.

In this study I have discussed a large number of plausible explanations for the death penalty. Throughout the work, however, I have found it necessary to return to the relation between democracy and capital punishment. Implicitly at least, these phenomena are not thought to be ideal playmates and quite so; the results have shown that democracy and an absence of capital punishment tend to go hand-in-hand. In the light of these results, it is natural to compare death penalty trends with trends in the process of democratization. In his seminal work, *The Third Wave: Democratization in the Late Twentieth Century*, Huntington (1991) identified three waves of democratization. Can similar waves be discovered with regard to the death penalty, and if so, how do these trends relate to Huntington's findings? If democracy and the death penalty are related, then trends in the abolition of the death penalty should correspond to waves of democratization.

According to Huntington, the first long wave of democratization occurred between 1828 and 1926. The wave began with the gradual transformation of the USA toward democracy and ended with the new democracies that erupted in Europe as a consequence of the First World War. The first wave was followed by a counter-wave, starting with the Fascist seizure of power in Italy in 1922. In the inter-war era, authoritarian regimes erupted all over Central and Eastern Europe. The second wave of democratization began at the end of the Second World War and ended in the early 1960s. During this phase, democracy was restored in Western Europe. The process of decolonization in Africa and Asia also gave birth to a number of new democracies in Asia. In Latin America a democratic form of government was introduced in a number of countries. Again, the wave of democratization was followed by a counter-wave. The global process of democratization stagnated at the beginning of the 1960s and, until the mid-1970s, very few democracies emerged. During the same time-period, many democratic regimes collapsed, especially in Africa, but also in Latin America and even in Western Europe (Greece). The third wave of democratization began with the fall of the authoritarian regimes in Portugal, Spain and Greece and has continued to date. During this phase, democracy conquered the American continent and the communist regimes in Eastern Europe have been replaced by democratic ones. Nevertheless, a substantial number of countries still have authoritarian forms of government (including the powerful example of China). In Africa and the Middle East, democracy has not yet managed to secure a foothold. Overall, the process of democratization has stagnated during the 1990s and this has even raised the question of whether the third wave of democratization has now come to an end (Diamond 1999: 24–63).

Can we, then, identify similar trends to the ones described above with regard to the attitude toward capital punishment, and if so, how do these trends relate to Huntington's waves of democratization? A quick glance at Table 1.1 reveals that, for more than a century, no trends regarding the popularity of the death penalty could be discerned. The abolitionist movement gained ground at an extremely slow rate. However, by the end of the 1980s, there was a huge increase in the number of countries which had abandoned the death penalty. In 1987 Haiti, Liechtenstein and the German Democratic Republic abolished the death penalty. In 1989, four countries (Cambodia, New Zealand, Romania and Slovenia[1]) abolished the death penalty. In 1990, no less than eight countries (Andorra, Croatia,[1] Czechoslovakia, Hungary, Ireland, Mozambique, Namibia and Sao Tome & Principe) abolished the death penalty for all crimes. During the time period 1991–2003, no less than 35 countries abolished the death penalty for ordinary crimes. On the basis of these figures, it is difficult to reach any conclusion other than that we are currently witnessing the first wave of abolition of the death penalty.

Having answered the first question in the affirmative, we must ask ourselves whether there is any correspondence between the waves of democratization and the waves of abolition of the death penalty. Again, the answer is undoubtedly yes. The pace of abolition of the death penalty increased rapidly at exactly the same time as the process of democratization reached its peak.[2] The connection between a newly installed democratic form of government and the abolition of the death penalty is strong, albeit not without exception. The abolition of the death penalty in countries such as Romania, Czechoslovakia, Hungary, Moldova, Poland, South Africa, Bulgaria, Estonia, Lithuania, Latvia, Albania and Chile are clearly linked to their transition from authoritarianism to democracy. In other cases the connection between the abolition of the death penalty and democratization is weaker. For instance, we find a category consisting of countries where abolition goes hand-in-hand with movements toward independence in the first place and democracy in the second (Slovenia and Croatia, for example). We also have a number of countries with a history of recent violence where a foreign intervention or international involvement in a peace process (along with movements toward democracy), coincide with the abolition of the death penalty (Bosnia-Herzegovina, Angola, Haiti and Namibia, for example).

Still, a number of cases cannot be explained by the waves of democratization. Liechtenstein, New Zealand, Ireland, Switzerland, Belgium, Canada and Cyprus had all been stable democracies for a long time before abolishing the death penalty. Likewise, the death penalty has been abolished in Turkmenistan, where the prospects for democracy were not and are not good.

The analyses have shown that democracy is an important determinant of the attitude toward the death penalty. Therefore, the finding that waves of democratization coincide with waves of abolitionism is not surprising. Nevertheless, we need to reflect on the finding, which shows that only the latter part of the third wave of democratization coincided with a wave of abolitionism. From a global perspective, the empirical evidence clearly tells us that general attitudes toward the death penalty remained unaffected by the first and second wave of democratization. In addition, the first (and only) wave of abolitionism started at the end of the 1980s; that is, more than a decade after the start of Huntington's third wave of democratization. We therefore must ask ourselves why waves of democratization did not provoke similar trends in attitudes toward the death penalty until now.

One plausible answer is, of course, that countries which move from authoritarianism to democracy do not adapt to all aspects of a democratic form of government immediately. In the beginning, many institutions are likely to be highly unstable. For instance, evidence suggests that there are fluctuations in the party system, and that government instability is high (Berglund and Dellenbrant 1994: 248). Therefore, a negative view of the death penalty is not created overnight. Instead, we can expect a rather long time lag between the introduction of a democratic form of government and the abolition of the death penalty. However, even with this in mind, it is clear that the first two waves of democratization did not give rise to a corresponding boost in the abolitionist movement.

I would say that the current wave of abolitionism is not exclusively a consequence of the third wave of democratization. Instead, I would argue that the general loss of popularity of the death penalty is a consequence of the combination of democratization and diffusion. If we take a look at the countries which have abolished the death penalty for all crimes, or only for ordinary crimes, during the period 1987–2002, we discover that not less than 17 countries are former Eastern European countries. These countries have undergone a rapid shift from socialism to democracy. At the same time, they have abandoned the death penalty. I have, however, argued that pressure from Western European countries is a very important explanation for the absence of the death penalty in the newly democratized countries in Eastern Europe. Without this pressure, it is doubtful whether the number of countries having abolished the death penalty in recent years would be that high.

My conclusion, then, is that, at least in the long run, waves of abolitionism similar to those of democracy cannot be identified. True, the last wave of democratization partly coincides with an abolitionist boom, but it is evident that diffusion also plays an important role. This finding notwithstanding, it is still necessary to reflect on what effects the current wave of democratization is likely to have for the death penalty. First, I would argue that the current wave shows no signs of abating. The number of countries that have abolished the death penalty grows each year. It is very likely indeed that the current wave of abolition is, to a large extent, a domino effect. The international pressure to abandon the death penalty is very strong, and the higher the number of countries that abandon the death penalty, the harder it is to uphold the punishment in other countries. At the same time, it is far too early to predict the complete extinction of the death penalty from penal codes all over the world. The future of the death penalty in the world largely rests on its future in the USA. As long as the world's only super power upholds the death penalty, regimes with a favorable attitude toward capital punishment can resist the pressure from abolitionists. We have seen that, in the USA, the number of executions has increased during the last decade and opinion polls continually show that the death penalty enjoys support from a vast majority of the population. Therefore, the death penalty will probably continue to exist in many countries, at least in the immediate future.

Nevertheless, history has shown that the situation in the USA can change fast. We must remember that the legal status of the death penalty in the USA is ultimately decided by the Supreme Court judges. What happens if the death penalty is suddenly declared unconstitutional in the USA, and if the American government starts to lobby in favor of its abolition worldwide? In this case, it would be very difficult for most regimes to retain capital punishment. This book, therefore, ends with the ironic assertion that the future of one of the most important and controversial political issues perhaps lies in the hands of a few hand-picked jurists in one single country.

Notes

1 Mapping the death penalty

1 Turkey, as well as the Caucasian border states, Armenia, Azerbaijan and Georgia are classified as European countries.

2 Explaining the death penalty

1 With the following exceptions: in the 1985 version of Freedom House's compilation, Kuwait and Tonga have an overall scoring of 8, while Morocco's score is 9. However, in these countries the ruler had far reaching powers at the time. In all countries parliaments existed, but they had/have very little legislative power. As the example of Kuwait illustrates, the parliament was allowed to work only as long as it did not threaten the authority of the Emir. Kuwait, Morocco and Tonga are consequently classified as absolute states in 1985. In 2000, Kuwait, Morocco and Tonga are again classified as absolute systems despite the fact that each country's combined degree of political rights and civil liberties is less than 10. For the year 2000, I include Fiji and Russia among the unstable democracies although they only just fail to meet the criteria. For the Vatican State, I have made use of the latest *Freedom House* figures available, which are from 1985.
2 Colonial heritage was thought to affect the death penalty in two different ways. For one thing, I assumed that the attitude to the death penalty was a consequence of diffusion from mother country to colony. The other theoretical argument departed from the view that being under foreign rule itself gave rise to frustration and a more accepting attitude toward violence and various forms of corporal punishment. These two differing views have some consequences for the operationalization of colonial heritage. The former theoretical base suggests that the mother countries are given the same values as their colonies, since it is not the colonial past in itself that is seen as the explanatory factor but constitutional devices and values found in the mother country. The latter argument, again, presupposes that former colonial powers are regarded as countries without a colonial past, since being subject to foreign rule is what is crucial. In Table 2.22, the latter strategy has been applied. However, I also conducted separate comparisons of means tests where former colonial powers were given the same values as their ex-colonies, but this strategy did not significantly change the results.

3 Contextual patterns

1 For obvious reasons, the seventh non-democratic country that does not apply the death penalty, the Vatican State, is excluded from the statistical analysis between infant mortality and the death penalty.

2 I am indebted to Professor Felix Bethel for raising these points during a discussion in March 2000, in Nassau.
3 The death penalty exists in the criminal code in Azerbaijan in the sense that, in time of war or threat of war, the passing of a law that allows the death penalty for "exceptional crimes" is possible (Fawn 2001, 9).
4 According to the sources used, there has been no executions in Samoa since the country gained independence. Strictly focusing on the formal judiciary system, this is true. However, alongside the formal legal system, an informal legal system persists. When introducing universal suffrage, the government was compelled to take measures that compensated the *matais* for the effective loss of power that this change created. Accordingly, the Village Fono Act was enacted in 1990. This act formally recognized traditional powers. The loose wording of the act effectively meant that it allowed "virtually unlimited scope for the imposition of punishment" (Lawson 1996: 156). In 1993, the effects of the Village Fono Act became evident, when a villager was shot to death in Samoa. The execution was apparently sanctioned by senior *matais*. Following the execution, there has been a vivid debate concerning the legitimacy of the execution. Whereas some people argue that the execution was justified under the Village Fono Act, others disagree (Lawson 1996: 155–157). This example is illustrative of the problems many countries in the Pacific are facing as laws clash with traditions and old values.

4 The death penalty in the USA

1 Which, inevitably, leads to the question of whether the term "case study" is appropriate at all in this context. Eckstein (1975: 85), for instance, would argue that this is not the case since his conception of case study implies a single observation only.
2 Prior to that, the death penalty was abolished for a short period in Iowa (1872–1878) and in Maine (1876–1883) (Bohm 1999: 5).
3 One exception is made from this rule. Missouri scores the value 2.97 and is situated in the ninth decile. However, its value is much higher than the values of the other states within the same category (2.00, 1.70 and 1.65) and very close indeed to the value of Florida (3.03), which is situated in the tenth decile. I therefore give Missouri the same value on the dependent variable as the states in the tenth decile, i.e. Texas, Virginia and Florida), i.e. 1.9.
4 The following states are excluded: Alabama, Arkansas, Florida, Georgia, Kentucky, Louisiana, Mississippi, Missouri, North Carolina, South Carolina, Tennessee, Texas, West Virginia, Virginia.

5 Determinants of the death penalty

1 Slovenia and Croatia were still part of Yugoslavia.
2 It is not unusual to regard the process of democratization after 1989 as a separate, fourth wave (see Karvonen 1997: 110).

References

Akehurst, M. (1987) *Akehurst's Modern Introduction to International Law*, 7th edn, London: Routledge.
Allardt, E. and Rokkan, S. (eds) (1970) *Mass Politics: Studies in Political Sociology*, New York, NY: The Free Press.
Allardt, E. and Starck, C. (1981) *Språkgränser och samhällsstruktur*, Stockholm: Almqvist & Wiksell.
Amnesty International (2000) *Death Penalty News, September 2000*, AI index: ACT 53/03/00, online, available at: http://web.amnesty.org/library/Index/ENGACT530032000 (accessed 11 December 2003).
Amnesty International (2000) *Death Penalty News, September 2000*, AI index: AFR 31/003/2000, online, available at: http://web.amnesty.org/library/Index/ENGAFR310032000 (accessed 11 December 2003).
Amnesty International (2001) *Abolitionist and Retentionist Countries*, online, available at: http://web.amnesty.org/pages/deathpenalty.countries-eng (last accessed 12 December 2003).
Anckar, C. (1997) "Size and Democracy: Some Empirical Findings", in D. Anckar and L. Nilsson (eds), *Politics and Geography: Contributions to an Interface*, Sundsvall: Mid-Sweden University Press, pp. 19–40.
Anckar, C. (1998) *Storlek och partisystem: en studie av 77 stater*, Åbo: Åbo Akademis förlag.
Anckar, C., Eriksson, M. and Leskinen, J. (2002) "Measuring Ethnic, Linguistic and Religious Fragmentation in the World", *Department of Political Science, Åbo Akademi University Occasional Papers Series* 18.
Anckar, D. (1997) "Federal and Bicameral Microstates: Gigantic Miniatures?", in D. Anckar and L. Nilsson (eds), *Politics and Geography: Contributions to an Interface*, Sundsvall: Mid-Sweden University Press.
Anckar, D. (1999) "Homogeneity and Smallness: Dahl and Tufte revisited", *Scandinavian Political Studies*, 22: 29–44.
Anckar, D. and Anckar, C. (1995) "Size, Insularity and Democracy", *Scandinavian Political Studies*, 18: 211–229.
Archer, D., Gartner, R. and Beittel, M. (1983) "Homicide and the Death Penalty: a Cross-National Test of a Deterrence Hypothesis", *Journal of Criminal Law and Criminology*, 74: 991–1013.
Aristotle (Aristoteles) (1991) *Politiikka*, trans. to Finnish A.M. Anttila, Jyväskylä: Gaudeamus.

Bachrach, P. and Baratz, M.S. (1972) *Makt och fattigdom: teori och praktik*, trans. to Swedish M. Mörling and G. Uddenberg, Stockholm: Wahlström & Widstrand.

Bedau, H.A. (ed.) (1982) *The Death Penalty in America*, 3rd edn, New York, NY: Oxford University Press.

Bell, W. (ed.) (1967) *The Democratic Revolution in the West Indies: Studies in Nationalism, Leadership, and the Belief in Progress*, Cambridge, MA: Schenkman Publishers.

van den Berghe, P.L. (1981) *The Ethnic Phenomenon*, New York, NY: Elsevier.

Berglund, S. and Dellenbrant, J.-Å. (1994) "Prospects for the New Democracies in Eastern Europe", in S. Berglund and J.-Å. Dellenbrant (eds), *The New Democracies in Eastern Europe*, 2nd edn, Aldershot: Edward Elgar, pp. 238–252.

Beristain, A. (1987) "La sanction capitale en Espagne: reference spéciale a la dimension religieuse Chrétienne", *Revue Internationale de Droit Pénal*, 58: 613–636.

Betts, R.F. (1991) *France and Decolonisation 1900–1960*, London: Macmillan Education.

The Bible, ed. with an introduction and notes by R.P. Carroll and S. Prickett (1997). Authorized King James version. Oxford: Oxford University Press.

Bienen, H.S. and van de Walle, N. (1991) *Of Time and Power: Leadership Duration in the Modern World*, Stanford, CA: Stanford University Press.

Blaustein, A. and Flanz, G.H. (eds). *Constitutions of the Countries of the World*, updated regularly, Dobbs Ferry, NY: Ocean Publications.

Bohm, R.M. (1999) *Deathquest: an Introduction to the Theory and Practice of Capital Punishment in the United States*, Cincinnati, OH: Anderson Publishing Co.

Bollen, K.A. (1979) "Political Democracy and the Timing of Development", *American Sociological Review*, 44: 572–587.

Bollen, K.A. (1983) "World System Position, Dependency and Democracy: the Cross-National Evidence", *American Sociological Review*, 48: 468–479.

Bollen, K.A. and Jackman, R.W. (1985) "Political Democracy and the Size Distribution of Income", *American Sociological Review*, 50: 438–457.

Bowers, W.J. and Pierce, G.L. (1980) "Deterrence or Brutalization: What is the Effect of Executions?" *Crime and Delinquency*, 26: 453–484.

Bratt, E. (1951) *Småstaterna i idéhistorien: en studie i äldre statsdoktriner*, Uppsala: Almqvist & Wiksell.

Braybrooke, M. (2003) *Religions and the Death Penalty*, Amnesty International, Dornbirn, Austrian Section, Group-5, online, available at: http://members.magnet.at/ai.dornbirn/rel-dp.htm (accessed 11 December 2003).

Cahen, M. (1991) "Vent des îles. La victoire de l'opposition aux îles du Cap-Vert et à São Tomé e Principe", *Politique africaine*, 43: 63–78.

Carr, R.K., Bernstein, M.H. and Murphy, W.F. (1963) *American Democracy in Theory and Practice: National, State, and Local Government*, 4th edn, New York, NY: Holt, Rinehart and Winston.

Catechism of the Catholic Church, 2nd edn, revised in accordance with the Official Latin text promulgated by Pope John Paul II (2000) United States Catholic Conference, Inc: Doubleday.

Cloninger, D.O. (1977) "Death and the Death Penalty: a Cross-Sectional Analysis", *Journal of Behavioral Economics*, 6: 87–106.

Collier, D. and Messick, R.E. (1975) "Prerequisites Versus Diffusion: Testing Alternative Explanations of Social Security Adoption", *American Political Science Review*, 69: 1299–1315.

Cutright, P. (1963) "National Political Development: Measurement and Analysis", *American Sociological Review*, 28: 253–264.

Dahl, R. and Tufte, E. (1973) *Size and Democracy*, Stanford, CA: Stanford University Press.

Death Penalty Information Center. Online, available at: www.deathpenaltyinfo.org (last accessed 13 December 2003).

Death Penalty Information Center, Summaries of Recent Poll Findings. Online, available at: http://www.deathpenaltyinfo.org/article.php?scid=23&did=210 (accessed 13 December 2003).

Decker, S.H. and Kohfeld, C.W. (1990) "The Deterrent Effect of Capital Punishment in the Five Most Active Execution States: a Time–Series Analysis", *Criminal Justice Review*, 15: 173–191.

Derbyshire, J.D. and Derbyshire, I. (1989) *Political Systems of the World*, Edinburgh: Chambers.

Derbyshire, J.D. and Derbyshire, I. (1996) *Political Systems of the World*, 2nd edn, Oxford: Helicon Publishing Ltd.

Derbyshire, J.D. and Derbyshire, I. (1999) *Political Systems of the World*, vols I–II, new edn, Oxford: Helicon Publishing Ltd.

Deutsch, K.W. (1961) "Social Mobilization and Political Development", *American Political Science Review*, 55: 493–514.

Diamond, L. (1992) "Economic Development and Democracy Reconsidered", in G. Marks and L. Diamond (eds), *Reexamining Democracy: Essays in Honor of Seymour Martin Lipset*, London: Sage, pp. 1–36.

Diamond, L. (1999) *Developing Democracy: Toward Consolidation*, Baltimore, MD: The Johns Hopkins University Press.

Dogan, M. (1994) "Use and Misuse of Statistics in Comparative Research. Limits to Quantification in Comparative Politics: the Gap Between Substance and Method", in M. Dogan and A. Kazancigil (eds), *Comparing Nations: Concepts, Strategies, Substance*, Oxford: Blackwell, pp. 35–71.

Eckstein, H. (1975) "Case Study and Theory in Political Science", in F.I. Greenstein and N.W. Polsby (eds), *Handbook of Political Science*, vol. VII, Reading, MA: Addison-Wesley.

"Election Watch", *Journal of Democracy*, 1998, 9, 4: 176–178.

"Election Watch", *Journal of Democracy*, 1999, 10, 1: 173–176.

Erlich, I. (1975) "The Deterrent Effect of Capital Punishment: a Question of Life and Death", *American Economic Review*, 65: 397–417.

Erlich, I. (1977) "Capital Punishment and Deterrence: Some Further Thoughts and Additional Evidence", *Journal of Political Economy*, 85: 741–788.

Europa World Yearbook 2003 (2003), 44th edn, London: Europa Publications.

Fawn, R. (2001) "Death Penalty as Democratisation: is the Council of Europe Hanging Itself?", *Democratization*, 8: 69–96.

Flanigan, W. and Fogelman, E. (1971) "Patterns of Political Development and Democratization: a Quantitative Analysis", in J.V. Gillespie and B.A. Nesvold (eds), *Macro-Quantitative Analysis: Conflict, Development and Democratization*, Beverly Hills, CA: Sage Publications.

Forst, B.E. (1977) "The Case Against Capital Punishment: a Cross-State Analysis of the 1960s", *Minnesota Law Review*, 61: 743–767.

Freedom in the World: the Annual Survey of Political Rights and Civil Liberties, various issues, New York, NY: Freedom House.

Gasiorowski, M.J. (1988) "Economic Dependence and Political Democracy: a Cross-National Study", *Comparative Political Studies*, 20: 489–515.

Gastil, R. *Freedom in the World: Political Rights and Civil Liberties*, various issues, New York, NY: Freedom House.

Ghai, Y. (1988) "Constitution Making and Decolonisation", in Y. Ghai (ed.), *Law, Politics and Government in the Pacific Island States*, Suva: Institute of Pacific Studies, University of the South Pacific.

Grant, A. (1991) *The American Political Process*, 4th edn, Aldershot: Dartmouth.

Gray, V. (1973) "Innovation in the States: a Diffusion Study", *American Political Science Review*, 67: 1174–1185.

Hadenius, A. (1992) *Democracy and Development*, Cambridge: Cambridge University Press.

Halperin, R. (1998) *Death Penalty News: Worldwide*, February 10. Online, available at: http://venus.soci.niu.edu/~archives/ABOLISH/jan98/0247.html (accessed 9 March 2001).

Hamilton, A., Madison, J. and Jay, J. (1961) *The Federalist Papers*, New York, NY: New American Library.

Hannan, M.T. and Carroll, G.R. (1981) "Dynamics of Formal Political Structure: an Event-History Analysis", *American Sociological Review*, 46: 19–35.

Heywood, A. (1997) *Politics*, London: Macmillan.

Hicks, J.D., Mowry, G.E. and Burke, R.E. (1971) *The American Nation*, 5th edn, Boston, MA: Houghton Mifflin Company.

Hofstadter, R., Miller, W. and Aaron, D. (1959) *The American Republic, Volume One: to 1865*, New Jersey, CT: Prentice-Hall Inc.

Hood, R. (1989) *The Death Penalty*, Oxford: Clarendon.

Hood, R. (1996) *The Death Penalty*, 2nd edn, Oxford: Clarendon.

Hood, R. (2002) *The Death Penalty*, 3rd edn, Oxford: Oxford University Press.

Horigan, D.P. (1996) "A Buddhist Perspective on the Death Penalty of Compassion and Capital Punishment", *The American Journal of Jurisprudence*, 41: 271–288.

Huntington, S.P. (1984) "Will More Countries Become Democratic?", *Political Science Quarterly*, 99: 193–218.

Huntington, S.P. (1991) *The Third Wave: Democratization in the Late Twentieth Century*, Norman, OK: University of Oklahoma Press.

Jeldres, J.A. (1993) "The UN and the Cambodian Transition", *Journal of Democracy*, 4, 4: 104–116.

Karvonen, L. (1981) *Med vårt västra grannland som förebild*, Åbo: Meddelanden från stiftelsens för Åbo Akademi forskningsinstitut nr 62.

Karvonen, L. (1997) *Demokratisering*, Lund: Studentlitteratur.

Kateregga, B.D. and Shenk, D.W. (1983) *Islam och kristen tro*, trans. to Swedish B. Sharpe, Älvsjö: Verbum Förlag AB.

Keesing's Record of World Events, various volumes, 1996–1999, Bristol: Keesing's Publications.

Lane, J.-E. and Ersson, S. (1994) *Comparative Politics: an Introduction and New Approach*, Cambridge: Polity Press.

Lawson, S. (1996) *Tradition versus Democracy in the South Pacific: Fiji, Tonga and Western Samoa*, Cambridge: Cambridge University Press.

Layson, S.K. (1985) "Homicide and Deterrence: a Reexamination of the United States Time–Series Evidence", *Southern Economy Journal*, 52: 68–89.

Lenski, G. and Lenski, J. (1974) *Human Societies*, New York, NY: McGraw-Hill.

Lerner, D. (1958) *The Passing of Traditional Society: modernizing the Middle East*, New York, NY: Free Press.

Lijphart, A. (1971) "Comparative Politics and the Comparative Method", *American Political Science Review*, 65: 682–693.

Lijphart, A. (1975) "The Comparable-Cases Strategy in Comparative Research", *Comparative Political Studies*, 8: 158–177.

Lijphart, A. (1977) *Democracy in Plural Societies: a Comparative Exploration*, New Haven, CT: Yale University Press.

Lipset, S.M. (1959) "Some Social Requisites of Democracy: Economic Development and Political Legitimacy", *American Political Science Review*, 53: 69–105.

Lipset, S.M. and Rokkan, S. (1967) "Cleavage Structures, Party Systems, and Voter Alignments: an Introduction", in S.M. Lipset and S. Rokkan (eds), *Party Systems and Voter Alignments: Cross-National Perspectives*, New York, NY: Free Press.

Locke, J. (1967) *Two Treatises of Government* (P. Laslett ed., 2nd edn), Cambridge: Cambridge University Press.

Lundell, K. (2000) *Religion och demokrati: en studie av 109 stater i tredje världen*, Åbo: Meddelanden från Ekonomisk-statsvetenskapliga fakulteten vid Åbo Akademi. Serie A: 510.

May, J.D. (1973) *Of The Conditions and Measures of Democracy*, Morristown, NJ: General Learning Press.

Medhanie, T. (1993) "The Patterns of Transition to Democracy", *The Courier*, 138, March–April: 63–66.

Mill, J.S. (1972) *Utilitarianism, On Liberty and Consideration on Representative Government*, London: Dent.

Mohrenschlager, M. (1987) "The Abolition of Capital Punishment in the Federal Republic of Germany: the German Experience", *Revue Internationale de Droit Pénal* 58: 509–519.

Montesquieu (1944) *De l'esprit des lois. Texte établi avec une introduction des notes et des variantes par Gonzague Truc*, Paris: Classiques Garnier.

Needler, M.C. (1967) "Political Development and Socioeconomic Development: the Case of Latin America", *American Political Science Review*, 62: 889–897.

Nikolainen, A.T. and Raittila, A.-M. (1970) *Religionerna i vår tid*, Vasa: FSF.

Nozick, R. (1974) *Anarchy, State and Utopia*, Oxford: Basil Blackwell.

Olsen, M.E. (1968) "Multivariate Analysis of National Political Development", *American Sociological Review*, 33: 699–712.

Olson, J.S. (ed.) (1991) *Historical Dictionary of European Imperialism*, Westport, CT: Greenwood Press.

Paddison, R. (1983) *The Fragmented State: the Political Geography of Power*, Oxford: Basil Blackwell.

Pastor, R.A. (1990) "The Making of a Free Election", *Journal of Democracy*, 1, 3: 13–25.

Peters, B.G. (1998) *Comparative Politics: Theory and Methods*, London: Macmillan.

Peterson, R.D. and Bailey, W.C. (1988) "Murder and Capital Punishment in the Evolving Context of the Post-Furman Era", *Social Forces*, 66: 774–807.

Peterson, R.D. and Bailey, W.C. (1998) "Is Capital Punishment an Effective Deterrent for Murder? An Examination of Social Science Research", in J.R. Acker, R.M. Bohm and C.S. Lanier (eds), *America's Experiment with Capital Punishment: Reflections on the Past, Present and Future of the Ultimate Penal Sanction*, Durham, NC: Carolina Academic Press.

Phillips, D.P. (1980) "The Deterrent Effect of Capital Punishment: New Evidence on an Old Controversy", *American Journal of Sociology*, 86: 139–148.

Phillips, D.P. and Hensley, J.E. (1984) "When Violence is Rewarded or Punished: the Impact of Mass Media Stories on Homicide", *Journal of Communications*, summer: 101–116.

Pinkney, R. (1993) *Democracy in the Third World*, Buckingham: Open University Press.

Powell, G.B. (1982) *Contemporary Democracies: Participation, Stability, and Violence*, Cambridge, MA: Harvard University Press.

Rae, D. and Taylor, M. (1970) *The Analysis of Political Cleavages*, New Haven, CO: Yale University Press.

Rawls, J. (1971) *A Theory of Justice*, Cambridge: Belnap Press of the Harvard University Press.

Regional Surveys of the World: Africa south of the Sahara 1997, 26th edn (1997), London: Europa Publications Limited.

Regional Surveys of the World: the Far East and Australasia 1997, 28th edn (1996), London: Europa Publications Limited.

Regional Surveys of the World: the Middle East and North Africa 1997, 43rd edn (1997), London: Europa Publications Limited.

Regional Surveys of the World: South America, Central America and the Caribbean 1997, 6th edn (1996), London: Europa Publications Limited.

Rhodes, J.F. (1949) "Antecedents of the American Civil War, 1850–1860", in E.C. Rozwenc (ed.), *Slavery as a Cause of the Civil War*, Boston, MA: D.C. Heath and Company.

Riker, W.H. (1964) *Federalism: Origin, Operation and Significance*, Boston, MA: Little, Brown and Company.

Rodriguez, J.P. (ed.) (1997) *The Historical Encyclopedia of World Slavery*, vols I and II, Santa Barbara, CA: ABC-CLIO.

Rodriguez, J.P. (ed.) (1999) *Chronology of World Slavery*, Santa Barbara, CA: ABC-CLIO.

Rothstein, B. (ed.) (1995) *Demokratirådets rapport 1995: demokrati som dialog*, Stockholm: SNS förlag.

Rousseau, J.-J. (1900) *Du contrat social. Ou principes du droit politique*, Paris: Flammarion.

Rozwenc, E.C. (1949) "Introduction", in E.C. Rozwenc (ed.), *Slavery as a Cause of the Civil War*, Boston, MA: D.C. Heath and Company.

Sartori, G. (1970) "Concept Misformation in Comparative Politics", *American Political Science Review*, 64: 1033–1053.

Sartori, G. (1991) "Comparing and Miscomparing", *Journal of Theoretical Politics*, 3: 243–257.

Sartori, G. (1994) *Comparative Constitutional Engineering: an Inquiry into Structures, Incentives and Outcomes*, London: Macmillan.

Sawyer, R. (1986) *Slavery in the Twentieth Century*, London: Routledge & Kegan Paul.

Schabas, W.A. (ed.) (1997a) *The International Sourcebook on Capital Punishment*, Boston, MA: Northeastern University Press.

Schabas, W.A. (1997b) "African Perspectives on Abolition of the Death Penalty", in W.A. Schabas (ed.), *The International Sourcebook on Capital Punishment*, Boston, MA: Northeastern University Press.

Schemmel, B. *Rulers*, online, available at: www.rulers.org (last accessed 17 December 2003).

Sellin, T. (1959) *The Death Penalty*, Philadelphia, PA: The American Law Institute.

Sellin, T. (ed.) (1967) *Capital Punishment*, New York: Harper & Row.

Stepan, A. (1999) "Federalism and Democracy: Beyond the U.S. Model", *Journal of Democracy*, 10, 4: 19–34.

Tarkiainen, T. (1959) *Demokratia: antiikin Ateenan kansanvalta*, Porvoo: WSOY.

Tvedten, I. (1993). "The Angolan Debacle", *Journal of Democracy*, 4, 2: 108–118.

van Trease, H. (1995) "The Colonial Origin of Vanuatu Politics", in H. van Trease (ed.), *Melanesian Politics: stael blong Vanuatu*, Christchurch: Macmillan Brown Centre for Pacific Studies, University of Canterbury.

Vanhanen, T. (1984) *The Emergence of Democracy: a Comparative Study of 119 States, 1850–1979*, Helsinki: Societas Scientarium Fennica.

Vanhanen, T. (1987) *The Level of Democratization Related to Socioeconomic Variables in 147 States in 1980–85*, Amsterdam: European Consortium for Political Research.

Vanhanen, T. (1990) *The Process of Democratization: a Comparative Study of 147 states, 1980–1988*, New York: Crane Russak.

Vila, B. and Morris, C. (ed.) (1997) *Capital Punishment in the United States: a Documentary History*, Westport, CT: Greenwood.

Walker, J.L. (1969) "The Diffusion of Innovations Among the American States", *American Political Science Review*, 63: 880–899.

Weber, M. (1978) *Den protestantiska etiken och kapitalismens anda*, trans. to Swedish A. Lundquist, Lund: Argos.

Weiner, M. (1987) "Empirical Democratic Theory", in M. Weiner and E. Özbudun (eds), *Competitive Elections in Developing Countries*, Durham, NC: Duke University Press.

World in Figures: Editorial information compiled by The Economist (1987), London: Holder and Stoughton.

Reports

Council of Europe

Convention for the Protection of Human Rights and Fundamental Freedoms (ETS No.: 005).

Resolution 1044 (1994) on the Abolition of Capital Punishment. Parliamentary Assembly of the Council of Europe 1994.

Protocol No. 6 to the Convention for the Protection of Human Rights and Fundamental Freedoms concerning the Abolition of the Death Penalty (ETS No.: 114)

United Nations

Capital Punishment: Report of the Secretary General, E/5616; E/1980/9; E/1985/43; E/1990/38.

Capital Punishment and Implementation of the Safeguards Guaranteeing the Protection of the Rights of Those Facing the Death Penalty: Report of the Secretary-General, E/1995/78; E/2000/3.

Universal Declaration of Human Rights, General Assembly resolution 217 A (III) of 10 December 1948.

Cases cited

Furman v. *Georgia, Jackson* v. *Georgia, Branch* v. *Texas* 408 U.S. 238 (1972) (per curiam).

Gregg v. *Georgia* 428 U.S. 153 (1976) (plurality opinion).

Jurek v. *Texas* 428 U.S. 262 (1976).

Proffitt v. *Florida* 428 U.S. 242 (1976).

Data sources

Global figures

Death penalty

1985 and 2000: Hood 1989, 1996, 2002; Schabas 1997a; United Nations: Capital Punishment, Report of the Secretary-General, E/5616; E/1980/9; E/1985/43; E/1990/38. United Nations: Capital Punishment and Implementation of the Safeguards Guaranteeing the Protection of the Rights of Those Facing the Death Penalty, Report of the Secretary-General, E/1995/78; E/2000/3; Amnesty International: Annual Reports 1976–2001.

Population

1985: Derbyshire, J.D. and Derbyshire, I. 1989.

2000: Central Intelligence Agency – *The World Factbook 1999*, CIA.

Area

1985: Derbyshire and Derbyshire (1989).

2000: Central Intelligence Agency – *The World Factbook 1999*, CIA.

Ethnic, linguistic and religious fragmentation

1985 and 2000: Anckar, Eriksson and Leskinen 2002.

Dominating religion

1985 and 2000: Central Intelligence Agency – *The World Factbook 1999*, CIA; *Europa World Yearbook 1998*, London: Europa Publications; *Regional Surveys of the World: Eastern Europe and the Commonwealth of Independent States 1997*: *Regional Surveys of the World: Africa South of the Sahara 1997*, 26th edn (1997), London: Europa Publications Limited; *Länder i fickformat nr. 210*, 1995. Stockholm: Utrikespolitiska institutet; Derbyshire and Derbyshire 1996: Helicon Publishing Ltd; *Harenberg Länderlexikon 1993–1994* (1993), Dortmund: Harenberg Lexikon-Verlag.

GDP per capita

1985: Derbyshire and Derbyshire 1989.
2000: Central Intelligence Agency – *The World Factbook 1999*, CIA.

Income inequality

1985: *Britannica Book of the Year 1986* (1986), Chicago: Encyclopedia Britannica Ltd.
2000: *Britannica Book of the Year 1999* (1999), Chicago: Encyclopedia Britannica Ltd.

Urbanization

1985: *World Urbanization Prospects 1990* (1991), New York: United Nations Publication; *Hela världen i fakta 1986* (1985), Stockholm: Bonnier Fakta Bokförlag; *Harenberg Länderlexikon 1993–1994*. Vatican State: estimation by the author.
2000: *Britannica Book of the Year 1999*; Vatican State: estimation by the author.

Infant mortality

1985: *World Population Prospects*: the 1998 Revision, vol. 1. Comprehensive Tables (1999), New York: United Nations Publications; *Hela världen i fakta 1986*; Kurian, G.T. (ed.) (1982) *Encyclopedia of the Third World*, vols I, II, III, New York: Facts on File; *Britannica Book of the Year 1994* (1994), Chicago: Encyclopedia Britannica Ltd.
2000: Central Intelligence Agency – *The World Factbook 1999*, CIA; *Britannica Book of the Year 1999*.

Literacy

1985: Derbyshire and Derbyshire 1989.
2000: Central Intelligence Agency – *The World Factbook 1999*, CIA; *Britannica Book of the Year 1999*; *Harenberg Länderlexikon 1993–1994*.

Human Development Index

1985 and 2000: *Human Development Report 1999* (1999), Published for the United Nations Development Programme, Oxford: Oxford University Press.

Number of Murders

2000: *Britannica Book of the Year 1999.*

Number of offenses

1985: *Britannica Book of the Year 1986.*
2000: *Britannica Book of the Year 1999.*

Conflicts

1985 and 2000: Database KOSIMO, *The Heidelberg Institute of International Conflict Research*, online, available at: http://hiik.de/de/index_d.htm (accessed February–March 2000).

Corruption

1985: *Transparency International*, Corruptions Perceptions Index, online, available at: http://www.gwdg.de/~uwvw/histor.htm (accessed February–March 2001).
2000: *Transparency International*, Corruptions Perceptions Index, online, available at: http://www.transparency.de/documents/cpi/index.html (accessed February–March 2000).

EC/EU trade

1985: *Britannica Book of the Year 1986.*
2000: *Britannica Book of the Year 1999.*

Trade dependency

1985 and 2000: *Handbook of International Trade and Development Statistics 1995*, New York: United Nations Conference on Trade and Development.

Degree of democracy

1985: Gastil, R. (1986) *Freedom in the World: Political Rights and Civil Liberties 1985–1986*, New York: Freedom House.
2000: Freedom House (2001) *Freedom in the World: the Annual Survey of Political Rights and Civil Liberties, 2000–2001*, New York: Freedom House.

State structure

1985: Derbyshire and Derbyshire 1989.
2000: Derbyshire and Derbyshire 1999.

Form of government

1985: Derbyshire and Derbyshire 1989; Gastil 1986.
2000: Derbyshire and Derbyshire 1999; Freedom House 2001.

Leadership duration

1985 and 2000: Bienen and deWalle 1991; Derbyshire and Derbyshire 1989, 1999; Schemmel *Rulers*, online, available at: www.rulers.org (last accessed 17 December 2003).

Regime stability

1985 and 2000: Arthur S. Banks Cross-National Time–Series Data Archive (CNTS) 7–2000.

Colonial heritage

1985 and 2000: Derbyshire and Derbyshire 1989; Olson, J.S. (ed.) *Historical Dictionary of European Imperialism*, Westport, CT: Greenwood Press.

Slavery

1985 and 2000: Rodriguez, J.P. (ed.) (1997), vols I and II, Santa Barbara, CA: ABC-CLIO; Rodriguez, J.P. (ed.) (1999).

State longevity

1985 and 2000: Derbyshire and Derbyshire 1999.

USA

Death penalty

Death Penalty Information Center, online, available at: http://www.deathpenalty-info.org (last accessed 12 December 2003).

Population

U.S. Census Bureau, online, available at: http://www.census.gov/datamap/www/maptxt.html (accessed February 2001).

Area

50 States and CAPITALS, created by R. Weber on July 16, 1996, online, available at: http://www.50states.com (accessed February 2001).

Ethnic fragmentation

U.S. Census Bureau, online, available at: http://www.census.gov/Press-Release/
state04.prn (accessed March 2001).

Gross state product

U.S Department of Commerce, Bureau of Economic Analysis, online, available at:
http://www.bea.doc.gov/bea/regional/gsp/gspsum_c.htm (accessed March 2001).

Infant mortality

U.S. Census Bureau, online, available at: http://www.census.gov/Press-Release/
state06.prn (accessed March 2001).

Murders

World Almanac and Book of Facts 2001 (2001), Mahwah, NJ: World Almanac
Books.

Number of offenses

World Almanac and Book of Facts 2000 (2000), Mahwah, NJ: World Almanac
Books.

Civil War and slavery

Hofstadter, R., Miller, W. and Aaron, D. (1959) vol. 1.

Governors (majority since the re-enactment of the death penalty)

Truhart, P. (1984) *Regents of Nations: Systematic Chronology of States and their
Political Representatives in Past and Present: a Biographical Reference Book,
Part I, Africa/America,* Munich: K.G. Saur; *World Almanac and Book of Facts,*
issues 1972–2001.

Governors (during re-enactment of the death penalty)

World Almanac and Book of Facts, issues 1972–2001.

*State legislatures during and since the re-enactment of the death
penalty*

World Almanac and Book of Facts, issues 1972–2001.

Index

Page numbers followed by a '*t*' indicates a table.

abolitionist movement, development of 2–4
absolute states 62, 70, *see also* non-democratic countries
Aden 80
Afghanistan 12*t*, 61
Africa 122–4; determinants of death penalty 166*t*; regime stability 167; regional figures for use of death penalty 18–19; slavery 84, 85, *see also specific countries*
Alabama (USA) 154
Albania 12*t*, 41*t*, 137
Algeria 12*t*
Aliyev, Heydar 114
Allardt, E. 31
Americas 124–7, 136; determinants of death penalty 166*t*; ethnicity and race 32; regional figures for use of death penalty 18, *see also specific countries*
Amnesty International 3, 4; colonial powers 77; Ivory Coast 117; numbers of executions 8
analyses, multivariate analyses 90–102
Andorra 12*t*, 78–9
Angola 12*t*, 20, 67, 112*t*; independence and civil war 113–14, 117–18
Antigua & Barbuda 12*t*, 61, 110*t*
Archer, D. 46
Argentina 12*t*, 20
Aristide, Jean-Bertrand 116
Aristotle 83
Arizona (USA) 154
Armenia 12*t*, 114, 118, 138
ASEAN (Association of Southeast Asian Nations) 115

Asia and the Pacific 127–32; determinants of death penalty 166*t*; regional figures for use of death penalty 18, *see also specific countries*
attention, murder seeking to obtain 47
Australia 12*t*, 20, 82–3
Austria 12*t*, 17, 24, 46
authoritarian nationalist states 61, 63, 70, *see also* non-democratic countries
Avril, Prosper 116
Azerbaijan 12*t*, 19, 39, 41*t*, 67, 112*t*, 114, 118, 121, 138, 180

Bahamas 12*t*, 110*t*
Bahrain 12*t*
Bailey, W.C. 46
Bangladesh 12*t*
Barbados 12*t*, 110*t*
Barbuda *see* Antigua & Barbuda
Beccaria, Cesare 17
Bédié, Henri Konan 117
Beittel, M. 46
Belarus 12*t*, 138
Belgium 12*t*, 110*t*, 140; colonial heritage and capital punishment 87*t*
Belize 12*t*, 110*t*
Benin 12*t*, 110*t*
Bhutan 12*t*, 40, 41*t*
Bienen, H.S. 70–1
Bohm, R.M. 46, 47
Bolivia 12*t*, 20, 110*t*
Bollen, Kenneth A 42, 54
Bosnia-Herzegovina 12*t*, 41*t*
Botswana 12*t*, 110*t*
Bowers, W.J. 47
Brazauskas, Algirdas 19

Brazil 12*t*, 20
Brunei 12*t*, 38, 41*t*
brutalizing effect (of death penalty) 47
Buddhism 36
Buddhist countries 39*t*, 40, 41*t*; Asia and the Pacific 128*t*, 129*t*, 130, 131*t*; multivariate analyses 91, 93, 93*t*, 94–5, 94*t*, 95*t*, 96*t*, 99, 100, 105*t*, 108*t*
Bulgaria 12*t*, 19, 137
Burkina Faso 12*t*, 41*t*
Burundi 12*t*

Cambodia 12*t*, 17, 20, 40, 41*t*, 67, 112*t*, 115–16, 117–18
Cameroon 12*t*, 78
Canada 12*t*, 20, 46, 82
Cape Verde 12*t*, 18, 20, 66, 112*t*, 118–19, 123
Caribbean 109–11, 125–7
Carr, R.K. 152
case studies, use of 141–2
Catherine II, Emperor of Russia 17
Catholic Church, attitude to slavery 84
Catholic countries 39*t*, 40; Americas 126
Catholicism 35
Central African Republic 12*t*
centralization, and federalism 63–5
Chad 12*t*
Chamorro, Violeta 120
Chile 12*t*, 20, 110*t*
China 12*t*, 130, 136, 138; compared to Iraq 9–10; and Mongolia 79, 82
Christian countries 38–9, 40; Asia and the Pacific 130, 132, 136; determinants of death penalty 170; multivariate analyses 91, 92, 97–8*t*, 98–100
Christianity 34–6, *see also* Catholicism; Eastern Orthodox; Protestantism
Cold War: civil war in Angola 113; impact of ending of 54–5
Colombia 12*t*, 17, 20, 119
colonial heritage 75–80, 179; Americas 125*t*; Asia and the Pacific 132; and capital punishment 87*t*; as determinant of death penalty 166–7; and independence 80–1; multivariate analyses 92, 93*t*, 94*t*, 95*t*, 96*t*, 101, 104*t*, 105*t*, 106*t*
communist states 62, 70
Comoros 12*t*, 38, 41*t*
conflicts 49–51, 53*t*; Africa 123*t*; Americas 124*t*; Asia and the Pacific

127–8, 131*t*; multivariate analyses 102, 108*t*
Confucianism 39*t*
Congo-Brazzaville 12*t*
Congo-Kinshasa 12*t*
corruption 52, 53*t*; Asia and the Pacific 130; Europe 134–5; multivariate analyses 91–2, 95–6, *see also* crime (level of)
Costa Rica 12*t*, 17, 20, 119
Council of Europe 19, 60, 111, 118, 138
coups, abolition of death penalty in Ivory Coast 117
crime (level of) 45–9, 53*t*, 109, 135*t*, 137; Asia and the Pacific 129*t*; determinants of death penalty 167; Europe 134*t*; multivariate analyses 93*t*; USA 151, 152*t*, 162–3, *see also* corruption; murders
Croatia 12*t*, 19, 137
Cuba 13*t*
culture, USA 149–50
Cutright, P. 42
Cyprus 13*t*, 20, 81
Czech Republic 13*t*, 19, 137
Czechoslovakia 13*t*

Dahl, Robert 25, 26, 27–8
deductive approach 20–2
democracy 102–21, 140, 165, 177; Americas 124*t*, 135*t*; Asia and the Pacific 128*t*, 129*t*, 131*t*; as condition of secession of former colony 77; countries with capital punishment 110*t*; determinants of death penalty 165, 166*t*, 167, 169; emergent democracies 61–2; Europe 133–4, 133*t*, 134*t*; former colonies 76–7; impact of ethnicity on 30; impact of insularity on 27, 28–9*t*; impact of territorial and population size on 24–9; leadership duration and regime stability 68–9, 73–5; multivariate analyses 91, 92, 93*t*, 94*t*, 95*t*, 96, 96*t*, 97–9*t*; and socioeconomic development 41–2; and state structure 65–7; waves of democratization 175, *see also* political institutions
Denmark 13*t*, 46
dependency theory, international relations 54–8
Derbyshire, Denis 61, 62, 71, 81
Derbyshire, Ian 61, 62, 71, 81

deterrence 46–9, 59, 167
development: socioeconomic
    development 41–5, *see also* GDP/cap
Diamond, Larry 42
diffusion 171–3; European democracies
    111
Djibouti 13*t*, 20, 38, 39, 41*t*
Dominica 13*t*, 110*t*
Dominican Republic 13*t*, 20
Duvalier, François 116
Duvalier, Jean-Claude 116–17

East Timor 17, 20
Eastern Europe (former) 19, 111;
    popular attitude to death penalty 171
Eastern Orthodox 39*t*
Ecuador 13*t*, 17, 20, 119
education 42
Egypt 13*t*
El Salvador 13*t*, 20
electoral systems 74–5
Elisabeth, Emperor of Russia 17
emergent democracies 61–2
Equatorial Guinea 13*t*
Eritrea 13*t*, 41*t*
Erlich, Isaac 46–7
Ersson, S. 63, 67–8, 71–2
Estonia 13*t*, 19, 137
Ethiopia 13*t*; colonial heritage and
    capital punishment 87*t*
ethnicity: definition 31; ethnic-religious
    fragmentation, multivariate analyses
    104*t*, 105*t*; impact of diversity on use
    of death penalty 29–33, 38–9*t*; and
    race 31; USA, fragmentation 149–50,
    159*t*, 161*t*, 162, *see also* race
Europe 132–5, 137; determinants of
    death penalty 166*t*; regional figures
    for use of death penalty 18
European Convention for Protection of
    Human Rights and Fundamental
    Freedoms 59–60
European Union (EU) 102, 114, 168–9;
    Council of Europe, and abolition of
    death penalty 19, 60, 111, 118, 138;
    dependency and the death penalty
    55, 56, 57–8; diffusion of abolitionist
    stance 111, 171–3; EU trade 132–3,
    133*t*, 134*t*; EU trade, multivariate
    analyses 105–6, 105*t*, 106*t*; popular
    attitudes to death penalty 169

Fawn, Rick 137

federalism 63–5
Fiji 13*t*, 20, 131–2, 179
Finland 13*t*, 46; semi-presidential
    system 69, 70
Flanigan, W. 42
Florida (USA) 148
Fogelman, E. 42
France 13*t*; colonial heritage and capital
    punishment 76, 87*t*; experience of
    democracy 77; semi-presidential
    system 69, 70; slavery 84
Freedom House 61, 62

Gabon 13*t*
Gambia 13*t*, 41*t*
Gartner, R. 46
Gasiorowski, Mark 54
GDP/cap 43, 44–5*t*; Europe 132;
    European and non-EC countries
    133*t*; multivariate analyses 91–2
Georgia 13*t*, 19, 138
Germany 13*t*
Germany (East) 13*t*, 137
Germany (West) 13*t*
Ghana 13*t*, 110*t*, 112
Gonzales, Filipe 71
Grant, A. 160
Greece 13*t*, 110*t*
Grenada 13*t*, 110*t*
Guatemala 13*t*
Guëi, Robert 117
Guinea 13*t*, 41*t*
Guinea-Bissau 13*t*, 20, 40, 118
Gulf War 55
Guyana 13*t*, 110*t*

Hadenius, Axel 42, 56, 57
Haiti 13*t*, 20, 67, 112*t*, 116–18
HDI (human development index)
    45–6*t*; Europe 132; multivariate
    analyses 91, 95, 105*t*
Heidelberg Institute of International
    Conflict Research 50
heterogeneity, impact on democracy 25
Heywood, A. 64
Hinduism 36, 39*t*
homicide *see* crime
homogeneity, impact on democracy 25,
    27
Honduras 13*t*, 17, 20
Hood, Roger 4; instability of category
    of de facto abolitionist countries 10;
    on UN survey 8

Houphouët-Boigny, Felix 117
human rights: human rights movement
　59; and slavery 83
Hun Sen 115
Hungary 13*t*, 19, 137
Huntington, S. P. 175
Hussein, Saddam 67

Iceland 13*t*, 17
income distribution 43, 44–5*t*
India 13*t*, 39, 110*t*, 130, 136
indigenous beliefs 39*t*
Indonesia 13*t*, 130, 136
inductive approach 21–2
infant mortality 44–5*t*; multivariate
　analyses 91–2, 93*t*, 107
insularity: Africa 123; impact on
　democracy 27, 28–9*t*; multivariate
　analyses 104*t*, 105*t*, 106
Iran 13*t*, 61, 62
Iraq 13*t*; compared to China 9–10
Ireland 13*t*, 110*t*
IRF (index of religious fragmentation)
　see religion
Islam 34; attitude to slavery 83, 84, 86
Islamic countries 38, 39*t*, 40, 41*t*
Israel 13*t*, 46, 122
Italy 13*t*, 46
Ivory Coast 14*t*, 20, 38, 39, 41*t*, 67, 112*t*,
　117–18

Jamaica 14*t*, 109, 110*t*
Japan 14*t*, 110*t*, 130, 138; colonial
　heritage and capital punishment 87*t*
Jeldres, J.A. 115
Jordan 14*t*
Joseph II of Austria 17
Judaism 35–6, 39*t*

Kampuchea *see* Cambodia
Kansas (USA) 156
Kazakhstan 14*t*, 138
Kendall, George 143
Kennedy, John F. 150
Kenya 14*t*
Kiribati 14*t*, 20
Korea (North) 14*t*
Korea (South) 14*t*, 110*t*
KOSIMO 50
Kuwait 14*t*, 179
Kyrgyzstan 14*t*, 138

Lane, J.-E. 63, 67–8, 71–2

languages, linguistic fragmentation 32,
　38–9*t*, 140
Laos 14*t*, 40, 41*t*
Latin American countries 126, *see also*
　specific countries
Latvia 14*t*, 19, 137
leadership duration: multivariate
　analyses 93*t*, 94*t*, 95*t*, 96*t*; and regime
　stability 67–75
Lebanon 14*t*
Lee, Robert E. 157
legitimacy 168–71
Leopold, Grand Duke of Tuscany 17
Lerner, David 54
Lesotho 14*t*
Liberia 14*t*, 61
Libya 14*t*, 78
Liechtenstein 14*t*, 110*t*
Lijphart, Arend 22; case studies 141,
　142; comparative research 139; size
　and democracy 25
Lincoln, Abraham 157
linguistic fragmentation 32, 38–9*t*, 140
Lipset, Seymour Martin 29, 42, 61
literacy 44–5*t*
Lithuania 14*t*, 19, 137
Luxembourg 14*t*

Macedonia 14*t*, 19, 137
Madagascar 14*t*, 40
Madison, James 25
Maine (USA) 156
Malawi 14*t*
Malaysia 14*t*
Maldives 14*t*, 38, 41*t*
Mali 14*t*, 41*t*, 100–1, 110*t*, 112
Malta 14*t*, 62
Marshall Islands 14*t*, 20
Marxism-Leninism 62
Mauritania 14*t*, 41*t*, 85, 86
Mauritius 14*t*, 20, 39, 110*t*
methodology 20–2
Mexico 14*t*, 20
Micronesia, Federated States of 14*t*, 20
Middle Ages 17
Middle East 122; regional figures for
　use of death penalty 18, *see also*
　specific countries
military states 70
Missouri (USA) 148, 156
modernization school 54
Moldova 14*t*, 19, 137
Monaco 14*t*

Mongolia 14*t*, 79, 82, 110*t*
Montenegro 19
Montesquieu, Charles de Secondat,
Baron de 24, 25, 83
Morocco 14*t*, 61, 179
Mozambique 18, 20, 40, 114
murders 53*t*; USA 159*t*, 161*t*, 163, *see
also* crime (level of)
Muslim countries 122, 135*t*; Africa 123*t*;
Americas 124*t*; Asia and the Pacific
128*t*, 129*t*, 130, 131*t*; Azerbaijan 114;
determinants of death penalty 170;
multivariate analyses 91, 92, 93*t*, 94*t*,
95, 95*t*, 98–9*t*, 99–101, 108*t*
Myanmar 14*t*, 40, 41*t*

Nagorno-Karabakh 114
Namibia 14*t*, 18, 20, 80, 114
Namphy, Henri 116
Nasser, Gamal Abd al- 67
nationalistic socialist states 62, 70
Nauru 14*t*, 20, 80, 110, 130, 131
Nebraska (USA) 156
Needler, M.C. 42
Nepal 14*t*, 20, 39
Netherland Antilles 46
Netherlands 14*t*, 17; colonial heritage
and capital punishment 87*t*; slavery
84
New Zealand 15*t*, 20, 82–3
Nicaragua 15*t*, 20, 66, 112*t*, 118, 119–20
Niger 15*t*, 41*t*
Nigeria 15*t*, 61
non-democratic countries: abolitionist
countries 112*t*; determinants of death
penalty 166*t*, 169–70; Haiti 116–17;
Islamic tradition 170; leadership
duration and regime stability 68, 70;
multivariate analyses 106–8
North Yemen 80
Norway 15*t*, 17, 46

Öcalan, Abdullah 55
Oceania 18, 131
Oklahoma (USA) 148
Olsen, M.E. 42
Oman 15*t*
Ortega, Daniel 120

Pacific 127–32
Pakistan 15*t*
Palau (Belau) 15*t*, 20
Panama 15*t*, 20, 112*t*, 118, 119

Papua New Guinea 15*t*, 20, 80, 110*t*, 140
Paraguay 15*t*, 20
parliamentary systems 69
Perons (Argentina) 67
Peru 15*t*, 20
Peterson, R.D. 46
Philippines 15*t*, 110*t*; reintroduction of
death penalty 7
Pierce, G.L. 47
Plato 24–5
Poland 15*t*, 19, 137
political actors 67–75
political institutions: forms of
government 58–63, 66–7; state
structure 63–7, *see also* democracy;
regime stability
population density: impact on
democracy 26, 28–9*t*; USA 148*t*
population size 136; Americas 124*t*;
Asia and the Pacific 128*t*, 129*t*, 130,
131*t*; as determinant of death penalty
165–6; impact on democracy 24–8,
28–9*t*; multivariate analyses 107, 108*t*;
USA 148*t*, 159*t*, 161*t*, 163, *see also*
territorial size
Portugal 15*t*, 17; colonial heritage and
capital punishment 87*t*; as colonial
power 114, 119; semi-presidential
system 69–70
Powell, Bingham 30
presidential systems 68–9; and semi-
presidential systems 69–70
Préval, René 116
Protestant countries, Americas 126
Protestantism 35, 39*t*, 40, 84

Qatar 15*t*

race: and ethnicity 31; tensions, USA
149, *see also* ethnicity
Rae, Douglas 32
Ranariddh, Prince 115
Reagan, Ronald 160
regime stability: Africa 123*t*; Americas
124*t*; Asia and the Pacific 128*t*;
determinants of death penalty 167;
and leadership duration 67–75;
multivariate analyses 93*t*, 94*t*, 108*t*,
see also political institutions; state
longevity
religion 91, 93*t*, 94*t*, 95*t*, 96*t*, 136; Africa
123*t*; Americas 124*t*; Americas, index
of religious fragmentation 125–6*t*;

religion *continued*
  Asia and the Pacific 128*t*, 129*t*, 131*t*;
  ethnic-religious fragmentation 104*t*,
  105*t*; multivariate analyses 91, 104–5,
  104*t*, 105*t*, 108*t*; religious
  fragmentation 33–41, 133*t*; USA 150,
  see also Buddhist countries; Christian
  countries; Muslim countries
René, Albert 121
Riker, William 63
Rogriguez, J.P. 85
Rokkan, Stein 29
Romania 15*t*, 17, 19
Rousseau, Jean Jacques 25, 83
Russia 15*t*, 17, 138, 179
Rwanda 15*t*, 50

Sachs, Albie 77
St. Kitts & Nevis 15*t*, 110
St. Lucia 15*t*, 110*t*
St. Vincent & Grenadines 15*t*, 110*t*
Samoa 20, 80, 131, 180
Samoa (Western) 15*t*, 110*t*
San Marino 15*t*, 17, 71
Sandino, Augusto César 120
São Tomé e Príncipe 15*t*, 18, 20
Sartori, G. 33, 140; case studies 142
Saudi Arabia 15*t*
Schabas, W.A. 114
Schemmel, B. 71
secularization 33
security, and leadership duration 68
Sellin, Thorsten 46
Senegal 15*t*, 38, 41*t*
Serbia 19
Seychelles 15*t*, 20, 66–7, 112*t*, 118,
  120–1, 123
Shintoism 39*t*
Sierra Leone 15*t*
Singapore 15*t*
slavery (history of) 83–8, 87–8*t*, 109–11,
  136; Asia and the Pacific 127, 128,
  128*t*, 129*t*; multivariate analyses 92,
  93*t*, 94, 94*t*, 95*t*, 96*t*, 97–9*t*, 101–2,
  105*t*, 107, 108*t*; USA 84, 156–9, 159*t*
Slovakia 15*t*, 19, 137
Slovenia 15*t*, 19, 137
socioeconomic development 41–5, 107;
  USA 150–1, *see also* GDP/cap
Solomon Islands 15*t*, 18, 20
Somalia 15*t*
Somoza family 119–20
South Africa 15*t*, 20, 82–3

South Yemen 80
Soviet Union (former) 15*t*, 19, 72, 79, 114
Spain 15*t*; Andorra 78–9; colonial
  heritage and capital punishment 87*t*;
  leadership duration 71; slavery 84
special circumstances, death penalty
  allowed under 5, 6
Sri Lanka 15*t*, 40, 41*t*
stability *see* leadership duration; regime
  stability
Stalin, Joseph 67
Starck, C. 31
state longevity 80–3; Americas 126*t*;
  and capital punishment 87–8*t*, *see
  also* leadership duration; regime
  stability
state structure: and democracy 65–7;
  federalism and centralism 63–5
Sudan 15*t*, 85
'suicide-murder syndrome' 47
Suriname 15*t*, 110*t*, 112
Swaziland 15*t*
Sweden 15*t*, 17, 46, 50; popular
  attitudes to death penalty 169
Switzerland 16*t*, 46, 50, 71
Syria 16*t*

Taiwan 16*t*, 110*t*
Tajikistan 16*t*, 138
Tanzania 16*t*
Taylor, Michael 32
territorial size: Asia and the Pacific
  130–1; influence on democracy and
  death penalty 24–9, 28–9*t*; USA
  148–9, 163, *see also* population size
Texas (USA) 148, 154
Thailand 16*t*, 110*t*
Third World dependency 54–7
Togo 16*t*, 78
Tonga 16*t*, 20, 179
trade dependency 54–8; Americas 124*t*
Transparency International 52
Trinidad & Tobago 16*t*, 110*t*
Tufte, Edward 25, 26, 27–8
Tunisia 16*t*
Turkestan 17, 41*t*, 138
Turkey 16*t*, 41*t*
Turkmenistan 16*t*, 19, 20, 39, 67, 112*t*,
  114–15
Tuscany 17
Tuvalu 16*t*, 18, 20, 130

Uganda 16*t*, 61

UK 16*t*, 46; and Canada 82; colonial heritage and capital punishment 75–6, 87*t*; democracy 77; slavery 84
Ukraine 16*t*, 19, 138
Ulmanis, Guntis 19
United Arab Emirates 16*t*
United Nations 4, 118, 168; Angola 113; Cambodia 115; Second Optional Protocol to the International Covenant on Civil and Political Rights 60, 137–8; survey on use of death penalty 8; Universal Declaration of Human Rights 59
urbanization 43, 44–5*t*
Uruguay 16*t*, 17, 119
USA 16*t*, 81, 110*t*, 138, 139–64, 168, 178; Civil War and slavery 84, 156–9; colonial heritage and capital punishment 87*t*; constitution 144, 152; crime (level of) 151, 152*t*; culture 149–50; dependency and the death penalty 56, 57–8; determinants of death penalty 166*t*; and diffusion 171, 172–3; federalism 64–5; *Furman* v. *Georgia* 144, 172; governors (party affiliation) 154–5, 159*t*, 160–1, 161*t*, 167; *Gregg* v. *Georgia* 144, 145, 146, 172; Haiti 116; historical overview 143–5; Kansas-Nebraska Act 156; Nicaragua 120; Panama 119; party dominance 152–4, 160–1; racial tensions 149; religion 150; size 148–9, 163; socioeconomic development 150–1; state legislatures 151–5;

Supreme Court cases 144, 145, 146; violence 157
Uzbekistan 16*t*, 138

van de Walle, N. 70–1
van den Berghe, P. L. 30
Vanhanen, T. 42
Vanuatu 16*t*, 20, 79
Vatican State 16*t*, 67, 107–8, 112*t*, 130
Venezuela 16*t*, 17, 20, 119
Vietnam 16*t*, 115
violence, and ethnic diversity 30
Virginia (USA) 148

war *see* conflict
wealth 42–3, *see also* socioeconomic development
Weber, Max 81
websites: deathpenaltyinfo.org 144, 148; gwdg.de/~uwvw/histor.htm 52; hiik.de/de/index_d.htm 50; transparency.de/documents/cpi/index.html 52
Western Europe 102; regional figures for use of death penalty 20, *see also* European Union

Yemen 16*t*, 79–80
Yugoslavia 16*t*; colonial heritage and capital punishment 87*t*; crisis 55

Zambia 16*t*
Zanzibar 85
Zimbabwe 16*t*